A REVOLUTION
OF THE MIND

Jonathan Israel

A REVOLUTION
OF THE MIND

Radical Enlightenment and
the Intellectual Origins of
Modern Democracy

Princeton University Press

Princeton and Oxford

Paperback ISBN 978-0-691-15260-8

Library of Congress Cataloging-in-Publication Data

Israel, Jonathan.
A revolution of the mind : Radical Enlightenment and
the intellectual origins of modern democracy /
Jonathan Israel.
p.   cm.
Includes bibliographical references and index.
ISBN 978-0-691-14200-5 (hardcover : alk. paper)
1. Political science—Europe—History—18th century.
2. Enlightenment. 3. Democracy—History—18th
century. I. Title.
JA84.E9187 2010
321.8—dc22   2009011137

British Library Cataloging-in-Publication Data
is available

This book has been composed in Minion

Printed on acid-free paper. ∞

press.princeton.edu

Printed in the United States of America

5 7 9 10 8 6

Contents

Preface

In recent years historians and philosophers have made rapid strides in uncovering the main stages and the general history of the Radical Enlightenment. An originally clandestine movement of ideas, almost entirely hidden from public view during its earliest phase (the late seventeenth century), and maturing in opposition to the moderate mainstream Enlightenment dominant in Europe and America in the eighteenth century, radical thought burst into the open in the 1770s, 1780s, and 1790s during the revolutionary era in America, France, Britain, Ireland, and the Netherlands, as well as in underground democratic opposition circles in Germany, Scandinavia, Latin America, and elsewhere. Radical Enlightenment is now widely seen as the current of thought (and eventually political action) that played the primary role in grounding the egalitarian and democratic core values and ideals of the modern world.

Radical Enlightenment is a set of basic principles that can be summed up concisely as: democracy; racial and sexual equality; individual liberty of lifestyle; full freedom of thought, expression, and the press; eradication of religious authority from the legislative process and education; and full separation of church and state. It sees the purpose of the state as being the wholly secular one of promoting the worldly interests of the majority and preventing vested minority interests from capturing control of the legislative process. Its chief maxim is that all men have the same basic needs, rights, and status irrespective of what they believe or what religious, economic, or ethnic group they belong to, and that consequently all ought to be treated alike, on the basis of equity, whether black or white, male or female, religious or nonreligious, and that all deserve to have their personal interests and aspirations equally respected by law and government. Its universalism lies in its claim that all men have the same right to pursue happiness in their own way, and think and say whatever they see fit, and no one, including those who convince others they are divinely chosen to be their masters, rulers, or spiritual guides, is justified in denying or hindering others in the enjoyment of rights that pertain to all men and women equally.

These principles, broadly accepted nowhere in the world before the American Revolution—and by no means fully implemented there whilst slavery persisted and many whites as well as blacks and Indians remained excluded from voting and political participation in the decades after 1776—are only very patchily accepted by societies and governments in much of the world today. But while in many places these core democratic values retain only a precarious foothold, they did finally triumph in much of the world after 1945. With the struggle against Fascism and Stalinism, and especially after the end of the Second World War and the commencement of decolonialization (beginning in the late 1940s), modern representative democracy and equality before the law have become generally entrenched in the legal and legislative apparatus not just of Western Europe, America, and the wider English-speaking world, but also, from the late 1940s, for the first time became firmly grounded in several key Asian countries, most notably India and Japan, at least at the level of officially approved policy, law, and education.

Surprising as it may seem, the history of this process—the gradual advance of the ideas underpinning democratic Enlightenment in the modern era—remains very little studied or known. Indeed, there exist scarcely any historical accounts that analyze and narrate the story of the origins and rise of modern equality, democracy, individual liberty, and freedom of thought in their intellectual, social, and political context. Until recently, historians of the French Revolution still thought of it (and many still do) as "inventing a new form of political discourse" rather than as a struggle between rival ideologies complexly evolving over the previous century. Of course, no one would deny that there exists an impressive mass of studies, especially by political and social scientists, analyzing the concepts of equality, democracy, and individual liberty as abstract propositions. But there are virtually none that describe in the contexts of history and culture the actual emergence of these ideas. As one scholar recently noted, the word "democracy" has (since 1945) generally been "a pretext for ideological endorsement rather than a term for a historically rooted process."[1] This is equally true of equality. While there is "plenty of work on equality," another commentator observes, "there is precious little in the modern literature on the background to the idea that we humans are, fundamentally, one another's equals."[2] The story of the emergence of modern democratic core values as a Western and global historical phenomenon before 1789 remains—in America, Europe, Africa, and Asia alike—a gigantic yawning gap.

The risk in considering our core values as purely abstract concepts that do not require examination in their historical context, or imagining the French Revolution invented them, is that we then remain blind to how, why, and where these concepts first emerged amid conflict and controversy, and the means whereby they slowly advanced in the teeth of widespread opposition and eventually became first intellectually and then politically hegemonic. Not only scholars but also the general reading, debating, and voting public need some awareness of the tremendous difficulty, struggle, and cost involved in propagating our core ideas in the face of the long-dominant monarchical, aristocratic, and religious ideologies, privileged oligarchies and elites, and in the face also of the various Counter-Enlightenment popular movements that so resolutely and vehemently combated egalitarian and democratic values from the mid-seventeenth century down to the crushing of Nazism, the supreme Counter-Enlightenment, in 1945.

Radical Enlightenment is the system of ideas that, historically, has principally shaped the Western World's most basic social and cultural values in the post-Christian age. This in itself lends the history of the movement great importance. But this type of thought—especially in many Asian and African countries, as well as in contemporary Russia—has also become the chief hope and inspiration of numerous besieged and harassed humanists, egalitarians, and defenders of human rights, who, often against great odds, heroically champion basic human freedom and dignity, including that of women, minorities, homosexuals, and religious apostates, in the face of the resurgent forms of bigotry, oppression, and prejudice that in much of the world today appear inexorably to be extending their grip.

It is perhaps this global dimension above all that lends the history of radical thought its continuing relevance in our time. Democratic, secular, and egalitarian ideas dismally failed to be accepted or officially sponsored in very many new countries emerging in the 1950s and 1960s through decolonization, desegregation, and the spread of anticolonialism. Consequently, there still exists relatively little understanding of the intellectual grounds of these ideals in most of the developing world while, even in the West, these values, being very recent as publicly and officially endorsed principles, remain only weakly embedded in education, the media, and in many people's minds. Besides the urgent need to strengthen democratic awareness, it is also vital to gather from the Radical Enlightenment's history how exactly the core ideas of modern Western secularism interconnect and function together socially and culturally as a set, and how, after nearly three centuries of constant and sometimes massive repression, they eventually came to be embraced (sometimes half-heartedly and incompletely) by ruling elites and the West's legal systems. Furthermore, key teachings of the Radical Enlightenment continue to offer pertinent and unsettling lessons. Who can doubt that ignorance and credulity, identified by the eighteenth-century radical enlighteners as the prime cause of human degradation and oppression, remain still the foremost foes of democracy, equality, and personal freedom; or that an informal aristocracy, like that which arose in America, eventually nurturing vast inequality of wealth, can endanger equality and individual liberty as much as any formal nobility based on lineage, rank, and legally anchored privilege?

Since Radical Enlightenment emerged in opposition to mainstream thinking, and still clashes with the traditions and cherished beliefs of many, it is hardly surprising that its perceived irreligion, libertinism, and subversiveness drew immense hostility and disapproval in the past, not least in Britain and America, and still excite fierce opposition in many quarters. In the nineteenth and early twentieth centuries, national narratives were particularly an obstacle to the study of the rise of democratic and egalitarian ideas. Unrelenting stress on the overriding importance of national identity frequently obscured the rise of modern democratic and egalitarian values or led to an exaggerated notion of the imagined uniqueness of individual countries' contributions. Thus, the Dutch supposed their golden age (in the seventeenth century) was far more tolerant than it really was, remaining unaware that when the modern concepts of individual liberty and freedom of thought were originally introduced by Enlightenment thinkers and publicists in the late seventeenth and eighteenth centuries, most of their countrymen (no less than the British and Americans) staunchly opposed them.

More recently, among the foremost challenges to Radical Enlightenment principles, and one particularly threatening to modern society, was the modish multiculturalism infused with postmodernism that swept Western universities and local government in the 1980s and 1990s. For this briefly potent new form of intellectual orthodoxy deemed all traditions and sets of values more or less equally valid, categorically denying the idea of a universal system of higher values self-evident in reason and equity, or entitled to claim superiority over other values. In particular, many Western intellectuals and local government policymakers argued that to attribute universal validity and superiority over other cultural traditions to core values forged in the Western Enlightenment smacks, whatever its pretensions to rational cogency, of Eurocentrism, elitism, and lack of basic respect for the "other."

Based on a lecture series delivered at Oxford between January and March 2008, in commemoration of the life and work of Sir Isaiah Berlin (1909–1997), one of the major intellectuals of the twentieth century, this small volume has been slightly expanded and in part substantially revised in response to questioning and debate with academic colleagues and students about its arguments. Among the chief features of Sir Isaiah's intellectual legacy were his valiant efforts to pull philosophy and history closer together (no easy task) and establish what in his time was the virtually new discipline of "intellectual history." Accordingly, I hope that what follows will stand as a small tribute to his memory and achievements, especially by again attempting to draw philosophy and history into a closer, more meaningful partnership.

A REVOLUTION
OF THE MIND

CHAPTER I

Progress and the Enlightenment's
Two Conflicting Ways of
Improving the World

That notions concerning "progress," "improvement of society," and what one now-forgotten radical-minded novelist of the 1790s termed the "amelioration of the state of mankind" were central to the Enlightenment is scarcely surprising.[1] Four out of six of the Enlightenment's philosophical founding figures—Descartes, Hobbes, Spinoza, and Bayle—held that most people's ideas about the most fundamental questions are wildly wrong and that were it possible to improve men's ideas about the world and about the structure of reality, this, in itself, would significantly improve human existence. For it would make society safer and more stable (Hobbes's main concern), more tolerant (Bayle's main concern), more rational in its approach to disasters and health problems (one of Descartes' aims), and also freer and more accepting of the dissenting individual.

All four of these philosophical founders shared in generating this "revolutionary" tendency in Western modernity and hence in forging the dramatically new way of viewing the world that began with them and with the more general cultural changes of the Enlightenment era. Spinoza, however, with his one-substance doctrine—that body and soul, matter and mind are not distinct substances but rather one single substance viewed under different aspects—extends this "revolutionary" tendency appreciably further metaphysically, politically, and as regards man's highest good than do Descartes, Hobbes, or Bayle. On Spinoza's principles, society would become more resistant to being manipulated by religious authority, autocracy, powerful oligarchies and dictatorship, and more democratic, libertarian and egalitarian. Thereby, he creates a sharper opposition than the rest between philosophy and theology, characteristics that make him the first major figure of the Radical Enlightenment.[2]

The reformation of ideas projected by these great thinkers, however, offered only the theoretical possibility of improvement, not the actuality, and both Hobbes and Bayle remained generally rather pessimistic. By the later eighteenth century, however, there had been a remarkable change. Now it appeared that such a revolution in thinking and circumstances was not just a theoretical possibility but something real. "The world," declared Richard

Price (1723–1791), a leading representative of the radical tendency in England, "has hitherto been gradually improving. Light and knowledge have been gaining ground, and human life at present compared with what it once was, is much the same that a youth approaching to manhood is compared with an infant. Such are the natures of things that this progress must continue."[3] His close friend Joseph Priestley (1733–1804) and most famous disciple, the feminist theorist Mary Wollstonecraft (1759–1797), were equally convinced God had a plan for the world's gradual improvement albeit not through direct divine action or miraculous happenings but through the ordinary processes of nature and society.[4]

In enlightened circles during the later eighteenth century, the concept of progress was broadly endorsed in Europe and America and became the general view. Theories of progress, however, contrary to what many have assumed, were usually tempered by a strong streak of pessimism, a sense of the dangers and challenges to which the human condition is subject. The notion, still widespread today, that Enlightenment thinkers nurtured a naïve belief in man's perfectibility seems to be a complete myth conjured up by early twentieth-century scholars unsympathetic to its claims. In reality, Enlightenment progress breathed a vivid awareness of the great difficulty of spreading toleration, curbing religious fanaticism, and otherwise ameliorating human organization, orderliness, and the general state of health and was always impressively empirically based. Its relative optimism rested on man's obviously growing capacity to create wealth, invent technologies capable of raising production, and devise stable legal and political institutions, as well as, it should be mentioned, the disappearance of the plague. Despite the slowness of our steps, urged the baron d'Holbach (1723–1789), one of the most radical of the *philosophes*, at the close of his *Système social* (1773), the evidence shows, without question, that human reason does progress. We are manifestly less ignorant, barbarous, and ferocious than our fathers and they in turn were less ignorant than their predecessors. Doubtless in times when ignorance and superstition are very strong there is little disposition to accept the light of reason. But who can deny, he demanded, that this resistance has significantly lessened in recent times?

By the 1760s, even the more cynical were convinced: progress was indeed occurring. Across Europe, ruling elites were "beginning to think," commented the "enlightened despot" Frederick the Great of Prussia (r. 1740–1786), in a letter to Voltaire in January 1766. Even in "superstitious" Austria and Bohemia, he remarked, the bigotry and fanaticism of the past were fading fast, at least in court and administrative circles, and leading men were "opening their eyes." While official censorship in Central Europe still banned many "good books," "the truth," as Frederick put it, was everywhere seeping through and "superstition" and veneration of images receding. Citing the example of the once notoriously puritanical and rigid Calvinist city of Geneva, Frederick applauded the advance of toleration and press freedom, among other obvious improvements. It all amounted, he thought, to a true modern "miracle" and one undeniably due to the Enlightenment and, especially, he suggested, to Voltaire.

François-Marie-Arouet de Voltaire (1694–1778), after some years residing in Germany and Switzerland, was no less persuaded that "a great revolution in men's minds was becoming manifest on all sides." Writing to Jean le Rond d'Alembert (1717–1783) in 1766 Voltaire averred that his fellow *philosophe* would scarcely believe what magnificent progress "reason" was now achieving in Germany. He did not mean, he explained, the advance of those "impious spirits" who embrace the ideas of Spinoza, with whom he carried on a kind of perpetual private battle throughout his career and deemed the quintessence of what he considered the wrong kind of Enlightenment, the radical ideas of Denis Diderot (1713–1784), the baron d'Holbach, and the German materialists; rather, he meant those with no fixed principles concerning the deeper nature of things and who did not pretend to know what ultimate truth is but instead knew what it is not and revered the true principles, as he saw it, of reason and toleration, namely those of Locke, Newton, and himself: "voilà mes vrais philosophes."[5]

But writing to another correspondent soon afterwards, Voltaire carefully qualified this optimism, pointing out that while reason had made great strides, this was occurring only amongst a tiny elite, "chez un petit nombre de sages," those few eager to understand the reality of things. Most men, he noted, prefer to be directed by authority than think for themselves and hence remain no less benighted than before; but then, he added, the remainder of humanity—some nine-tenths of mankind, he calculated—do not deserve to be enlightened (les autres ne méritent pas que l'on les éclaire).[6] Throughout his career, Voltaire consistently opposed radical thought and its egalitarian aims.

The later Enlightenment's greatest philosopher, Immanuel Kant (1724–1804), teaching at the university of Königsberg (today Kaliningrad) in what was then East Prussia likewise had no doubt that mankind was experiencing "progress" and that this evident amelioration was driven by the advance of "reason." Hence, while man's improvement, as he saw it, was manifest in all spheres— legal, political, moral, commercial, and technological—it was in the first place a progression of the human mind and the impact on mankind of nature (or Providence) that was driving the process. In a famous essay of 1795 he asserted that European states were gradually becoming more "republican," and more "representative" of the general will of their people, through their assemblies, laws, and institutions. Politically, the ultimate end of human progress would be an international federation of powers to resolve disputes, leading ultimately, he envisaged, to "perpetual peace." The final goal, or "telos" of human progress, in his view, was the full flowering of human rationality and moral capacity, conceivable only on the basis of republican legislation and perpetual peace; all this, however, would come about almost automatically, through the working of Providence, without any specific human intervention.[7]

Yet while nearly all Enlightenment thinkers were inspired by notions of progress, however diffusely, it was Anne-Robert-Jacques Turgot (1727–1781), one of the founders together with Adam Smith (1723–1790) of the science of economics, who first formulated a coherent, systematic doctrine of progress. A leading reformer of the last decades of the *ancien régime* who served as Louis XVI's controller-general of the royal finances during the years 1774–1776, Turgot was fiercely critical of Diderot, d'Holbach, and the other radical thinkers.[8] He, too, championed toleration and especially a sweeping program of economic liberalization and rationalization but strictly within the framework of monarchy, aristocracy, and the existing order. Like Voltaire, he rejected equality as a principle and thoroughly repudiated atheism, determinism, and materialism.

An avowed providential Deist but one who attributed to Christianity a broadly positive role in the world, Turgot delivered two doctoral lectures at the Sorbonne, in Paris, in 1750, which together, as has been said, "framed a new conception of world history from remotest antiquity to the present and constituted the first important version in modern times of the ideology of progress."[9] Turgot, linking epistemology, economics, and administration, argued that man's capacity to receive new impressions from the outside world—and to sift, combine, and analyze them—had opened a path by which experience absorbs and builds an unending sequence of material improvement, technological advancement, and better organization. The empirically proven fact of progress in the past, furthermore, he construed as proof that retrogression would also be impossible in the future. It was this cumulative unidirectional process embracing all aspects of social development—something he viewed as divinely driven, and hence irreversible—that he designated "progress."

The Enlightenment's idea of progress, then, was invariably conceived as being "philosophical," a revolution of the mind. But it was undoubtedly economic, technological, political, medical, and administrative as well, in addition to being legal, moral, educational, and aesthetic. Enlightenment "progress" was thus very wide-ranging and multifaceted. Moreover, it was also inherently unstable, a feature historians have by no means sufficiently focused on in the past. For it is apparent that Enlightenment progress could take specifically Christian, Deist, or atheistic forms; it could be conceived as endorsing or opposing the existing order of society, as being reversible or irreversible, God-ordained or purely natural.

These differences were certainly not national in character, though the French possibly put more emphasis on the advance of reason than the rest, and Adam Ferguson (1723–1816), the only major Enlightenment figure to hail from the Gaelic-speaking part of Scotland, followed his fellow Scot Lord Kames (1696–1792) in developing what might be deemed a distinctively Scottish perspective. This he did in several works, including his *Essay on the History of Civil Society* (1767), which is among the most remarkable and innovative works of the (moderate) Enlightenment in the British Isles. Here Ferguson envisages the entire panorama of civil society as a process of development from primitive beginnings to higher stages, but higher only in the sense that they were later, more intricately differentiated parts of the same coherent sequence. His progress was a collective attainment, a development toward increasingly complex social structures, but also increasingly complex problems that did not necessarily produce a higher—that is, more developed—kind of individual and, still less, a more equal one.

Divine design, for Ferguson, was equally manifest in small and large things and evident, as he put it, "throughout the whole system [. . .] of nature."[10] For him, as for Kames and Adam Smith, divinely ordained design infuses all features and the successive stages of civil society itself. Everywhere one discerns "a chain of connection and mutual subserviency, which renders the vestige of intelligent power the more evident, that parts are so various, while they are so happily ranged and connected."[11] Sharing with Montesquieu the idea that manners, attitudes, and morals, reflect and are "adapted to the constitution of the state,"[12] and hence like him, stressing the necessity of aristocracy and rank in a mixed monarchy like Britain, Ferguson did not doubt that different institutions and moral and social systems are appropriate to different societies: "human nature no where exists in the abstract."[13] Hence he defended the particular and emerged as an early opponent of the French Revolution, claiming that when opting between rival forms of government, any "fortunate people" will, like the British, adopt some mixed system, combining elements of monarchy and aristocracy, rather than embrace full democracy.

If one had to choose between British mixed monarchy and the republican democracy lately established by the Revolution, he remarked in 1792, it is easy to see which would be better. "Under one species of establishment, we observe the persons and possessions of men to be secure, and their genius to prosper" while under the other (that is, in France), we see "prevalent disorder, insult and wrong, with a continual degradation or suppression of all the talents of men."[14] Here, he diverged dramatically from English Radical Enlightenment writers, such as Richard Price, Joseph Priestley, John Jebb, William Frend, William Godwin, Mary Wollstonecraft, and the humbly born, irrepressible autodidact Tom Paine (1737–1809). In

Paine's opinion, given in 1792, England had not yet entered the democratic age of "reason" at all. "Conquest and tyranny," he wrote, "transplanted themselves with William the Conqueror from Normandy into England, and the country is yet disfigured with the marks. May then the example of all France," he fervently hoped, "contribute to regenerate the freedom which a province of it destroyed!"[15]

With regard to social and political life, the positions of Ferguson and Paine were diametrically opposed, with only the latter seeing the advent of democratic politics, and getting rid of monarchy and aristocracy, as properly an integral part of progress. Indeed, Paine, like the other philosophical radicals seeking to introduce democracy and equality into an essentially monarchical-aristocratic-imperial society (but with a strong commercial underlay), such as Britain was in the eighteenth and early nineteenth centuries, had an altogether more far-reaching conception of progress than Ferguson, not just politically and socially but also philosophically. To him, progress was inseparable from transforming attitudes as well as overturning the prevailing monarchical-aristocratic-ecclesiastical order, and not only in one country but universally. "The insulted German and the enslaved Spaniard," averred Paine, in 1792, "the Russ and the Pole, are beginning to think. The present age will hereafter merit to be called the Age of Reason, and the present generation will appear to the future as the Adam of a new world."[16]

This striking contrast between the progress of the radical democratic thinkers and that of defenders of mixed monarchy like Ferguson and Burke exactly mirrors the contrast between opposing broad tendencies running throughout the Western Enlightenment as a whole and making this clear is the chief aim of this chapter. For these two fundamentally different conceptions of progress—the radical democratic and, in metaphysics, materialist-determinist, or alternatively Christian-Unitarian, on the one hand, and the "moderate" and positively providential (Deist or religious), championing the monarchical-aristocratic order of society, on the other—were diametrically opposed to each other in their social and political consequences. They were also from the outset philosophically and theologically incompatible, and indeed opposed, which, on the whole, Enlightenment historians have failed to engage with.

A diffuse, highly complex and wide-ranging phenomenon such as the Enlightenment, we are apt to think, must reflect a great variety of shades of opinion and so it does. But when it came to the most crucial questions, as we shall see, both logic and circumstances precluded any real spectrum of opinion. On the main points, bridging the gulf between Radical democratic Enlightenment and moderate antidemocratic Enlightenment was literally inconceivable both philosophically and practically. The only thinker who seriously tried to bridge this antithesis conceptually, though even he does not really manage it, was Kant. Kant, as he often did, sought an ingenious, but perhaps overly subtle, synthesizing middle position between the "providentialists" and the "Spinozists." Building resolutely on his celebrated division of reality into the "phenomenal sphere" of sense, which we actually experience, and the "noumenal sphere" of reality-in-itself, which we know exists but the content of which is closed to us, he showed that a middle position is just about conceptually possible.

His great innovation, splitting reality into two distinct spheres of knowing sealed off from each other, was crucial in the history of metaphysics and epistemology, but far less so in the history of moral, social, and political ideas. It enabled him to steer adroitly between the physical order of "Nature," which he not infrequently designates the driving force behind "progress," and the "regular order which we observe in the course of events of this world" and "call Providence, as we discern in her the profound wisdom of a superior cause, which predetermines the course of fate, and makes it tend to the final purpose of human existence." By entrenching himself in this way in a highly ambiguous position located between blind fate and knowing Providence, the later post-1789 Kant, abandoning his earlier more conservative stance, stood firm with a foot in both camps, unfurling the banner of a pervasive liberalism, and qualified support for the French

Revolution, while at the same time expressly rejecting democracy and insisting that his philosophy was not anti-aristocratic or antimonarchical or opposed to religion.[17]

By postulating divine planning and "the finger of God" as the force behind both progress and the existing order, Ferguson, Kames, and Adam Smith, along with Voltaire and Turgot, effectively resigned all prospect of viewing the existing order of institutions and social relations as basically defective, as diverging unacceptably from equity and the natural path. If morality is God-ordained, held Voltaire in his *Essai sur les moeurs*, written in the early 1740s, then the moral ideas we discover through experience must be the correct ones; if the course of history is guided by divine Providence, then men's basic institutions must have been established upon the right lines. The great limitation of the Moderate Enlightenment was that it was not open to its theorists (assuming that temperamentally they had so wished) to repudiate the existing hierarchical structure of society, or portray society as it had evolved as inherently defective, oppressive, and systematically unjust, and hence wrongly organized for the purpose of advancing human happiness. They could not, like John Jebb (1736–1786), an academic who endeavored to reform Cambridge University in the 1770s but had been forced out in 1775,[18] acknowledge the need for across-the-board reform in all of a country's institutions, even in a flourishing society like Britain's. Though he died before the Revolution, by the 1780s Jebb had come to see the British House of Commons as an appallingly corrupt body: "the majority of that House are no longer the representatives of the Commons; they are," he deplored, "the dependents of the nobles, the creatures of the crown."[19] Neither could the moderate mainstream offer the kind of devastating critique of the European colonial empires embodied in the writings of the Abbé Guillaume-Thomas Raynal (1713–1796), Diderot, d'Holbach, Paine, and other radical thinkers, including the German philosopher Johann Gottfried Herder (1744–1803).

The Moderate Enlightenment was not opposed to reform as such, but did reject sweeping programs of reform like those envisaged by Paine, Priestley, and Price. Ferguson, like the foremost Scottish philosopher of the Enlightenment, David Hume (1711–1776), urged extreme caution—though admittedly not outright conservatism—when evaluating plans for the future depending on any "derangement in the only scenes with which we are acquainted."[20] Among the first theorists to analyze the phenomena of rank, social classes, and class exploitation, he was indeed a highly original thinker. His work continued to attract the attention of social theorists, including Hegel and Marx, during the nineteenth century. Yet he has remarkably little to say about the conflicts—economic, moral, and political—generated by the social divisions he was among the first to investigate. His prime criticism of the French *philosophes* as social critics, significantly enough, was that they were too prone to exaggeration of the evils of present and past society.

Hume, no less unreceptive to radical ideas, was viewed in conservative circles as a particularly useful philosophical resource against egalitarian and democratic ideas and was also invoked against colonial rebellion. Among his conservative admirers was one of the leading American "Tory" publicists who in 1776, under the pseudonym "Candidus" [William Smith?], published a tract insisting on the benefits of rule by Britain and glorying in the fact that "this beautiful system (according to Montesquieu), our constitution is a compound of monarchy, aristocracy and democracy," an empire dominating the Atlantic and the trade of the entire world. Implacably opposed to independence, "Candidus" went so far as to claim that "independence and slavery are synonymous terms," repeatedly citing "the profound and elegant Hume" against the subversive elements attempting to "seduce the [American] people into their criminal designs."[21]

At the close of his *Principles of Moral and Political Science* (1792), Ferguson memorably summed up the difference between the radical kind of Enlightenment he roundly rejected, and the sort of Enlightenment he endorsed, the empirically grounded path of moderation advocated by Turgot and Voltaire and most British and American participants in the Enlightenment.[22] The radical conception he repudiated (in France then variously termed *la philosophie nouvelle, philosophisme,* or simply *la philosophie moderne*)—the thought of Diderot, d'Holbach, Claude-Adrien Helvétius (1715–1771), the marquis de Condorcet (1743–1795), and such British and American radicals as Paine, Jebb, Joel Barlow, and Robert Coram—he compared to that of an ambitious architect who aspires to tear down the entire existing edifice of institutions and then rebuild it from scratch on purely rational principles. The intentions of these confident architects, as he saw it, were not in themselves bad though they betrayed a considerable lack of respect for the divinely fashioned order of things; the consequences, however, were to his mind catastrophic. He did not deny the need for improvements or to make society better. Indeed, he was convinced God wants us to strive for amelioration: even "the walls," he says, "may be renewed or rebuilt in parts successively." But his Enlightenment insisted on retaining most of the existing foundations, walls, and roof in place at any one time, making only marginal changes without altering the building's basic shape or removing so many "of your supports at once as that the roof may fall in."[23] The basic structure of government, law, and administration, as he and his Scottish colleagues and allies— Hume, Kames, Smith, William Robertson (1721–1773), and Thomas Reid (1710–1796) saw it—should remain always in place.

Between these two opposed conceptions obviously no compromise or half-way position was ever possible, either theoretically or practically. Throughout the Enlightenment's history it is this irresolvable duality—rooted in the metaphysical dichotomy of one-substance doctrine (Spinozistic monism) and two-substance dualism, the latter as upheld by John Locke (1632–1704) and Voltaire, as well as other providential Deists and (most) Christians and Jews—that was always the principal and overriding factor shaping its course.

Thus, while in the last two or three decades scholars have mostly fastened their attention on national or confessional differences between shades of Enlightenment in different parts of Europe, embracing the "family-of-enlightenments" idea developed by John Pocock (a notion still widely in vogue today), such an approach is largely inapplicable to the Enlightenment's most basic and far-reaching questions and controversies. For the "family-of-enlightenments" concept deflects attention from the most fundamental disputed points of thought, morality, and social action, among them the scope of reason, the possibility or impossibility of miracles, and the status of divine Providence, as well as the place of ecclesiastical authority and the split for and against democracy, equality, a free press, and separation of church and state. For all these were essentially either/or questions. Either history is infused by divine providence or it is not, either one endorses a society of ranks or embraces equality, one approves representative democracy or opposes it. On these questions it was the polarization, the division of opinion, that shaped developments.

Beyond a certain level there were and could be only two Enlightenments—moderate (two-substance) Enlightenment, on the one hand, postulating a balance between reason and tradition and broadly supporting the status quo, and, on the other, Radical (one-substance) Enlightenment conflating body and mind into one, reducing God and nature to the same thing, excluding all miracles and spirits separate from bodies, and invoking reason as the sole guide in human life, jettisoning tradition. There was a closely allied variant to the latter, also part of the Radical Enlightenment, in the shape of philosophical Unitarianism, a variant almost as relentless in proclaiming reason as the sole guide, rejecting tradition as a source of authority and denouncing the existing order more or less in toto. The essence of the Radical Enlightenment both in its atheist and Christian Unitarian modes was that "reason, and law founded on reason," as the point was expressed by Nicolas-Antoine Boulanger (1722–1759) in a classic text of radical philosophical literature, "should be the only sovereigns over mortals."[24]

To correctly grasp this basic dichotomy, without which the key points about the Enlightenment cannot be understood, it is essential to avoid simply equating the split (as many tried to do at the time) with the difference between theists and atheists. Many "atheists" and thoroughgoing skeptics—including Thomas Hobbes (1588–1679), Julien Offroy de La Mettrie (1709–1751), Hume, and the marquis de Sade (1740–1814)—were not at all "radical," in the sense the term is employed here, since they did not base morality on reason alone, or on the principle of equality, or link their conception of progress to equity and democracy. Neither did they possess that sense of being the heads of a "faction" in society, of an underground movement, opposing a dominant bloc and evincing that clandestine, proselytizing spirit and impulse to convert others to their way of thinking that, as Jean-Jacques Rousseau (1712–1778) stresses in his last work, *Les Rêveries du promeneur solitaire* (1777–1778), was a typical—indeed, he thought the prime — characteristic of the radical thinkers whom he, too, mostly labels simply the *philosophes modernes*.[25] These were the men (principally Diderot, d'Holbach, and their disciples) whom Rousseau, following his bitter and enduring quarrel with Diderot that began in 1757, came to perceive as "mes persécuteurs" and principal enemies.

"Radical Enlightenment" cannot in any way simply be equated with "atheism," or, still more vaguely, with freethinking or with libertinism or irreligion. As many contemporary critics stressed, the sort of ideas diffused by Diderot, d'Holbach, and their disciples in the 1770s and 1780s had an essentially "Spinozist" philosophical underpinning in that they envisaged philosophical reason as the only guide in human life, sought to base theories about society on the principle of equality, and separated philosophy, science, and morality entirely from theology, grounding morality (as Bayle notably also did, but Hume, equally notably, refused to do) on secular criteria alone and especially the principle of equality. Radical Enlightenment was further quintessentially defined by its insistence on full freedom of thought, expression, and the press, and by identifying democracy as the best form of government, features again specifically Spinozistic and in no way Hobbesian or, in the latter case, Humean. Neither did radical thought ever have anything concretely to do with Locke and still less (despite the continuing efforts of some to argue this)[26] with the English Commonwealth tradition or Freemasonry. Without classifying radical thought as a Spinozistic tendency, combining one-substance doctrine or philosophical monism with democracy and a purely secular moral philosophy based on equality, the basic mechanics of eighteenth-century controversy, thought, and polemics cannot be grasped.

However, classifying Radical Enlightenment as "Spinozistic" does not mean all believing Christians, Jews, and Muslims were excluded from participating in the radical tradition. In his clandestinely published *Tractatus Theologico-Politicus* of 1670, Spinoza holds that all the main churches had betrayed true Christianity by perverting it with humanly concocted "mysteries," dogmas, and ecclesiastical authority, though Christ's moral teaching remains the highest ethics and the purest tradition of moral teaching. He claimed that "disputes and schisms have ceaselessly disturbed the church ever since Apostolic times, and will surely never cease to trouble it, until religion is firmly separated from philosophical theories and reduced to the extremely few, very simple dogmas that Christ taught his own."[27] These boiled down, according to Spinoza, to the principles of justice based on equality, and charity.

Teaching "true" Christianity was something the Apostles and the church fathers failed to do, held Spinoza, "because the Gospel was unknown to people" then, so that "to avoid offending" the populace "with the novelty of its teaching, they adapted [Christianity], so far as they could, to the minds of their contemporaries and built upon the basic principles most familiar and acceptable at the time."[28] The result was a great heap of "superstition" piled on by theologians and the churches since Apostolic times, all of which, contends Spinoza, must be stripped away if one wishes to grasp the precious core. This Spinozistic doctrine opened the way for Spinoza's Christian Socinian Collegiant friends to join him and these "philosophical" Unitarians—men such as Pieter Balling (d. 1669), who translated much of his early work into Dutch; Jarig Jelles (c. 1620–1683), who wrote the preface to his *Opera Posthuma* (1677); and the Amsterdam publisher Jan Rieuwertz (c. 1616–1687), who published his writings clandestinely (despite all the mature works of Spinoza being banned by decree of the Dutch States General in 1678)—figured among his most important allies in late seventeenth-century Holland.

These men were sincere in their Christianity, yet also deeply influenced by the moral teaching expounded in Spinoza's *Ethics* (1677). By forging an alliance with them, Spinoza gained important adherents for his campaign of philosophical renewal and social reform. But the Socinians, too, gained much from their alignment, especially a new methodology of Bible criticism of unparalleled sophistication at the time, and one that seemingly undermined the authority of all established churches as well as rabbinic Judaism (while leaving open the possibility of a reformed Judaism), and that powerfully reinforced their own arguments against the doctrine of the Trinity and Christ's divinity. Spinozism also equipped them with a much more incisive and broader argument for toleration than any other thinker had yet come up with (and much broader than that of Locke), something of practical consequence to them since Socinianism was then banned practically everywhere, in theory even in Holland and post-1688 England. It also afforded them a system of ethics that not only eliminated all ecclesiastical authority but removed all dependence on theological notions that they eschewed, such as Original Sin, Spinozism rendering primitive man neither good nor bad morally but merely neutral and morality itself purely a function of society.

Remarkably, the alliance between Spinozism and Socinianism (or at least some Socinians) persisted not just through Spinoza's lifetime but virtually throughout the eighteenth century. In the enormously influential *Encyclopédie ou Dictionnaire raisonné des sciences, des arts et des métiers* (17 vols.; Paris, 1751–1765) of Diderot and d'Alembert, the powerful seventeen-page entry "Unitaires," pronounced by Voltaire the most *terrible*—meaning the most formidable—of all the articles in the later volumes, a piece penned by Diderot's disciple Jacques-André Naigeon (1738–1810) clearly states that what he, too, calls *la philosophie moderne*, itself materialist, had one major ally within the religious fold—the Christianity of the Unitarians. This needs emphasizing not just because Spinoza would not have achieved the impact and diffusion he did without the help of the Dutch Collegiants but because in the later eighteenth century—particularly in Britain, America, and Holland—Unitarianism and the Dissenting fringe infused with Socinianism produced some of the most effective spokesmen of the Radical Enlightenment and helped inject the radical tradition into many provincial and local groups, charities, and societies.

In the early eighteenth century, the very term "Socinian" still elicited general and intense disapproval. The beautifully illustrated *Cérémonies et coûtumes religieuses de tous les peuples du monde* (7 vols.; Amsterdam, 1723–1735), edited by the radical Jean-Frédéric Bernard (c. 1683–1744) and illustrated by Bernard Picart (1673–1733), the world's first real encyclopedia of religion, styles Socinianism a doctrine "so odious and dangerous," as the English version puts it, "with its subtle arguments and objections proposed," as to be little better than atheism. While "both Arians and Socinians deny the Trinity," the *Cérémonies* explains, only the Socinians refused to worship Christ and declared him a man, hence treating "Christ with much more indignity than the Arians ever did."[29] The *Cérémonies* summarized the key points of the Socinian (Unitarian) creed as rejection of Christ's divinity and the Trinity and the claims that "there is no such thing as Original Sin" and that "God might have forgiven the sins of mankind, and reconciled Man with divine justice, and pardoned them, without the satisfaction of Christ."[30]

While stressing the sect's allegedly dangerous character, the *Cérémonies* informs readers of the "astonishing progress that [Socinianism] has made through Europe."[31] Astonishing progress it certainly made: by the middle of the eighteenth century, Socinianism had spread dramatically both as an open church movement where this was permitted de facto—in some places in Holland, England, and Germany—and also privately within other churches, including the state churches. Consequently, France was by no means the only country where incredulity and religious subversion were perceived to have made huge inroads by 1750. As the Devon-based liberal Presbyterian minister Micaiah Towgood observed in 1755, there was "now a present prevailing scepticism" and such "a mighty prejudice, with some men of sense and consideration, against Christianity [as traditionally understood]" that many took seriously the unbelievers' claims that the established Church, the Church of England, showed "plain marks of imposture"; indeed, there were "violent and strong suspicions that it could not possibly come from God." Moreover, it was now only a "little less notorious in Britain, so strong was this scepticism," observes Towgood, that in their own thoughts the Anglican "clergy are, generally, gone far from the religious sentiments which the Articles [of the Church] expound and are many or most of them either Unitarian or Arian."[32]

The signs of the time, Towgood admonished the English bishops, showed that "Christianity is now passing a strict examination" and while, as far as he was concerned, his religion stood ready to undergo "the most critical search," the "consequence of this search, there is little question, will be that superstition must totter; and that all claims and pretensions of a spiritual kind not founded on truth, nor supported by right, must fall before the axe laid at the root." He implored the bishops to act—that is, thoroughly purge their theology of irrational, unfounded and unnecessary accretions—whilst there was still time to prevent those "having broken from the chains of gloomy superstition" from going from one extreme to the other, and from rushing "headlong into the wilds of disconsolate infidelity," Socinianism, and atheism.[33] The choice the bishops faced, he insisted, was to align with or be conquered by the force of reason.

If the evidence of book acquisitions in the college libraries at Harvard, Princeton, Yale, and Philadelphia (College of Pennsylvania) is anything to go by, there were scarcely any "philosophical Unitarian" works extant in America before the 1776 Revolution. After 1780, though, interest in such texts grew, a process accelerated from 1791 when the outspoken former New England Calvinist minister Eliahu Palmer (1764–1806) caused a great scandal in Philadelphia by publicly admitting his Unitarianism (he later became a militant Deist, opponent of Christianity, and fervent admirer of the French Revolution),[34] and from June 1794 with the arrival in America of Priestley himself.[35] The more intellectually minded wing of the Socinians, moreover, combined their Unitarianism with an emphatic linking of Unitarian doctrine with philosophy, on the one hand, and democracy and egalitarianism, on the other. The officially Arian but privately Unitarian Richard Price, described by one leader of eighteenth-century English Unitarianism, Theophilus Lindsey, as someone who "though an Arian [. . .] is one of the firmest Unitarians I know,"[36] when celebrating the fall of the Bastille in London in 1789, linked Enlightenment, civil emancipation on the basis of equality, and so-called Rational Dissent in the clearest terms. "Why are the nations of the world so patient under despotism?—Why do they crouch to tyrants, and submit to be treated as if they were a herd of cattle?" His unequivocal answer is because they lack Enlightenment. "Ignorance," he wrote, "is the parent of bigotry, intolerance, persecution and slavery." Enlighten mankind and it will not only get rid of tyrants and institute equality, a principle for which he was passionate, but also abandon the prevailing forms of Protestant and Catholic religion, grasping that true religion resides not in theology, or indeed, "in any rites and ceremonies, but in worshipping God with a pure heart and practicing righteousness."

Price, like Priestley, dismissed all conventional forms of Protestantism, including Presbyterianism and Baptism, as well as Anglicanism and Catholicism, as so badly corrupted as to be not truly "Christian" at all. In addition to the many among the higher ranks of men who "not distinguishing between the religion they see established and the Christian religion, are generally driven to irreligion and infidelity," there was also, he thought, great peril in England from undesirable forms of evangelical fervor spreading in society via new and disturbingly popular "irreligious" church movements welling up among "the lower orders." Very many "are sinking," as Price styled it, "into a barbarism in religion lately revived by Methodism."[37]

Unitarianism, then, is a vital part of the fundamental dichotomy characterizing the play of intellectual forces, and hence the history of philosophy in the period, and, also crucial, reflected in the interaction between social forces and ideas. For it was above all social forces that drove the polarization between Radical Enlightenment and the moderate mainstream until by 1770 it had reached boiling point, culminating in what Voltaire called a "guerre civile entre les incrédules." If one wished to attract the support of governments, churchmen, and magistrates in the eighteenth century one had to couch proposals for reform in terms of support for monarchy, for the existing social hierarchy based on privilege, and for the existing moral norms—in other words, propose only slight repairs to the existing edifice. Every Enlightenment writer had to choose either broadly to endorse the existing structure of law, authority, and privilege, whatever incidental repairs he proposed, or else denounce them more sweepingly. If he or she, as in the case of Mary Wollstonecraft or the feminist republican historian Catherine Macaulay (1731–1791), chose the latter course, circumstances inevitably pushed such would-be reformers into the arms of the out-and-out rejectionists and into the direction of democracy, equality, and revolt. For once spurned by those in authority, the only way to gain any support at all was to become a mouthpiece for social grievance and resentment.

Given the prevailing vast disparities of wealth in England as in the rest of Europe, the conspicuous lack of protection for the poor or unprivileged individual, extremely inadequate and archaic structure of the law and the penal code, the oligarchic, corrupt character of politics, and disabilities still applying to Dissenters,

Catholics, and Jews, social grievance was bound, in Britain, too, to be a broad impulse in the late eighteenth century. No doubt, as has been frequently observed, ordinary British folk were predominantly hostile to radical ideas. In Britain, the "sheer volume and the social and geographical distribution of [. . .] conservative propaganda was much greater than that disseminated by the radicals in the 1790s." But the very relentless and overwhelming character of the loyalist campaign—eulogizing the governing elite and constantly invoking "the rampant xenophobia and virulent anti-gallicanism that had long been a feature of British society"—and continual efforts "to arouse a profound loathing of British radicals and deep hatred of French revolutionaries" also reveal the scale of the perceived challenge.[38] The distinction between mainstream and Radical Enlightenment, driven by legal and social conditions, including gender discrimination, as much as by ideas, was thus both intellectually and socially an unbridgeable, polarizing dichotomy that no one could evade.

Finally, to define Radical Enlightenment fully and accurately one further distinction is necessary: that between the British Radical Enlightenment as part of the wider philosophical-ideological movement in the Western world and late eighteenth-century English radicalism in its narrower, more exclusively political and parochial sense. For there remained a hard core of often highly motivated radicals in late eighteenth-century Britain who cultivated the old seventeenth-century Commonwealth tradition. Typically these men were ardent for what they considered the "true" English constitution, a legacy revived but, as they saw it, not fully restored by the Glorious Revolution of 1688.[39] The leading reforming activist, John Thelwall (1764–1834), for instance, agreed with Price, Priestley, Paine, and Jebb that eighteenth-century British parliamentary monarchy, thoroughly corrupted by crown interference and "rotten-borough mongers," was really just a "usurped oligarchy," but, unlike them, took no interest in the philosophical grounding of human rights, in turning radical ideas into a universal ideology, or even in establishing a full democracy in Britain, being quite willing to accept that even when the "corruption" was corrected, Britain would still be what Thelwall termed a "limited democracy," with a House of Lords embodying its aristocratic element and an hereditary chief magistrate— namely, the king—acting as the country's chief magistrate. True Commonwealthmen, like Thelwall, were inclined to disapprove of those, like Paine and Priestley, whom they suspected were ready to plunge society "into commotion for speculative opinions."[40] In this respect they shared some of the distaste shown by Edward Gibbon (1737–1794), the foremost eighteenth-century English historian, and Edmund Burke (1729–1797), England's preeminent conservative philosopher, for what the latter labeled Priestley's and Price's "democratic fanaticism."[41]

Not only were radical enlighteners intellectually better placed than their Moderate Enlightenment opponents and nonphilosophical radicals to give expression to broadly based social discontent, grievance, and resentment; they were also driven by circumstances to repudiate the existing system of social hierarchy. This they denounced, along with its accompanying structures of law and institutions, as oppressive, rapacious, and fundamentally unjust. Priestley, who was well known on both sides of the Atlantic for his researches into electricity and chemistry, called for the total abolition of the aristocracy on the grounds that this would prove a moral blessing not only for society but also for the nobility themselves.[42] With the yawning divide extending in this way to social theory and politics, the split inevitably also generated conflict between competing factions at the local level, as in Ireland, for example,[43] and in late eighteenth-century Liverpool. It was an antagonism encompassing all major issues—totally indefinable along national, ethnic, or religious lines—even though by 1789 France had opted, for the time being, for radical solutions and by the mid-1790s Tom Paine, Godwin, Wollstonecraft, Coleridge, Price, Priestley, Frend, and the poet William Wordsworth (1770–1850) had all either been ejected from Britain or effectively silenced.

The struggle was between sweeping reformism versus a gradualist, conservative approach. It was also a battle between amelioration purely natural, on the one side, and supernaturally ordered and divinely guided progress, on the other, a fight between progress that drives toward equality and democracy and seeks to enlighten everyone, and marginal reform of the existing order of monarchy and privilege, backed by theological criteria, content (or even preferring), especially in Voltaire's and Frederick the Great's case, to enlighten only the few. The "revolution of the mind" the Radical Enlightenment had engineered among sections of society by the 1770s and 1780s through the clandestine spread of new ideas aspired one day to carry through a successful revolution of fact, leading to an entirely new kind of society. Such a perspective was roundly rejected by those who understood progress as divine Providence at work. Even the two opposed enlightenments' respective conceptions of "reason" were distinct and, before long, fiercely competing ideas. For the moderate mainstream, reason is immaterial and inherent in God, a divinely given gift to man, and one that raises him above the rest. In radical thought, by contrast, man is merely an animal among others with no specially privileged status in the universe while "la raison," as one radical text expressed it in 1774, far from being something beyond and above matter, is nothing but "la nature modifiée par l'expérience."[44]

Opposition and struggle, then, were inherent in the radical conception of history. Tom Paine summed up the story of human progress as a progression in three main stages. First, mankind evolved from the "government of priestcraft" in remote times to states based on "the uncivilized principle of governments founded in conquest" in more recent eras, a system in which aristocracy is the essential element and the whole edifice rests on schemes "to govern mankind by force and fraud, as if they were all knaves and fools." And, finally, the culmination of human progress, developing "in contradistinction" to life under rule rooted in "superstition and conquest"—that is, under the government of "reason," statecraft based on "the common interest of society, and the common rights of man."[45]

Hence the divide between Radical and Moderate Enlightenment is far more fundamental and also more enduring than distinctions within the Enlightenment that were national or confessional in character. But the dialectics of Enlightenment were also a shifting balance of intellectual forces in the course of which, from the 1760s down to the early 1790s, especially in Holland and France, the moderate mainstream were increasingly thwarted and repulsed and the radical wing increasingly preponderant. This occurred first intellectually and, then, for some years, in France and the Western European countries conquered by the French revolutionaries, especially the Netherlands and Italy, also politically. It was precisely this and the frustration and failures of the moderate mainstream after 1770 that lent formidable new vigor to both the loyalist anti-intellectualism that flourished in Britain and the general Counter-Enlightenment, the system of ideas that rejected both kinds of Enlightenment, insisting on the primacy of faith and tradition, not reason, as the chief guides in human existence. This reaction reared its head on all sides after 1770, and still more after 1789, as moderate mainstream Enlightenment, both in its Christian and Deist modes, was more and more humiliated and weakened.

The modern reader might be surprised by this outcome, as the existing historiography strongly suggests that the political cards were always stacked heavily against the radical wing. Admittedly, all the nobilities and monarchical courts of Europe opposed radical thought and, after 1789, became much more strident and aggressive in doing so, whether in Russia, Prussia, Austria, or Britain. It is worth noting that in Britain the bulk of the lower and middle orders of society proved entirely willing to unite under crown and Parliament in decrying radical activity and seditious writings.[46] But this was because, behind the scenes, democratic and egalitarian ideas were gaining ground and a fierce defensiveness, even signs of desperation, were taking hold of the *ancien régime*'s defenders. Nor should the sheer cumulative effect of the diffusion of radical ideas—that is, the impact of plain intellectual cogency fortified by genuine resentment against social injustice—be underestimated. The dramatic rise of the Counter-Enlightenment and the vehemence of the British public's loyalism and anti-intellectualism by the 1780s and 1790s are probably symptoms that the moderate mainstream, in the tradition of Montesquieu, Hume, and

Voltaire, was losing the fight to block radical intellectual arguments.

The last three decades of the eighteenth century were an age of much turmoil, instability, and revolutionary violence. But they were also an age of promise. The emancipation of man via forms of government promoting the "general good" and life in a free society that accords protection to all on an equal basis, argued d'Holbach in 1770, is not an impossible dream: "if error and ignorance have forged the chains which bind peoples in oppression, if it is prejudice which perpetuates those chains, science, reason and truth will one day be able to break them" (si l'erreur et l'ignorance ont forgé les chaines des peuples, si le préjugé les perpétue, la science, la raison, la vérité pourront un jour les briser).[47] A noble and beautiful thought, no doubt, but was he right? That perhaps, is the question of our time.

CHAPTER II

Democracy or Social Hierarchy?
The Political Rift

The Atlantic democratic revolutions of the later eighteenth century, then, were certainly caused by deeply rooted, complex "structural" change, a full-scale "revolution," but one of a kind that later nineteenth-century and twentieth-century historians and philosophers have found exceedingly difficult to come to grips with. The mistake in the historiography, arguably, has been to assume that developments driven by powerful social forces must have clear recent changes in social structure, some dramatic transformation of conditions, as their primary cause. This seems to be a fallacy and one that would seem to account for the confusion and frustration evident in the historiography of the French Revolution (as well as that of the British Counter-Revolution) over the last half century or so.

The real structural shift before 1789 has been broadly missed because it was a "revolution of the mind"; an intellectual transformation, bringing with it a huge cultural shift, the essential revolution that preceded the revolutions of fact. What proved to be the great strength of the Radical Enlightenment was that it was an ideological system that answered to long-standing and intrinsic grievances and needs of large portions of society, especially but by no means only on the European side of the Atlantic. Its great weakness was that it had to combat strongly held popular traditional beliefs and attitudes as well as *ancien régime* institutions and authority. For the great majority, in Europe no less than in Britain, believed, as Hume liked to stress, that the most fundamental features of society derive from age-old tradition, faith, and belief and have nothing to do with "reason" or principles. Very widely disapproved of and condemned throughout the eighteenth and nineteenth centuries, not least in Britain and America, the sweeping democratic egalitarianism of the Radical Enlightenment after 1770 has, curiously, not found much favor with modern historians either.

But however baffling the Enlightenment's "revolution of the mind" has so far proven for historiography, the fact remains that the most decisive phase in the rise of democracy, individual liberty, and egalitarian values to centrality within the Western World's value system was clearly the period from immediately prior to the American Revolution, say from around 1770, down to 1789. Neglected in the past, the astounding intellectual victories of the radical *philosophes* during these two fraught, bitterly

contested decades, as well as the ensuing torrent of egalitarian ideology engulfing France and Holland before
(even more crucially than after) 1789, were inseparably
linked to the revolutionary process that followed, a historical reality that must eventually assume a preeminent
place in all serious inquiry into the origins of modern
equality and democracy.

Arguably the French Revolution, preceded by and en-
twined as it was with both the American (1776–1783) and
the Dutch (1780–1787) revolutions, was no local occurrence happening in a particular country, as has generally
been assumed by historians and philosophers. For like the
rest of the revolutionary wave in the transatlantic world,
this great upheaval stemmed chiefly from a general shift
in perceptions, ideas, and attitudes gathering pace in the
1770s and 1780s that persuaded much of the reading elite
on either side of the Atlantic that "the wretched condition
of Man under the monarchical and hereditary systems of
government," as Paine expressed it, was incontrovertible
evidence "that those systems are bad, and that a general
revolution in the principle and construction of governments is necessary."[1]

In essence, the ideas driving the French Revolution,
and especially the Radical Enlightenment ideology of
"reason" infusing the rhetoric of key democratic revolutionary leaders (figures such as Mirabeau, Sieyes, Brissot,
Condorcet, Cloots, Volney, Maréchal, Cabanis, and other
anti-Rousseauist opponents of Robespierre), were no

different from those inspiring the Anglo-American Radical Enlightenment, or the more radical fringe of the important Dutch democratic movement of the 1780s and 1790s (figures such as Cerisier, Paape, Paulus, Vrede, or Irhoven van Dam). It was thus with considerable justification that the French Revolution was designated the "General Revolution" by Paine and by the Connecticut-born American radical Joel Barlow (1754–1812), who likewise personally participated in events in France: for actually there was little that was inherently French about the democratic ideology permeating the Revolution of 1789–1792.

The American Revolution was a crucial inspiration for the French, Dutch, German, and British democrats alike. But from the radical standpoint, it was also a disturbingly defective, truncated revolution. As Jacques-Pierre Brissot de Warville (1754–1793), the future French revolutionary leader, noted in 1783, no country had ever been so favorably placed as America now was to transform the previously prevailing order, where laws were fixed by those who ruled to buttress their own power and interests, rather than regulate society for the good of all. But would the Americans, asked Brissot, take the bold steps needed to erase the system of rank and privilege and the religious intolerance extended to the New World by the European colonial empires? Would they abolish the religiously sanctioned oppression of the past and only follow "the principles adopted by reason" (les principes adoptés par la raison)? [2]

The American Revolution's perceived shortcomings were widely broadcast by radical authors such as Mirabeau, Brissot, Cloots, Cerisier, Chastellux, Condorcet, Volney, and Paine, and Americans such as Benjamin Rush, Barlow, and Robert Coram, as well as, in part, Jefferson. Their reservations were neither few nor inconsiderable. Most glaringly, the revolution in the thirteen colonies had failed to emancipate the slaves, either at all, as in the southern states, or only in a qualified, partial manner, as in the north, though Condorcet at least expected abolition to come soon to New York, New Jersey, and other northern states and that "this stain would not long sully the purity of American laws."[3] Even in Pennsylvania, the home of abolitionism, where the Quakers who initiated the antislavery movement in the 1760s were strongest and where the work of abolition proceeded fastest, under the legislation of 1780 emancipation extended wholly only to future generations, existing slaves being eligible for freedom only from the age of twenty-eight.[4]

In New York, most existing slaves remained enslaved and even the slave trade continued for the time being.[5] In New Jersey, as late as 1790 John Witherspoon (1723–1794), philosopher and president of the College of New Jersey (today Princeton University) and one of the signatories of the Declaration of Independence, refused to back immediate and categorical emancipation of the remaining slaves.[6] Meanwhile, the Unites States' first president, George Washington, instead of giving an unequivocal example by publicly supporting abolition and freeing his own contingent of slaves on his Virginia estates, kept his slaves (and continued pursuing runaways) until he freed them under his will, after his death. Meanwhile, he quietly supported the idea of future emancipation but only privately, in a lukewarm fashion, standing aside from the bitter public quarrel that erupted during his presidency between abolitionists and slave owners.[7]

Philadelphia-born Benjamin Rush (1746–1813) was the earliest activist, broadly ideological advocate of equality and general opponent of slavery in America. He began attacking the institution of slavery well before the onset of the Revolution with his *Address to the Inhabitants of the British Settlements in America, upon Slave-Keeping* (1773). Co-founder and president of the "Pennsylvania Society for Promoting the Abolition of Slavery and the Relief of Free Negroes Unlawfully Held in Bondage" of 1774, he had been a fervent Evangelical as a young man. Yet his radical libertarianism stemmed not from this religious background (which he soon abandoned for a highly unconventional kind of Christianity), but from Enlightenment ideas that he avidly absorbed as a student in Edinburgh and in London and Paris in the years 1766–1769, when he met Hume, Ferguson, Diderot, the celebrated feminist Catharine Macaulay, and other eminent Enlightenment figures. He switched to radical ideas because skepticism, having destroyed his confidence in conventional political notions, led him to suspect, as he put it, "error in everything" he had previously been taught in America.[8]

A reader of Locke, Sidney, Montesquieu, and Helvétius, and (like Priestley and Price) an admirer especially of David Hartley's philosophy, Rush became an advocate of worldly progress based on liberty, equality, and fraternity in which all men would share. Like Price, though, he never accepted that unaided reason alone is the exclusive source of truth. After returning to his homeland, Rush became a famous medical and political reformer, and in religion, from 1780, for some years an advocate of "Universalism"—that is, the doctrine of universal salvation of souls irrespective of belief or behavior, the only theology that renders all souls equal and considers union between all the Christian denominations a necessity if "corrupted" Christianity is to be eradicated and mankind's interests promoted.[9] Like the Unitarians, to whom he was close, Rush stressed one's obligations to the entire human race, opposing all theology dividing Christians into separate denominations. Aspiring to unify reason with religion, he proposed stripping away practically all traditional theology.

Abolishing slavery topped the list of radical desiderata in America, but the Revolution's failure to emancipate the slaves struck Paine, Rush, and others as only its most obvious blemish. It had also overlooked the Amerindians in

a way that seemed deplorable to some and notably failed
to bring full toleration and liberty of conscience to small-
town America, a frequent complaint in moderate as in
radically enlightened circles at the time.[10] The new federal
constitution appeared to radical critics to assign excessive
power to the presidency, an arrangement they deemed a
deliberate bid to check the Revolution's democratic tendency. In addition, Rush and Coram complained that the
colonies had lamentably failed to foster a system of universal primary education to promote levels of literacy and
awareness indispensable to the proper exercise of democratic rights. Education was needed, urged Rush, to har-
monize "the wills of the people," "produce regularity and
unison in government," and further propagate the true
principles of the Revolution.[11] Like John Adams (1735–
1826) and Alexander Hamilton (1755–1804), most Americans deemed the Revolution complete once Britain recognized American Independence in 1783. Not so the Revolution's radical critics: "it remains yet to effect a revolution
in our principles, opinions, and manners," Rush assured
Price, "so as to accommodate them to the forms of government we have adopted."[12]

From early on, moreover, American society showed
distinct signs—highly disturbing to Diderot, Brissot,
Mirabeau, Rush, and Barlow—of deliberately encouraging the emergence of an informal aristocracy. In a passage
penned for the Abbé Raynal's *Histoire philosophique des
deux Indes*, lines written shortly after the Revolution's

onset in 1776, Diderot, confident that they would succeed, urges the insurgents to remember in building their new world not to allow inequality of wealth to become too great. He admonished them to "fear a too unequal division of wealth resulting in a small number of opulent citizens and a multitude of citizens living in misery, from which there arises the arrogance of the one and the abasement of the other."[13] This, he thought, would ruin what Mirabeau later called "la plus étonnante" of all revolutions, and the only revolution "philosophy" could endorse, since it would assuredly undermine the equality that is the fundamental principle of the democratic republic.

By 1784 there were even worries that formal, let alone informal, nobility might surreptitiously creep back in via the initiative among Washington's veteran officers, backed by the ardently anglophile Hamilton, to set up a permanent officers' association, the Order of Cincinnatus, with its own insignia, ranks, and marks of distinction. Initially welcomed by Washington himself (who for a time agreed to be the society's first president until he saw how much opposition it provoked), this proposal stirred up a considerable controversy. Despite the outcry against it, Mirabeau complained that there was insufficient awareness in the newly born United States of the danger inherent in plans to recreate the trappings of nobility. Military prowess and land ownership should never be permitted to become the basis for privileged social status in an enlightened republic.[14] Performance in reason and virtue, he claimed, is the only veritable "nobility" that exists on earth and the only "nobility" admissible by the truly enlightened.

Mirabeau held that the basic source of the threat to equality in the United States were the traditions and much cherished "prejudices" Americans had inherited from the English. The most damaging of these, in his opinion, were the Americans' inexplicable love of aristocracy, formal and informal, and their boundless respect for (and willingness to pay high fees to) lawyers.[15] Deference to men of rank and noble birth, however fundamental to *ancien régime* society, Mirabeau dismissed—five years before the onset of revolution in his own country—as rooted in pure "préjugés absurdes et barbares."[16]

Given the Moderate Enlightenment's commitment to upholding privilege, rank, and monarchy, as Hamilton made clear, even in America, there is adequate reason to identify the mainstream of the American Revolution, and the Constitution's Founding Fathers other than Jefferson, broadly with Moderate rather than Radical Enlightenment. They were content to work within one country. The Radical Enlightenment of the late eighteenth century, by contrast, developed as an active force on both sides of the Atlantic opposed not just to the European, Caribbean, and Ibero-American *ancien régime* but also offering a comprehensive critique of the "General Revolution" as it had thus far progressed in North America. Its spokesmen objected in particular to slavery in the Caribbean and also to the new situation in Canada, where, after 1763, the new British government had preserved intact the system of noble and ecclesiastical privileges and exemptions introduced originally under the previous French regime. Radical writers hoped that the American Revolution would not just continue internally but also accelerate the process of democratization in Europe, the West Indies, Spanish America, and elsewhere.[17]

Radical Enlightenment was a transatlantic phenomenon. But the quarrel between moderate and Radical Enlightenment ideas extended much further than this. All the European colonial empires—those of Russia, Portugal, Denmark, and the Dutch, as well as those of Britain, Spain, and France—had not only propped up old forms of social hierarchy but were actively creating robust and domineering new ones. The Russian crown and nobility were extending their grip over vast tracts. Sir William Jones (1746–1794), one of the chief figures of British moderate mainstream Enlightenment, himself stressed that the aim of the British judiciary in Calcutta in the 1780s was to ensure that the "British subjects resident in India be protected, yet governed by British laws; and that the natives of these important provinces be indulged in their own prejudices, civil and religious, and suffered to enjoy their own customs unmolested."[18] This meant preserving the caste system, amongst much else. That such hierarchies of customs, morality, and law were being extended in the world were anathema to the radical thinkers.

The central tenet in politics of the radical *philosophes* was that a good government is one where legislation and the lawmakers lay aside all theological criteria and ensure by means of laws that education, individual interest, political debate, and society's moral values "concourir," as Helvétius, a leading French materialist, expressed it, to the general good "au bien général."[19] This meant creating a common, universal framework of morality and law for all. Since privilege, vast inequality of wealth and status, and the prevalence of monarchy, aristocracy, and ecclesiastical authority were then the foremost features of European societies—as well as of Canada, the Caribbean, Brazil, Spanish America, China, and British India—no one applying the radical *philosophes'* criterion of what constitutes good government could evade their electrifying conclusion that therefore hardly any satisfactory governments existed and that only "la philosophie moderne" could demonstrate what an adequate government and set of social values would actually look like.

Radical Enlightenment, then, was the primary intellectual source of the dynamic rhetoric of democratic egalitarianism propagated during the twenty years before 1789 by the numerous disciples of Diderot, Helvétius, and d'Holbach, most obviously Mirabeau, Brissot, Condorcet, Cerisier, Raynal, Maréchal, Cloots, and Volney, besides

Jefferson, Paine, Priestley, and Price, but also including numerous other British, American, Dutch, and German as well as French writers. Their writing and speeches represented a vast flow of democratic ideology, filling hundreds of tracts and pamphlets, and engendered an entire new language of freedom, combating tyranny, and human rights. It was this outpouring of thought and writing, the evidence shows, that was the most active and chief factor in shaping the democratic tendency contained within the American Revolution and the Dutch *Patriottenbeweging* (1780–1787) and culminating in the French Revolution.

While a perplexing notion for us, it seemed perfectly obvious to most contemporaries that "modern philosophy"—as it was (usually disparagingly) named in England in the 1790s—was the chief engine of the revolutionary process. Condorcet, for instance, held that "philosophy" caused the Revolution and that only philosophy could cause the kind of revolution that entails (and yet simultaneously depends on) a rapid, complete, and thorough transformation in thinking about the basic principles of politics, society, morality, education, religion, international relations, colonial affairs, and legislation all at the same time. Although this view remained broadly current from 1789 down to the mid-nineteenth century, later it came to be completely obfuscated by the dogmas of Marxism, which insisted that only changes in basic social structure can produce major changes in ideas, as well as by the kind of dogmatic anti-intellectualism promoted in the

1950s and 1960s by Alfred Cobban and others, and then latterly by Postmodernism. All insisted on the impossibility of intellectual debates and ideas playing a fundamental role in shaping societal change.

However, as we have seen, it was not ideas on their own that did the work. The late eighteenth-century *ancien régime* world, still extending, even after American independence, to large parts of the New World, was one ruled by princes and nobilities, and characterized by huge inequalities of wealth and legally buttressed privilege besides highly archaic legal systems and institutionalized discrimination, including legalized penalization of religious minorities and homosexuals. Newspapers, writers, and the book-trade were fettered by severe censorship in France and even stricter controls in Italy, Spain, Portugal, and Ibero-America, as well as the Austrian Habsburg Empire. Serfdom prevailed in much of Eastern Europe. In Holland hundreds of men were executed for the "crime" of homosexuality during a wave of fierce persecution in the 1730s. Women were everywhere held by law in strict subordination, first to their fathers and then to their husbands, and "still reckoned" by men, as Wollstonecraft put it, "a frivolous sex, and ridiculed or pitied by the writers who endeavor by satire or instruction to improve them."[20] Marriage, for propertied upper-class women, was such a trap of legal subordination to husbands that Wollstonecraft judged it "a melancholy truth, yet such is the blessed effect of civilization! the most respectable women are the most oppressed; and, unless they have understandings far superior to the common run of understandings, taking in both sexes, they must, from being treated like contemptible beings, become contemptible."[21]

To demolish such an edifice of oppression and prejudice was a staggeringly vast undertaking. American developments were suggestive, though, of what such a "revolution of the mind" might deliver. European writers visiting America in the 1780s and 1790s, Brissot and Volney among them, noted that practically everyone in the United States enjoyed at least a modicum of dignity and prosperity, as well as liberty, whereas most men and women in Europe eked out their lives in hardship and destitution. This appeared to signify that most lives were avoidably and unnecessarily impoverished, miserable, dependent, and oppressed, a conclusion the moderate mainstream Enlightenment indignantly denied. For a divinely ordained order cannot be one that reduces the majority to avoidable degradation. Certainly, some are rich and command while most have nothing and obey, Voltaire granted in 1771, but this did not mean, in his view, that they are unjustly exploited. Ranks, nobility, and inequality of wealth are simply inherent in human life. Most must toil to live and while toiling, he contended, have no time to be miserable. Only when jolted out of their usual prejudices do men become unhappy; and it is then that serious trouble starts.[22] Hence he maintained that "philosophy" ought not try to enlighten the majority.

Unquestionably, the moderate view was by far the more widely embraced everywhere and at all social levels: the world and everything in it were created by God and the social order is divinely sanctioned. According to the many infused with the ideas of Leibniz and Christian Wolff in Germany, Scandinavia, and Russia, God had ordered the world in the best way possible. Yet by the 1770s not a few concurred in the prime Radical Enlightenment premise— that existing society presented a scene of chronic deprivation and disorder—and demanded to know why and how to change it. What remedy can there possibly be, asked d'Holbach in 1773, for "la dépravation générale des sociétés," where so many factors combine to perpetuate the prevailing disorder and misery? There is only one way, he urged, to cure such a mass of ills: abolish the whole corrupt system of rank, privilege, and prejudice and substitute a more equitable society. And there is only one way to undertake such a task: namely, attack "error" and proclaim "the truth." "If error, as everything shows, is the source of all the evil on earth," held d'Holbach, if men are vicious, intolerant, oppressed, and poor because they have totally wrong ideas about "their happiness" and about everything else, then it can only be by fighting "error" with courage and resolution, by showing men their true interests and propagating "des idées saines" that society's defects can be tackled. When these are structural and deeply rooted in credulity, trust in authority, and ignorance, then "philosophy" is not just the aptest but only agent potent enough to precipitate a rapid, all-encompassing revolution.[23]

Re-educating the public, accordingly, seemed the crucial first stage toward renewing society in a fairer way. Helvétius, who was a strong advocate of education as a tool, realized that instituting the right kind of general education was an unattainable goal without its being accompanied by a thoroughgoing political revolution, the best outcome of which in a large country like France, he thought, being either a federal republic or else a league of around twenty small republics linked together for mutual defense. Once suitable forms of government exist, and good laws are adopted, these will naturally direct the citizenry to the general good while simultaneously leaving each individual free to follow his or her own personal quest for their own particular happiness.[24] Helvétius's ultimate aim was to forge a system of legislation and institutions binding private interest to the public interest and "establishing virtue on the advantage of each individual."[25]

This implies that the radical *philosophes* were more than just "chefs de parti," as Rousseau disparagingly labeled them,[26] seeking influence and to change opinion. They were also deliberate, conscious revolutionaries. Like Helvétius (and also Voltaire), d'Holbach remarks that the defenders of throne, altar, and privilege—those he calls "the enemies of human reason"—constantly accused the radical *philosophes* of being subversives, rebels, "des factieux," enemies of all authority. But where Voltaire denied that his kind of *philosophe* was in any way subversive, d'Holbach countered that "tyrants and priests were the 'true rebels,'" that those who forge the oppression provoke the aware, honest and well-intentioned to turn against the false sway that they illegitimately usurp. It is those who hold power in *ancien régime* society who render authority "détestable" and force good men to "contemplate its ruin." He declared that to flatter despots, burn incense to tyranny, endorse those whose business it is to destroy the common good—courtiers, aristocrats, magistrates, and priests—is not rightful submission to legitimate authority but betrayal of one's fellow men and country, and complicity in the outrages everywhere committed against the human race.[27]

D'Holbach argues that real treason is not subversion of the existing order, but rather the flattery and "pious" conduct of sycophants and intriguers who, helped by priestcraft and superstition, facilitate the tyranny of princes and aristocrats. It is despotism itself, buttressed by ignorance and credulity, that harasses people to the point that they feel compelled to retaliate, and, while most understand neither why nor how they are cheated, drives them to seek the ruin of the existing order. Certainly, the radical *philosophes* hesitated to condone violence: "revolt is a terrible recourse," agreed Diderot, "but it is the only one that works in humanity's favour in lands oppressed by despotism" (mais c'est la seule qui reste en faveur de l'humanité dans les pays opprimés par le despotisme).[28] Radical Enlightenment, aiming to correct what d'Holbach calls the "peu de sagesse," the negligence and perversity of teachers and "guides of men,"[29] and finally discredit those responsible for filling the world with prejudice, superstition, bad laws, and bad institutions—that is, instigate an intellectual and moral revolution designed to render society and individuals happier—from the 1770s came to be heavily infused with political revolutionary expectations and denunciations of tyranny.

Originating in the 1750s with Diderot's and Rousseau's widely noticed political articles in the *Encyclopédie*, the then (already) partly politicized propaganda war waged by the radical *philosophes* against *ancien régime* institutions in general, rapidly gained momentum. This was reflected in a growing stream of clandestine, and from the 1760s, increasingly politically radical books, such as Boulanger's posthumous political masterpiece *Recherches sur l'origine du despotisme oriental* (1761), edited by d'Holbach, which plausibly recounts how and why, for most of recorded history, society had been ruled by forms of theocracy, and then divine-right monarchy, with the result that individual rights and personal liberty had been systematically trampled upon. This was followed by d'Holbach's key article for the *Encyclopédie*, entitled *Représentants*, a stepping-stone in the development of democratic revolutionary political thought that roundly rejects the claims of the nobility and clergy to speak in the nation's name.[30] Penned around 1763, the piece contained important input from Diderot,[31] and was followed in 1766 by Boulanger's influential *L'antiquité dévoilée.*

The pace quickened from 1770, when d'Holbach's *Système de la nature*, despite appearing clandestinely, achieved an unprecedented degree of penetration throughout Western Europe and was widely perused, notes Voltaire, by artisans and women as well as by *savans.*[32] This text, with its one-substance monistic metaphysics drawn from Hobbes and Spinoza, in part via the writings of Toland,[33] proved highly subversive politically, as well as philosophically and religiously, and was later invoked by one enthusiastic radical, under Napoleon, as "the most beautiful monument which philosophy has erected to reason" (Le *Système de la nature* est le plus beau monument que la philosophie ait élévé à la raison).[34] Radical political thought eventually swelled into an astonishingly broad torrent of revolutionary literature that penetrated everywhere in the 1770s and 1780s with the openly egalitarian, democratic, and anti-colonial late works of Diderot, Raynal, d'Holbach, Helvétius, and Mably, soon further expanded upon by Mirabeau, Brissot, Cerisier, Cloots, Condorcet, Volney, and the rest.

D'Holbach, in his *Essai sur les Préjugés* (1770) and *Système social* (1773), identifies two great "powers"—namely, organized religion and government—that have traditionally combined to preclude enjoyment of the benefits that society ought to confer on all men. Government has done this, he contends, by dividing men according to their vested interests and advancing the happiness of those who rule at the expense of the rest. Society in his day performed its job of harmonizing the interests of all under the protection of the law so wretchedly that certain "penseurs découragés"—that is, Rousseau—had concluded that life in society is "contrary to the nature of man" and the wisest course is to renounce society altogether. This was indeed Rousseau's position in his last works. But such a recourse, held d'Holbach, is wholly misconceived and immoral.[35] Men have not degenerated in society, he argued; it is simply that reason has not yet developed sufficiently for them properly to take advantage of it. "La corruption des peuples" is the necessary effect of powerful causes that conspire to blind men and retain them in an eternal infancy.[36]

This new ideology that held that the moral, social, and political transformation of man, striving for amelioration or renewal on a better basis, can only be generated by a universal revolution driven by the active agent of *la philosophie*, was, of course, totally incompatible with the social and moral conservatism of a Montesquieu, Voltaire, Ferguson, or Hume. None of the latter thought in terms of a comprehensive or polarized struggle, or of one forced on those capable of enlightenment by what Diderot and d'Holbach called the truly brutal, destructive, and savage ignorance of men "and those who govern."[37] "A morally blind politics," proclaimed d'Holbach, "guided by interests entirely contrary to those of society does not allow men to become enlightened either about their own rights, or their true duties, or about the true ends of the association which it continually subverts."[38] Eventually, even such supposedly "enlightened" despots as Frederick the Great and Catherine the Great had somehow to be supplanted or pushed aside. As for rank, privilege, and aristocratic fiscal exemptions, these contradicted every principle of equity, justice, and morality and were the very contradiction of the "general will." In fact, concludes d'Holbach, here preceding Mirabeau and Priestley by some years, all distinction of orders, privilege, and forms of legal discrimination should be abolished.[39]

The chief problem of politics, as Diderot and d'Holbach understood it, was to prevent those being governed from becoming the prey of those who rule.[40] In the eighteenth century Britain was frequently alleged to be much better governed than most countries. Conservative Enlightenment authors such as Ferguson were adamant that "notwithstanding the disdain of [Price]," as the former put it in his tract of 1776 opposing the American Revolution, the British constitution remained superior to "any other constitution in the known world; and notwithstanding the high ideas of liberty with which it is contrasted does actually bestow upon its subjects higher degrees of liberty than any other people are known to enjoy."[41] But Radical Enlightenment writers viewed matters very differently.

Price deplored the absurdly narrow and undemocratic electorate—a mere 300,000 out of seven million, even suggesting, to Ferguson's indignation, that a pure monarchy might be better than the corrupt aristocratic oligarchy that was the result.[42] In a letter of September 1785 Jebb averred that the British had become "helpless prey to the depredations of ministers of state."[43]

Unlike Voltaire, Montesquieu, Ferguson, and Hume, Radical Enlightenment writers characteristically rejected British-style mixed monarchy on principle as a recipe for dividing sovereignty, introducing unnecessary forms of corruption into politics, manipulating an electoral system that did not provide elected representatives in remotely equal ratios to electors, and preserving what was effectively a modified monarchy encased in aristocracy. Gabriel Bonnot de Mably (1709–1785), an austere republican hostile to Voltaire, had already severely criticized British-style mixed monarchy in his *Observations sur les Romains* (1751).[44] But the trend intensified during and after the American Revolution. Unlike the moderate mainstream that always remained emphatically anglophile, the Radical Enlightenment grew increasingly antagonistic to Britain's global preponderance, attitude to foreign nations, mercantilist economic system, and mixed constitution, a hostility that proved entirely mutual.

But if they rejected mixed monarchy neither did Diderot, d'Holbach, Paine, Jebb, or Priestley—unlike

Rousseau—see the solution in Athenian-style direct democracy. The rooted instability and dismal failure of the direct democracies of ancient Greece had been analyzed by Boulanger in his *Recherches* with a thoroughness that convinced many that a people's republic on the classical model, or that of Rousseau, must revert to theocracy—a form of government considered worse than any other in radical eyes—since only theocracy accords popular religion and popularly venerated priests the principal role in formulating legislation and managing public affairs.[45] Since the common people—being credulous, fanatical, and illiterate—cannot escape the tyranny of superstition, priestcraft, and demagogues on their own, Boulanger concludes that humanity must opt either for constitutional monarchy or else a system of elected representatives.

Like the Dutch democratic Patriots of the mid-1780s— Pieter Paulus, Gerrit Paape, Irhoven van Dam, and Pieter Vrede—the French radical thinkers simultaneously wanted all to be free in the sense of enjoying equal protection under the law and equal liberty to pursue their own ambitions and goals while refusing to accept that this necessarily entails direct participation of all in the business of lawmaking and government, on the model of the ancient democracies. Direct democratic government appeared to them, no less than to Kant, an impossible "chimère," an invitation to the worst demagoguery, tumult, and license, a form "totally incompatible with our nature" and the general will.[46]

How then could democracy and equality be truly based on justice, reason, and genuinely enlightened ideas? Pieter Paulus (1754–1796), after becoming pensionary of Rotterdam at an early age, developed into one of the foremost intellectual as well as political leaders of the Dutch democratic revolution. His egalitarian theorizing culminated in his 216-page *Verhandeling over de Vraag: in Welken Zin kunnen de Menschen gezegd worden Gelijk te zijn* (1793) (Treatise Concerning the Question: In What Sense Can People Be Said to Be Equal), mostly written in 1791, which, though referring frequently to Montesquieu—and to a lesser extent Price, Paine, Locke, and the seventeenth-century English republican political thinker Algernon Sidney (1623–1683)—is chiefly based on the radically egalitarian strand in Rousseau's political thought and especially the un-Hobbesain, Spinozistic idea that the equality of man in the state of nature, far from being dissolved, is carried over and reinforced in society. In this way, equality becomes, as it was not before (in the state of nature), a moral and legal equality firmly grounded in the social compact itself.[47] It is true that following his radicalization in the mid-1780s, Paulus still admired and cited Rousseau. But in crucial respects he, like Cloots and many other democratic theorists of the 1780s, also became an outspoken critic of Rousseau. For the inestimable freedom and equality of the individual proclaimed by Rousseau seemed to them to be directly contradicted by his peculiar conception of "volonté générale" that stressed the particularity and distinctiveness of nations, the oneness of the nation's "general will," and urged loyalty to traditional sentiment and a strong version of patriotism.

To assert, as Rousseau does in the *Social Contract* (1762), objected Paulus in 1791, that each of us places his or her person and all his power under "la suprême direction de la volonté générale," each becoming indivisibly a part of the whole, so that where any individual refuses to obey the "general will" that person "must be forced to be free," is to invite terrible abuse, suppression of the rights of the individual, and the sort of tyrannical behavior that Paulus thought the French national assembly was already becoming complicit in by 1791.[48] Fiercely opposing the conservative Enlightenment philosophy of Burke but warmly concurring with Paine, Paulus expounded the rights of man, as he understood them, under sixteen headings, taking great care to delimit the power of the sovereign and safeguard the rights of the individual, in this way defusing what he saw as the wrong-headed totalitarian dimension of Rousseau's thought.

Rejecting direct or "simple democracy," as Paine called it, of the sort Rousseau recommended, the early architects of the philosophical democratic revolution, in Holland as in France and Britain, searched for a convincing solution to the problem of how to organize a workable and effective democracy. The key political tool they devised was that of representation as a way of organizing large-scale democracies on a viable and stable basis and of democratizing mixed monarchies. A concept clearly sketched by Diderot, d'Holbach, and their Parisian "synagogue" in around 1763 for the article *Représentants*, in the *Encyclopédie*, it henceforth figured prominently in the work, among others, of d'Holbach and Mably. It also constituted one of the prime differences between what we might call mainline European radical republican ideology in the 1760s and 1770s, with its plea for an unregulated, free press, and the republican deviationism of Rousseau, with its very different conception of the "general will" and its plea for strong press censorship.[49] For it remained one of Rousseau's cardinal doctrines that popular sovereignty, being unlimited, cannot be delegated and that representatives must therefore always be supervised, strictly mandated by their constituents, and subject to censorship.[50]

Rousseau's conception later developed into the revolutionary rhetoric of "will," sentiment, and undivided popular sovereignty, which stood in opposition to the Radical Enlightenment impulse within the French Revolution, or the discourse of "reason," as it has been aptly termed.[51] Rousseau's notion of sovereignty as "indivisible and inalienable," something that "could be neither delegated nor represented," required strong press censorship not least to check the influence of the *philosophes modernes* whom he blamed for propagating views about God, the soul, patriotism, and women entirely contrary to those of the common people.[52] Consequently, Rousseau's political goals all tended to an agenda that the radical *philosophes*—d'Holbach, Diderot, Helvétius, and Mably, and all the major Dutch Patriot spokesmen—in varying degrees deplored and consciously strove to avoid. D'Holbach and Diderot, furthermore, denied that their model entailed any diminution of individual liberty when compared with Rousseau's model. Sovereign in appearance, in reality the common people in a direct democracy are the slaves of "perverse demagogues" who know how to manipulate and flatter them. In direct democracy the people often have no real conception of what liberty is and their rule can be harsher than that of the worst tyrant. Liberty without reason, held d'Holbach, is of scant value in itself; consequently, the "history of most republics," he admonished, "continually conjures up the gruesome picture of nations bathed in their own blood by anarchy."[53]

Radical Enlightenment, then, is partly defined by an emphatic, anti-Rousseauist preference for representative democracy. The revolutionary character of the summons to transform government on an egalitarian and democratic basis—whether in its French, Dutch, British, Irish, or American version—was by the 1770s manifested in a steadily louder and more insistent call for a system of democratic elections, participated in by all qualified citizens, designed to produce experienced and qualified representatives of the people who would be regularly changed through elections, a procedure from which the hereditary and aristocratic principles would be entirely excluded. Here was a concept approximating far more closely to what we today would call "democracy" than the originally medieval system of representation by "estates" that still lingered in Europe in the eighteenth century. The essential difference between representation according to the traditional "estates" model and the new conception of *assemblée nationale,* or "senate," propounded by radical *philosophes,* Dutch democrats, and American Founding Fathers was the elimination of hereditary or privileged access together with the inalienable right to convene whenever the representatives saw fit, along with effective control of the state revenues to ensure these were expended "to serve the true needs of the state" and not used by the king to corrupt the "representatives of the people," or sustain, in d'Holbach's words, "la splendeur et la vanité d'une cour."[54]

The *assemblée nationale,* d'Holbach's term for this new representative gathering, would also be empowered to establish regional assemblies and, last and most crucial, would control the armed forces. This *assemblée nationale* could never be dissolved by a monarch but could be annulled by the people if it no longer faithfully performed its task of legislating and governing in the "public interest." Meanwhile, provided this body did represent "the general will" of society faithfully, it would always be justified in forcibly overpowering and disarming aristocratic cliques, religious factions, royal pretenders, or would-be dictators conspiring to unseat or violate the "general will." If every individual of our species has "the right" to defend himself against aggression, contended d'Holbach, by what strange jurisprudence do apologists for monarchy and priestcraft deny to entire nations the right to resist their tyranny?[55]

If neither the hereditary principle, nor high office, nor royal favor, qualified individuals for election to the *assemblée nationale*, what did? Here we encounter what some might regard as the Achilles' heel of the radical program. Those who should "naturally" have the right to represent the nation, argued Diderot and d'Holbach, were those "citizens" best informed about its affairs, needs, and rights, "persons of superior education and wisdom," as the English radical William Godwin later styled them, who were therefore "the most committed to the public well-being" (les plus intéressés à la félicité publique).[56] D'Holbach's answer to those who questioned whether, in democratic elections, the people would in fact elect the best-informed and intentioned sounds to our ears naïvely optimistic: "I reply that the people rarely makes mistakes about the character of citizens which it scrutinizes."[57] Provided corrupt practices were eliminated from the electoral process, the deputies chosen, he trusted, would be "enlightened," honest, and virtuous.

This blueprint for democracy was then widely taken up by Dutch and other publicists in the 1780s. While denouncing the Orangist court at The Hague, the Dutch democrats at the same time decried the corrupt regent oligarchy monopolizing the city governments in the United Provinces, whom they designated self-seeking "Aristokraten." The Dutch Patriots' key ideologues—Schimmelpenninck, Paulus, Cerisier, Vrede, and Paape—tended to follow Mably, Rousseau, Diderot, d'Holbach, Condorcet, Paine, and Mirabeau in criticizing the British constitution, Parliament, and "mixed monarchy," and avowing "equality" and democracy the overriding principles in an enlightened politics.[58] They also roundly rejected Montesquieu's central theses that different forms of government suit different societies according to their particular character and moral systems, and that democracy as well as aristocracy "are not by their nature free governments," indeed, as Ferguson states, agreeing with Montesquieu, "are inferior in this respect to certain species of monarchy, where law is more fixed and the abuses of power are better restrained."[59]

Interested as they were in developing a universal system of rights and egalitarian values, the Dutch democrats disliked both Montesquieu's relativism and his aristocratic preferences, enthusiasm for constitutional monarchy, praise of Britain, and antipathy to the Dutch Republic (where nobility played scarcely any role). Hence, in the Dutch political battles of the day, Montesquieu's thought proved far more conducive to Orangist than to the democratic ideology of the radical Patriots.[60] Nevertheless, he was much respected, especially by those of moderate and conservative views, so that in the Dutch political debates of the 1780s he was no less frequently cited than Rousseau and Mably, and far more so than Locke, or even Price and Priestley, though both the latter appeared in Dutch translation and were avidly read by those to whom democratic ideology appealed—that is, to the more radical Dutch *Patriotten* of the 1780s.

Among the theoretically more accomplished *Patriotten* was Rutger Jan Schimmelpenninck (1761–1825), a gifted young lawyer of Mennonite background, from Deventer, later to be the last Grand Pensionary of the Batavian Republic (1805–1806). In 1784 he published, first in Latin and the following year in Dutch, his ardently republican and democratic *Verhandeling over eene wel ingerichte volksregeering* (Treatise Concerning a Well-Constituted People's Regime). Schimmelpenninck proclaimed representative democracy, through regular elections, the best way to extend democratic principles to large and medium-sized countries, and also complex federal entities like the United Provinces. Representative democracy was embraced by Schimmelpenninck once again in the context of a thoroughgoing critique of Rousseau and expressed with an incisiveness matched later by Paine but one that had few parallels in the Europe of the early 1780s.[61] His footnotes suggest that he, too, figured among the many Dutch democrats moving to radical positions before 1787, who did so primarily under the stimulus of French republican theory rather than British ideas.[62]

Before long the same call for representative democracy was taken up no less forcefully in Britain itself by Paine, Godwin, Bentham, and their followers, as well as by Price and Priestley. "By ingrafting representation upon democracy," wrote Paine in 1791, "we arrive at a system of government capable of embracing and confederating all the various interests and every extent of territory and population; and that also with advantages as much superior to hereditary government, as the republic of literature is to hereditary literature."[63] Scholars have generally assumed that the response was much weaker in Germany. Recent research shows, however, that there are grounds for qualifying this assumption. Admittedly, in Germany the network of princely courts, imperial and ecclesiastical tribunals, and ecclesiastical authorities—along with a thick overlay of overlapping jurisdictions, legal mechanisms, and customary law—staffed by jurists and officials churned out in awesome quantity by an academic machine of over thirty universities prioritizing theology, law, and scholastic versions of Wolffian philosophy looked denser and more intractable than anywhere else. Here moderate mainstream Enlightenment seemed impregnable. But precisely because the *ancien régime* edifice of the Holy Roman Empire was so tightly linked to princely authority, privilege, nobility, and ecclesiastical authority, it generated a robust clandestine intellectual reaction that, from the later 1770s, fed a widespread social and cultural rebellion "of the mind" partly organized in the form of underground subversive networks.

The two foremost figures of the German Radical Enlightenment, Gotthold Ephraim Lessing (1729–1781) and Johann Gottfried Herder, it must be granted, steered clear of the secret societies as well as most forms of practical involvement; they needed to watch their step. As it was, Lessing, director in his last years of the great library at Wolfenbüttel, was debarred by his local prince, Ferdinand, duke of Brunswick, from publishing various of his late writings. Behind the scenes, though, both Lessing and Herder labored to establish a viable basis for a pervasive German intellectual and cultural radicalism that was political as well as moral, religious, and literary. Like the young Goethe, both drew their deepest inspiration, as scholars have often remarked, from Spinoza (whom Lessing and Herder both studied more intensively than they did the other great philosophers and with particular care at certain stages of their careers); also, among contemporary French thinkers, both rated Diderot most highly.[64]

At the end of Lessing's life, Friedrich Heinrich Jacobi (1743–1819)—the writer who in the 1780s strove to alert German opinion to the "dangers" posed by Spinoza's system and alarm the public—challenged him in a personal encounter, remarking, "I certainly did not expect to find in you a Spinozist or pantheist, and you put it to me so bluntly! I had come chiefly hoping to receive your help against Spinoza." Lessing replied, "Then you really know him?" On hearing that Jacobi, too, had made a particular study of Spinoza's ideas and believed "hardly anybody has known him as well as I," Lessing famously retorted, "There is no other philosophy than the philosophy of Spinoza" (es gibt keine andre Philosophie, als die Philosophie des Spinoza), meaning there was no other system so fully cogent and consistent. With this judgment, as it happened, Jacobi fully concurred. This was why he had decided to combat all Enlightenment philosophy without exception, insisting that reason cannot serve as mankind's principal guide. In his view, a leap to faith alone affords a viable escape from the crisis into which German culture and society had been thrust by "philosophy."[65]

On receiving Jacobi's report of his encounter with Lessing, Herder rejoiced at finding in the latter such a distinguished "fellow believer in my philosophical credo." He, too, considered Spinoza the only fully coherent philosopher.[66] These details are well known to Enlightenment scholars, but few have noted the implications of Lessing's and Herder's neo-Spinozism with regard to their cultural and intellectual reform proposals. Lessing, not least through his last and most famous play, *Nathan der Weise* (1779), advanced the most comprehensive toleration plea of the German Enlightenment and the only one expressly to place Muslims and Jews on the same basis of citizenship under the law as Protestants and Catholics. During the so-called *Fragmentenstreit* of the mid-1770s, he also tried to undermine the authority of mainstream Protestant theology in German culture, while in his *Ernst und Falk* (1778–1780), he offered his century's most scathing critique of Freemasonry.

Lessing held that the highest goal, theoretical and practical, of those striving to bring enlightenment to humanity, and philosophy's supreme gift to mankind, is to minimize as far as humanly possible the three principal causes of strife and division among men: religious differences, class differences, and national differences.[67] The common people, ignorant and superstitious as they are, are usually fervent about all three: fiercely chauvinistic, blindly deferential to rank, and believing unquestioningly in their religion. The philosopher, by contrast, knows that none of these pivots of difference matter at all and while he cannot break their iron grip on popular thinking, he can help minimize their effect. If Freemasonry truly could fulfill its function, this is what the Freemasons would strive for. But Lessing asserts that Freemasonry had become so corrupted by love of ritual and "mysteries," along with deference for rank, that in Germany at least it everywhere betrayed the Enlightenment's essential ideals.

Lessing's disapproval of Freemasonry as it actually existed was fully shared by the German "left" underground societies that emerged and flourished for a few years, particularly during the 1780s, in the German court capitals and thirty university towns. These associations grew by concealing themselves within the distended body of German and Austrian Freemasonry, this having become thoroughly amorphous and divided, being infiltrated not only from "the left" but equally by reactionary right-wing opponents of radical thought, such as the Rosicrucians, zealous reactionaries who penetrated the lodges with equal ease. The widest ranging and most important radical secret organization was the order of the *Illuminati*, founded by the Bavarian professor Adam Weishaupt (1748–1830) at Ingolstadt in 1776. This organization—it eventually spread all over Central Europe, including Prague and Budapest, with a peak membership of around 2,000, including (rather passively) Herder, Goethe, and various friends of Schiller, most of whom had no idea how radical the veiled core principles of the society really were—clandestinely aspired to carry out a general "Weltreformation" (world reformation) based on philosophical reason, *Freiheit* (freedom), and *Gleichheit* (equality).[68] Still more tightly organized and more radical was another, and slightly later, organization, the *Deutsche Union*, founded at Halle, Prussia, by the former theologian Carl Friedrich Bahrdt (1741–1792), who likewise represented "the radical rationalist turn and politicization of the late Enlightenment" in Germany.[69] By 1789 this association had around 600 members.

While both the *Illuminati* and *Deutsche Union* utilized Masonic methods of organization, both simultaneously despised the crassness, "mysteries," and unintellectual attitudes of most Freemasons. Since the *Illuminati* kept their core doctrines, or "highest mysteries," hidden even from the lower grades of their own membership, it only slowly emerged, shortly before the French Revolution, that these secret concepts were merely "das Weishaup- tische System," Weishaupt's egalitarian and materialist philosophy. Contemporary observers, like the ultra- reactionary court official Ludwig Adolf Christian von Grolman (1741–1809)—who published a well-known collection of secret documents of German Illuminatism, *Die neuesten Arbeiten des Spartacus und Philo* in 1793— protested that the highest grades of the order were, in effect, a clandestine vehicle for the propagation of materialist and atheistic ideas and that at the core of the highest mysteries of the organization's first grade, the so-called *Philosophengrad* (philosophers' grade), lay un- adulterated *Spinozismus* (Spinozism), or at any rate con- cepts based on the Spinozistic *Grundsätze* (basic princi- ples): that everything that exists is matter, that God and the universe are the same, and that all organized religion is a political deception devised by ambitious men.[70] Con- servative detractors like Grolman depicted these societies in a shrill, virulently hostile fashion, but the documents they published were authentic, and whatever his harsh epithets, Grolman's basic philosophical characterization of Weishaupt and other leaders of the *Illuminaten* was not inaccurate.

Weishaupt evinced no particular interest in Spinoza di- rectly. What he felt drawn to, we see from his letters, texts, and other evidence, were the moral and social ideas of

d'Holbach's *Système de la nature, La Politique naturelle,*
and *Système social,* as well as to Helvétius's *De l'homme,*
and Jean-Baptiste Robinet's *De la nature* (1761).[71] These,
together with Raynal's *Histoire philosophique*—a favorite
work also of Adolf Freiherr von Knigge (1752–1796), son
of a prominent Hanover official and, for a short but crucial period, Weishaupt's chief ally propagating *Illumina-
tismus* in Protestant Germany—were their core books
and, in effect, the true intellectual inspiration of German
moral, political, and social revolutionary awareness in
the pre-1789 period. This is a point that needs stressing.
For while scholars have often claimed, not without reason, that many leading figures of the *Aufklärung,* including Kant, disliked French materialism while admiring
British thinkers such as Locke, Shaftesbury, Newton,
Hutcheson, ·Hume, and the "Common Sense" School,
especially Reid, German radical thought, no less clearly,
preferred French materialism as well as the early
eighteenth-century British radical tradition of Toland,
Collins, Tindal, and Bolingbroke.

The centrality of French radical ideas in the evolution
of German radical thought is further reflected in the intel-
lectual formation of other leading radical writers such as
Bahrdt, Georg Forster (1754–1794), and Anarcharsis
Cloots (1755–1794), as well as Johann Friedrich von
Struensee (1737–1772), a Halle-trained, radical-minded
physician who caused a great sensation in Scandinavia.
Son of a Lutheran general superintendent of Schleswig-

Holstein, Adam Struensee, it was through tending the mentally sick Danish monarch, Christian VII (r. 1766–1808), that Johann Friedrich first came to prominence in Copenhagen and came to be entrusted by the ailing monarch with autocratic power in the Danish-Norwegian monarchy. For eighteen extraordinary months in 1770–1771, Struensee strove to push through an astonishingly ambitious program of political and social reform, including the first state edict in history (4 September 1770) proclaiming freedom of the press a universal principle that benefits society and promotes the advancement of knowledge.

Detested by the clergy and decried as a Spinozist in a campaign of bitter vituperation in the very press he himself had emancipated from state censorship,[72] Struensee was overthrown by court opponents in 1771, tried for "treason," and executed. The chief element in the intellectual formation of this extraordinary personality, as he explained in interviews prior to his execution, was the thought of Helvétius and other French materialists whose ideas he sought to apply to reforming Danish-Norwegian society.[73] Among his closest associates had been the son of the Sephardic Jewish "Spinozist" David Gerson, in whose house at Altona (adjoining Hamburg) in the years 1742–1744 Spinoza's *Ethics* had for the first time (and with great competence) been translated into German by the much-hounded radical philologist and Bible scholar Johann Lorenz Schmidt (1702–1749).

Several Danish-Norwegian pamphlets published during the period of unrestricted press freedom reflect not just the resonance of Spinoza's name in Scandinavian and German popular folklore at the time but also a vivid awareness of the fundamental rift in the European Enlightenment more generally. One pamphlet deploring the new freedoms and negative impact of certain kinds of "philosophy" on morals, religion, and society was the *Alvorliger Betragtninger over den almindelige Tilstand* (Serious Observations on the Common Condition] of 1771. It denounced the spread of irreligious ideas but entirely endorsed the "Christian" philosophy of moderate thinkers like "Grotius, Pufendorf, Leibniz, Wolff, Locke, Newton, Boyle, Boerhaave, Haller, Hoffmann, Sulzer." These thinkers, according to the text, understood the workings of nature much better than the materialists. Earlier, in "dark times" prior to the Enlightenment, "true religion" had been attacked by the reputed Italian "atheists" Bruno and Vanini, but this had had little impact, so that, hitherto, most people had not needed to worry about philosophical irreligion. But a far more serious challenge had now emerged under the mask of "philosophy" and the sciences, a challenge anchored, it says, in the writings and ideas of "Tindal, Spinoza, Collins, and Bolingbroke."[74]

Weishaupt's key critical concepts—"despotism," designating monarchy, aristocracy, and *ancien régime* institutions generally, and "slavery," denoting the current condition of humanity—derive more particularly from d'Holbach than Helvétius, though the latter's name was far more widely known in Germany at the time.[75] The same is true of his special emphasis on bringing freedom and equality to all mankind, and notion of a universal morality and set of human rights as "ein allgemeines Recht" (a universal right) to which all other laws, morality, and institutions should in the future be subject. Also characteristic of d'Holbach is Weishaupt's replacing divine providence in his "philosophical history of mankind" with Nature and reason as the overriding factors shaping human history and society.[76] Whether men will, in the future, live in a despotic state or under a *Democratie* is, for Weishaupt as for d'Holbach, essentially a question of changing the thinking, values, and morality of the people, and thus depends on the success of the Enlightenment.[77]

According to Weishaupt, the "immanent revolution of the human spirit" (die bevorstehende Revolution des menschlichen Geistes), driven by *Aufklärung*, will return mankind to its pristine state of equality and freedom. Enlightenment, as conceived by him, is the only force strong enough to break the chains of tyranny and engineer such a revolution.[78] The sole effective engine of human progress, agreed Weishaupt and Knigge, is *Aufklärung*, by which, like d'Holbach and Diderot, they meant not Voltaire's or Kant's limited Enlightenment, but a "widely propagated universal Enlightenment" (*verbreitete allgemeine Aufklärung*) curtailing the power of superstition and ignorance among the common people. In their view, the "realm of reason" (*das Reich der Vernunft*), the "capacity to conduct one's life as an independent being" for the greater part of humanity, will always be a mere dream, an impossibility, without continual assistance from philosophers and philosophy.[79] Even where meaningful steps toward Enlightenment were being achieved, society still needed "secret philosophy schools" to serve as what Weishaupt saw as the eternal "archive of Nature and of human rights" (Archiv der Natur und der menschlichen Rechte).[80]

In defining *Aufklärung* Weishaupt was fiercely critical of what he saw as the excessively narrow, petty, word-spinning conception generally prevalent in Bavaria, Austria, and the rest of the German-speaking world at the time. True *Aufklärung*, he declares, can never be just knowledge of words and concepts. Rather it must be knowledge of realities, especially social and political realities.[81] "Whoever wishes to introduce general freedom spreads general Enlightenment," but Enlightenment here means "understanding of things, not knowledge of abstract, speculative, theoretical sciences which inflate the mind and do nothing to improve the heart."[82] For Weishaupt, in contrast to Kant, Enlightenment is ultimately a process of getting rid of priests, aristocrats, and kings. But though hostile to monarchy and the churches, Weishaupt denied being "irreligious" or subversive in the true senses of these words.[83] The *Aufklärung* of German Illuminism was committed to transforming the human condition by a comprehensive revolution in human knowledge and awareness. Weishaupt goes so far as to include traditional university scholasticism and education, or what he calls unenlightened "learning"—together with political oppression, social oppression, and theology—among the four pillars underpinning *ancien régime* social hierarchy and tyranny.[84] Enlightening a few, he objects, merely to keep others in error (like Voltaire's and Frederick the Great's Enlightenment), generates power and actively promotes social subordination. Only Enlightenment to enlighten others generates freedom: only "Aufklärung um andere wieder aufzuklären, giebt Freyheit."[85]

Bahrdt, meanwhile, yielded nothing to Weishaupt and Knigge as an underground propagator of radical ideas. His organization was similarly a vehicle for advancing *Aufklärung*, defined in a manner very different from Kant, seeing it as not just the opposite to "superstition" and *Fanatismus* but, above all, as the application of reason to the extension of mankind's earthly happiness.[86] *Naturalisten* and *Atheisten* were freely admitted to his secret society, albeit mockery of Christ and Christianity were forbidden. More coherently than the *Illuminati*, Bahrdt's organization expressly excluded princes and state ministers, and the general tone, though no less erudite and literary—Bahrdt, too, was a university professor—was more specifically republican in character.[87] In the thought-world of the late Bahrdt, the connection with the ideas of Boulanger, d'Holbach, Helvétius, and the mature Diderot was again strongly evident. After around 1780, Bahrdt, despite himself having long been a professional theologian, maintained, like Weishaupt, that revealed religions divide men. He, too, contended that miracles are impossible and belief in them harmful to the individual and society by masking the true nature of physical and social relations and serving as building-blocks for "Priestertirannei" (priestly tyranny).[88] He especially deplored that revealed religion teaches men to believe that faith not morality is the path to salvation, whereas the truth, to him, was precisely the reverse.[89] Because churchmen threaten with damnation those who lack faith in incomprehensible mysteries, Bahrdt, from the 1770s, viewed Christianity as an immoral as well as objectionable faith, an enemy of all truly universal moral values.

All the radical enlighteners held that liberty of thought and expression (de parler et d'écrire) benefits society, promotes knowledge, and also serves, in d'Holbach's words, as a "powerful dike against the plots and intrigues of tyranny" and religious fervor.[90] No particular religion should be sponsored by the state and the semi-toleration then prevailing in England, North America, and Holland, they agreed, should be transformed into a full toleration so that there would no longer be any sects or points of view suffering disabilities for refusing the sovereign's faith. By this measure, the famous toleration decree issued by the "enlightened" Emperor, Joseph II, in 1781 for the Habsburg lands fell markedly short since not only did Catholicism remain the official religion of the crown in Austria, Bohemia, Galicia, and Hungary but Unitarians, atheists, and freethinkers, along with other fringe sects, were excluded and continued to be persecuted.[91] Granting a degree of formal or informal toleration while still subjecting certain religious minorities to disabilities and marks of inferiority, as was usual throughout Europe at the time, is unjust, insists d'Holbach, and altogether incompatible with the general will. Nothing is more contrary to humanity and justice than theologies claiming the "exclusive approbation of heaven." Such pretensions should never be endorsed by society; rather, all who proclaim such spiritual authority should be declared enemies of the liberty of man.[92]

It is "liberty," argues d'Holbach, that ennobles man, raises his soul, and inspires generosity and love of the "bien public." But what he, like Diderot, Helvétius, and Weishaupt, meant by "liberty" was the "philosophical" principle of liberty, not particular liberties enshrined in countless ancient laws, codes, and digests. Since only equity, reason, and freedom can ground just constitutional principles, rational laws, and upright government, nothing is more absurd, they avowed, than the tradition of venerating ancient charters and privileges and basing everything on remote precedent, as the English do in designating the Magna Carta the foundation of their liberty. According to d'Holbach, this was merely an "obscure and crude charter," extorted many centuries ago from a despotic king by unruly barons at a moment of weakness.[93] Ferguson and Burke might enthuse over the sort of liberty that rests on "those very charters, statutes and precedents which are now to be set aside [by the Americans],"[94] but to radical minds like d'Holbach and Paine charters were irrelevant and, worse, detrimental to the majority. To them universal principles were what counted, the state's purpose being to procure for all its citizens true justice, security, and liberty, goals that have nothing to do with medieval charters and "liberties."[95]

From the early 1770s when Diderot and d'Holbach began propagating their fully fledged democratic republican ideology, it was plain what the radical thinkers intended. Their contention that the consent of the governed is the only source of legitimacy in politics was widely conceived, at least from the publication in March 1770 of the *Essai sur les Préjugés* onwards, to imperil the entire edifice of Europe's *ancien régime* institutions. Royalty and the hereditary principle, it was strongly implied, were mere prejudices. The astonishing fact that the peoples of the world readily allow themselves to be oppressed, exploited, robbed, pillaged, and forced to fight senseless wars on behalf of rapacious dynasts, asserts the *Essai*, is primarily due to superstition and credulous religion that cloud men's minds with "error," transforming even the most oppressive autocrats into divinities.[96] If priests everywhere are pampered by kings, it is because despots need "their lies to keep their subjects under their yoke."[97]

Reading the *Essai sur les Préjugés* a month after publication in his palace at Potsdam, Frederick the Great was so appalled, he immediately took up his pen to refute it. The unnamed author (d'Holbach) he deprecated as an "enemy of kings" intent on rendering monarchical government "odious" and a rabid hater of the nobility whose military code and values he himself had always cherished and protected.[98] Circulating his reply to selected allies (including d'Alembert and Voltaire), the incensed monarch denounced his opponent as a pillar of "philosophic pride" engaged in a hopelessly naïve quest, an undertaking bound to agitate the people needlessly and end in disaster. Adding a second refutation, this time of d'Holbach's *Système de la nature,* Frederick attacked d'Holbach's determinism and fatalism and especially condemned his contention that subjects "should possess the right of deposing when disgusted with their sovereigns."[99] No likelier formula for instigating civil wars and supporting ambitious upstarts, retorted the king, could possibly be devised.

Applauded by Voltaire and d'Alembert, Frederick probably saw little of the necessarily masked response of the radical camp. But their responses were as sharply worded as his own sallies. Diderot scathingly demolished the king's counterarguments denouncing him as a "tyrant," but only in private, unpublished writings.[100] Herder likewise kept his bitter criticism of the Prussian monarch to himself and his friends. Some loudly protest, commented d'Holbach in subsequent clandestine publications, that in striving for comprehensive change, the (radical) *philosophes* were causing turmoil and disturbance just as, in the past, the English, Dutch, and Swiss had curtailed absolute monarchy and papal jurisdiction only via "des troubles et des révolutions."[101] But it is not those who protest and fight back, he retorted, but rather the tyrannical ambition of princes and great nobles and the "fanaticism" and persecution fomented by the clergy that provoke a degree of violence that would be far less, moreover, were the people more enlightened.

D'Holbach and Diderot conceded that political revolution is apt to entail fearful upheaval and slaughter.[102] Even so, averred d'Holbach six years before the outbreak of the American Revolution, the English, Dutch, and Swiss through revolutionary upheaval and long years of strife and bloodshed had in earlier centuries incontestably gained in the end and so would others in the future. Were not a few temporary disturbances more beneficial to humanity than languishing eternally under endless tyranny? Where men's fundamental rights are systematically violated it is always justified for the citizenry to revolt.[103] This is only one of numerous passages where d'Holbach and Diderot offer a qualified but clear justification for mass armed resistance to tyrannical government where initiated by responsible leaders. The *Histoire philosophique* and its spin-off publications, stiffened by Diderot and several of his disciples, had no doubts on this score: "never will tyrants freely consent to the extirpation of servitude and to bring them to this point, it will be necessary either to ruin or exterminate them" (jamais les tyrans ne consentirent librement à l'extinction de la servitude, et pour les amener à cet ordre de choses, il faudra les ruiner ou les exterminer).[104]

This revolutionary tendency was an aspect of d'Holbach and Diderot's thought that outraged Voltaire and was rejected by Kant, who ruled that resistance to despotic power by those subjected to it is never justified.[105] The legislative power should reflect the general will, agreed Kant, and represent the needs and interests of everyone on an equal basis and help promote a true republican spirit. But "republicanism," in his view, entails separating the executive power (the government) from the legislative. "Where the legislator executes his own laws causing the private will of the ruler to be substituted for the will of the public," despotism ensues.[106] This formula enabled Kant simultaneously to oppose democracy as a form of "despotism" while combining enlightened absolutism on the German model, or at least some forms of it, with the principle of (limited) representation and legislative non-executive republicanism. Frederick himself meanwhile denounced d'Holbach's stance as immoral, treasonable, and unworthy of a philosopher. Someone who insults his own and other kings, calling them "despots" and "tyrants," he retorted, regardless of the laws of his own country, "is neither wise nor a philosopher."[107] Citing the slaughter of the French Wars of Religion (1562–1594), he reminded opponents of the terrible havoc that rebellion against legitimate kings can precipitate.[108]

In recent years, skepticism as to whether "books cause revolutions" has proved both influential and pervasive in university history teaching. But without the unprecedented surge of egalitarian literature during the 1770s and 1780s there would have been no grounding for a "General Revolution" such as swept North America and Europe in the late eighteenth century. This does not mean that the whole emphasis should be placed on books and ideas. Rather, the interpretation proposed here envisages revolution as a complex interaction of thought and action emerging by stages at a particular moment in history. But while great revolutions are always fueled by pre-existing social grievances, to create genuine revolution these grievances must be articulated in new, forthright, and much broader terms than previously such as were actually propounded in the 1770s and 1780s through a veritable deluge of subversive literature in continental Europe, Britain, and the New World alike. Embodying a whole new revolutionary consciousness, this outpouring included texts that were literary, satirical, and journalistic, as well as philosophical, but everywhere it was the new "philosophical" content that chiefly counted. "Philosophy" was what lent

form and a sharp edge to a powerful emotional upsurge of deeply felt poetic and dramatic aversion to oppression clearly discernible from the 1760s onward in the
work of Lessing, Schiller, Goethe, Alfieri, Beaumarchais,
Marmontel, Coleridge, Shelley, and other key poets and
playwrights of the age, as well as in philosophical and
other theoretical texts.

During the two decades before 1789 a revolutionary
ideology of completely unprecedented power, intensity,
and scope established itself firmly on both sides of the
Atlantic. Revulsion against the autocracy and militarism
of enlightened despotism became powerfully infused with
the literary sensibility of the age. "On entering the states
of the great Frederick [king of Prussia] which appeared
to me like a vast guard-house," recalled the Italian poet
and playwright Alfieri in 1769, "my hatred was still more
increased of the infamous trade of soldier, the sole basis
of all arbitrary authority, which must always rely on so
many thousand hired minions. On being presented to His
Majesty, I experienced not the slightest emotion either of
surprise or respect, but on the contrary, a rising feeling
of indignation which became daily strengthened in my
mind on beholding oppression and despotism assuming
the mask of virtue."[109]

Not only revolutionary movements inspired by the new
egalitarian and democratic ideas, but also old-fashioned
traditional-style popular rebellions against lordly oppression, such as the Pugachev Revolt (1773–1775) in Russia,
came to be viewed in these circumstances through the

spectacles of radical ideas. Even if not everyone went as far as d'Holbach in claiming "popular revolts are always the result of oppression and tyranny,"[110] rebellion in these years indubitably assumed a new image, one dramatically different, and in the former case more positive, than it had possessed in the past. This was a shift fed by the generally favorable reaction in Europe to the American Revolution. Armed intervention by the citizenry in defense of their own "rights" now seemed to be the order of the day. If Jebb called on the English people to agitate for parliamentary reform, and on the Irish and Canadians to resist the British ministry and crown, which, he warned, aspired to impose "arbitrary government" on them,[111] Dutch Patriot leaders during the years 1780–1787 openly summoned the citizenry to arm and form new militia units as a means to further the democratic cause. Political subversion, sanctioned by radical philosophy, acquired a degree of legitimacy and prestige never witnessed before.

"Tyranny," as both word and concept, plainly changed its meaning in European political usage and high culture in the 1760s and 1770s. In the past, "tyranny" had denoted legally unconstrained rule violating previously established constitutional procedures, laws, privileges, and legally defined rights, especially those of nobles, churchmen, and city corporations. The late eighteenth-century broadening of the scope of the term had no justification in traditional usage or statute. To this extent Ferguson was correct to insist on the "undoubted right of this country [Britain] to require from America some share in the supplies which are necessary to support the Imperial Crown and the Empire of Great Britain."[112] Judged on the basis of tradition and precedent the Americans had no right to rebel. By contrast, in Diderot, Helvétius, Mably, Raynal, and d'Holbach, as well as in Price, Priestley, Paine, Weishaupt, Knigge, Forster, and Bahrdt, "tyranny" denotes the exercise of any authority, legitimate or illegitimate in constitutional terms, not grounded "on advantages procured for those on whom it is exercised."[113]

According to older notions, absolute monarchs were free to act as they wished, provided they observed the fundamental laws of their realms. But under the new dispensation, no ruler was entitled to do anything other than for the good of society: this, for d'Holbach, was the "loi primitive et fondamentale" nature imposes on all who rule over men.[114] Courtly pomp, upholding nobility and rank, privilege, hereditary office-holding, granting monopolies to particular groups of merchants, as well as empire building, imposing imperial restrictions and tariffs on colonies, legalized discrimination, waging foreign wars not authorized by self-defense, and religious intolerance—suddenly all became by definition aspects of tyranny, while at the same time nothing now seemed more vital for humanity's happiness than "la liberté."[115]

"Tyranny," contended the radical thinkers, is whatever is not in the best interest of the people, including all forms of hereditary power and ecclesiastical authority, and the confessional standpoints and ascetic morality taught by churchmen; what Price and Priestley called "corrupted" Christianity. "Tyranny," in their view, is anything that contravenes basic morality and justice; hence everything obstructing the progress of democracy and equality is tyrannical.[116] The scope of "tyranny" was decisively extended not only horizontally but also vertically through society. For Diderot and his colleagues the "tyrant" was just the apex of a pyramid, a figurehead powerless to do anything much on his own who presided over a hierarchy of ranks and orders composed of unenlightened subjects all constantly striving mutually to oppress each other. Apart from a few nomads, islanders, and mountain people, practically all humans had in this sense fallen victim to superstition and despotic oppression; tyranny was virtually everywhere.[117]

"Government on the old system," as Paine summed it up, "is an assumption of power, for the aggrandizement of itself; on the new, a delegation of power, for the common benefit of society."[118] This "revolution of the mind" of the 1760s and 1770s was plainly one of the greatest and most decisive shifts in the entire history of humanity and one that cannot be comprehended without investigating the content of the great philosophical controversies of the age and the way these impacted, especially after 1770 and on both sides of the Atlantic, on society and culture.

CHAPTER III

The Problem of Equality and Inequality: The Rise of Economics

T he principle of equality, we have seen, was crucial to the Radical Enlightenment from the outset. This was because in Spinoza, Bayle, and the clandestine philosophical literature of the early Enlightenment, moral and social theory is grounded on the principle that every person's happiness, and hence worldly interests, must be deemed equal. Thus, the toleration of these philosophers, and uncompromising plea for freedom of expression and the press, were integrally linked to the notion that every person's needs and views are of equal weight. The radical thinkers wholly erased the distinction (retained by Locke) between an individual's theological status—or what Locke conceives as everyone's responsibility to save his or her soul—on the one hand, and, on the other, a person's civil status. Locke's more traditional and theological conception of "equality" was framed in such a way as to block the wider social and political role equality plays in the Spinozistic systems. He deemed individuals "spiritually" equal before Christ but not equal in civil status. Hence, Locke speaks of spiritual equality while simultaneously upholding a society of ranks, indeed even slavery—he was an investor in the Royal Africa Company and the Bahamas Adventurers Company, both major slaving concerns, as well as, late in his career, commissioner of the London Board of Trade.[1]

Locke's purely spiritual equality, distinguishing spiritual from civil status, accommodated the new nobility instituted by him in his draft constitutions for the English colony of the Carolinas (for which he was rebuked by Diderot in the *Histoire philosophique*). It was a doctrine resting on an assumed or implied philosophical dualism, distinguishing body from soul, that is rejected outright in Spinoza and, by implication, in Bayle. Their purely secular moral philosophy, excluding theological notions, depended crucially on the idea of reciprocity and equity in social relations and, ultimately, also in political relationships. Hence, we can say the special status and functions of democracy in radical thought originated in large part as the logical consequence of a socially orientated system of moral philosophy and toleration anchored (in contrast to Locke's) in equality. It was no accident, therefore, that

Spinoza was the first major philosopher in the history of philosophy to proclaim democracy the best form of government.

But if equality as a moral and political principle was foundational from the outset, only during the third quarter of the eighteenth century did Diderot, d'Holbach, and their disciples develop a broad critique of social inequality. Clashing as it did with the mainstream Enlightenment's comprehensive opposition to the principle of equality, this then provoked a lively controversy about social and economic inequality that became pivotal to all intellectual discussion about society and politics from the 1760s onward down to the present. Here was an intellectual encounter of paramount importance in modern history and one that accompanied, or rather tensely paralleled, the rise of economics. Classical free-market economics emerged directly from the context of the moderate, mainstream Enlightenment, and can rightly be declared one of its chief intellectual triumphs. The new science, however, was subject to immediate suspicion and opposition from among the radical bloc.

On the terrain of economic life, no less than in moral theory and politics, we encounter a fundamental divergence between the two enlightenments. Moreover, since inherited wealth and inequality extended far beyond the purely economic sphere, the growing rift over free-market economics tended to infuse and exacerbate the whole of the wider argument about privilege, social structure, and rank. It is useless to strive for the moral improvement of men and society, insisted Diderot, Helvétius, and d'Holbach, as long as the material interests and prejudices of the strongest are organized in such a way as to pervert both morality and society, as d'Holbach put it.[2] The radical enlighteners considered ruinous socially, morally, politically and culturally the hereditary principle as applied to land, high offices, wealth, and rank. By reserving prestigious posts and the best rewards for those whose only qualification is their lineage and who have done nothing "useful" for the state, sovereigns discourage all endeavors on behalf of society of the other categories of citizen. Yet the common people, so scorned by princes and their courtiers, often produce more gifted and "noble" minds than the "gilded crowd" congregating around princes and kings.[3] "It is from the bosom of poverty," urged Helvétius—rather simplistically but striking a wholly new note in the history of philosophy—that we generally see "science, genius and the talents emerge."[4] It is education not lineage, held Helvétius and d'Holbach, that "produces persons suited to high office and merit not birth which is the criterion for judging them."[5]

Precisely as the principle of equality, and the moral theory based on equity and reciprocity, anchored democracy in the moral and political philosophy of the Radical Enlightenment, so it was "equality" that grounded its entire social theory. Radical Enlightenment sought, especially from around 1770 onward, to undermine and vilify the principle of aristocracy. What was the origin of the modern European nobility, asked Mirabeau in 1784. Were not its ancestors mere ruffians, warrior chiefs whose original titles were those of usurpation and brigandage?[6] No one, contended d'Holbach, knows better how to pervert the true meaning of the ancient word "liberty" and subvert the true aims of the republic than the modern descendants of ancient nobilities. Were not the Polish nobility continually mouthing this word "liberty" when what they meant by it was the right to tyrannize over their serfs unhindered and subject their dependents to the cruelest oppression?[7] (That Rousseau in his proposed legislation for Poland encourages young Poles to immerse themselves in the history, laws, and "glorious deeds" of their nation, and take only Poles for their teachers—advice typical of him—shows how far removed he was from the radicals on such issues.)[8] Diderot and d'Holbach held that in the ancient aristocratic republics of Venice and Genoa an entire institutionalized culture of so-called liberty existed that actually involved subjecting the common people to the "atrocity" of despotism as oppressive as that of the most tyrannical prince.[9] With the stadholderate's restoration in the Dutch Republic at the point of Prussian bayonets in 1787, the hereditary principle and court culture, it seemed, had finally subjugated the republican legacy of the Dutch.

While championing egalitarianism, however, Diderot, Helvétius, and d'Holbach firmly disavowed any intention of leveling society or seeking to impose full economic equality, which, they appreciated, would inevitably establish a new form of tyranny. Thus, d'Holbach expressly warns against all doctrinaire and rigid zeal for economic equality as inherently dangerous, and likely to stifle freedom and destroy the republic.[10] "A perfect equality between the members of a society," ruled Helvétius, in 1773, "would be an *injustice véritable*," a true injustice.[11] According to d'Holbach it is right that the most useful should be the best rewarded and most respected. Not everyone works equally hard, or is equally deserving, or contributes as much to society, as the most diligent, ingenious, or benevolent. Men are only altogether equal in their moral obligation to be good and useful to other men, all groups being united in this, the moral law being "à tous également imposée."[12]

Rather than establish an exact equality, they aspired to demolish the existing hierarchy of social orders and attack the huge imbalance in the distribution of wealth. In Helvétius's *De l'homme* (1773)—a work composed over many years and one whose text was continually revised in the light of conversations held at the regular gatherings at his house—the pivotal idea of "a just equilibrium" between the fortunes of the citizens is introduced.[13] Any and every responsible government should concern itself principally with the well-being of the greatest number, treating all as morally equal and deserving of their right to happiness.[14] If men can never be equal in ability and it is right that some should be remunerated and rewarded by society more than others, nature made all men equal in rights, desires, in wanting to be happy, and in liberty. Acknowledging this, consequently, and attacking the gross disproportion of influence and property affording the few disproportionate leverage over the rest, must be the bedrock of any just and internally consistent political theory.

According to the radical *philosophes*, the rules of the new secular morality stripped of theology have always been and will always remain—even if they are only now becoming understood—the same for all, rich and poor, European and non-European, black, white, and yellow. Kings, nobles, merchants, and laborers all being subject to the same ethical goals and standards, moral conduct must begin by recognizing all men's equal "rights."[15] Hence, while no immediate levelers of incomes and property, Helvétius, d'Holbach, and their German disciples actively fought social inequality by denying the legitimacy of ancient distinctions between "orders" and urging the transformation of the existing distribution of wealth in favor of greater fairness.[16] In the 1760s and 1770s they did not yet call unambiguously, as radical writers did in the early 1790s, for mankind to "exterminate," in Paine's words, "the monster aristocracy root and branch";[17] but the eventual elimination of social hierarchy was both presupposed by their ethical system and inherent in their utilitarian social theory.

Always a consistent disciple of French radical thought, Paine no more proposed to eliminate aristocracy and inequality by confiscation, execution, or violence than did Weishaupt or Knigge. Abolishing aristocracy, which d'Holbach, Mirabeau, Brissot, Priestley, and Paine all explicitly urged, remained in Paine's mind a process of overthrow by ridicule, through changes in perception and ideas, through ensuring aristocrats lose "ground from contempt more than hatred." He longed to see aristocracy "jeered at as an ass" rather than "dreaded as a lion."[18] But would reason and ridicule suffice to strip nobles of their power, privileges, and inherited wealth? A society can be "happy," according to the radical thinkers, only when it places all those who compose it in a position equally to enjoy its benefits, rendering participation in it advantageous while in doing so eschewing violence as much as possible. Precisely here, though, lay a dilemma that proved irresolvable and deeply divisive, a formula almost bound to breed violence. Already in the *Histoire philosophique*, the most widely read radical text of the late eighteenth century, Diderot and his co-authors urge the downtrodden peoples of the world to rise against their oppressors in terms of an almost frightening militancy.

The Radical Enlightenment, then, aspired to forge a new kind of society and by the early 1770s deemed this conceivable only by means of what Paine and Barlow termed a "General Revolution." But since the "General Revolution" they strove to engineer was not intended to be one of violence, killing, and destruction, radical thought had to present itself as a war of "reason" and persuasion against crass "superstition" and cruel oppression, hoping this would suffice for success. It was a dogma of the radical thinkers that reason, and only reason, can raise man's dignity from the depths of degradation, error, and ignorance.[19] For a time, it seemed that reason *was* gaining ground and monarchy, nobility, and church power *were* crumbling under its assault. It was not hard to see "from the enlightened state of mankind," wrote Paine triumphantly in 1791, "that hereditary governments are verging to their decline, and that revolutions on the broad basis of national sovereignty, and government by representation, are making their way in Europe." Consequently, he added, "it would be an act of wisdom to anticipate their approach, and produce Revolutions by reason and accommodation, rather than commit them to the issue of convulsions."[20] Embracing revolution, while seeking to minimize disruption and violence, was a classic exhortation of the Radical Enlightenment.

As part of their "General Revolution," Diderot, Helvétius, and d'Holbach strove to transform notions about the different social ranks. Diderot had begun to dignify artisanship and the crafts during the 1750s in the *Encyclopédie*, via the numerous long and detailed entries describing artisanal techniques. The transformation in the theater that he and Lessing tried to bring about in France and Germany principally involved substituting for the characters of princes and aristocrats those of more ordinary men and women. Later, the impulse to elevate workmen's skills was taken further. Is not an industrious laborer more useful to society, asked d'Holbach, than the common run of useless aristocrats? And the impoverished *homme de lettres* who dedicates his energies to the edification of his fellow citizens: is he not worthier of being generally esteemed than the "opulent imbecile" of high birth who affects to disdain the arts and talent? Compassion is more easily aroused, he observed, in those who know destitution at first hand than in those whose wealth guarantees they will never suffer deprivation.

Occasionally, Diderot's and d'Holbach's later writings imply that if there is ever a better, more equitable society in the future, it is more likely to arise from the efforts of the poor than of the rich. Certainly, it seemed easier to demonstrate the advantages of fairness, equity, and equal right to protection to those whose weakness exposed them to oppression rather than to the wealthy and powerful whose well-being and glory, it would seem, lies in their ability to oppress. However arduous the lesson, the peoples of the world must learn to observe the rules of justice toward each other and respect the rights of all. Exactly the same applies to the different social classes.[21]

D'Holbach was not a particularly original philosopher. His "verbiage," protested the Abbé Bergier, "is borrowed from Spinoza."[22] Yet his materialist metaphysics, theory of mind, and moral philosophy were skillfully combined with a potent political theory expressed chiefly in the *Système de la nature* and his *La politique naturelle* (1773), a work reissued later in 1773, again in 1774, and then in 1790.[23] Like Diderot's contributions to the *Histoire philosophique,* these works refined in new ways Spinoza's anti-Hobbesian principle that the "natural right" of man in the state of nature carries over into the state of society and that there is no intrinsic gap between the equal status and condition of man in the state of nature and in society.[24] Drawing on the entire clandestine philosophical tradition originating in Spinoza, and running via Boulainvilliers, Fontenelle, Fréret, d'Argens, Du Marsais, and Boulanger to the radicals of the 1760s and 1770s, these authors forged an entirely new ideology offering social theories with undoubted revolutionary resonance and achieving, as the book-historical evidence abundantly proves, unparalleled success in propagating their ideas broadly in society, a process that accelerated rapidly with the onset of the Revolution.

By the early 1770s (hence prior to the American Revolution), the many editions and translations—French, Dutch, Swiss, English, and German—of works such as the *Système de la nature* and the *Histoire philosophique* (circulating under Raynal's name) were spreading the ideas they contained everywhere and to all social categories, from the court down to the humblest hamlets. In 1770 the chancellor of the French judiciary, Antoine-Louis Séguier, in a *réquisitoire* laid before the *Parlement* of Paris, prior to the public burning of seven radical texts—including d'Holbach's *Système de la nature* and Fréret's *Examen critique des Apologistes de la religion chrétienne*—broadcast, as he was to do again several times subsequently,[25] a remarkably pessimistic appraisal of what he considered France's fast deteriorating cultural and moral environment. The country was inundated with the writings of a "secte impie et audacieuse" and this *cabale philosophique* undermining religion and government was injecting its subversive ideas everywhere via clandestine printed literature, swaying even serving women, ordinary country cottagers, and the laboring poor in remote parts of the realm, a fact of which the *anti-philosophes* in France had indeed complained continually since the late 1750s. This unprecedented deluge of subversive text constituted, to use his exact word, a "revolution" in ideas and attitudes.[26]

The principles propagated by "cette ligue criminelle," warned Séguier, are designed to "destroy the close harmony" that has prevailed between the social orders and that "has always existed between the Church's doctrines and the laws of the state": subversion all the more insidious, he added with remarkable prescience, because their arguments appeared to many to tend "au Bonheur de l'humanité."[27] Nor did he doubt the capacity of this *cabale philosophique* to instigate serious trouble and commotion throughout France and beyond: "The people were poor but consoled [by religion]; now it is overwhelmed with its toil and its doubts" (le peuple étoit pauvre, mais consolé [. . .]; il est maintenant accablé de ses travaux et de ses doutes).[28] The agitated minds of the destitute, unsettled by philosophy, he suggested, must mean growing unrest.

The radicals' justification was that the alleged "harmony" men like the *avocat-général* and Voltaire imagined had always prevailed and formerly been uncontested was actually a barely veiled tableau of oppression, misery, and destitution. Why should people not be told the truth about how they are deceived? Diderot, d'Holbach, and their disciples considered the moral qualities of the peasantry estimable and their hatred of the *seigneurs* perfectly natural in light of their being perpetually scorned and oppressed by them and their plots being routinely ravaged by noblemen's hunting rights. Peasants become marauding pilferers and thieves because the rich and powerful despise and mistreat them while hardly ever extending them a helping hand.[29] The way to ameliorate the moral qualities of the peasantry, urged d'Holbach, in 1773, is to start by thoroughly reforming the nobility and especially abolishing the unjust privileges, onerous usages, and feudal "rights" that reduced rural life to unending misery for the poor.[30]

A truly enlightened moral philosophy, held the radical enlighteners, must focus on the downtrodden and impoverished. Here, the radical tradition, and Diderot and d'Holbach in particular, sought to indict almost the entire history of previous moral thought, which seemed to them to neglect precisely this dimension and concern itself exclusively with the aspirations of the privileged. This tendency they considered the outcome of a cultural environment in which the common people were routinely assumed to be "a vile rabble" scarcely "made to reason or to learn" and whom the aristocracy seemed to think must be "constantly duped and deceived so that they could oppress them with ease and impunity."[31] The object of the "General Revolution" envisaged by Diderot and d'Holbach was precisely to end this state of affairs by making equality the supreme principle of human morality and organization; by 1789 their efforts had begun to have startling results.

For a brief period, there was a remarkable flurry of optimism in radical circles in Britain, Holland, Germany, and France. "I do not believe," wrote Paine—as convinced as any of the radical enlighteners that a "revolution of the mind" had indeed taken place—in February 1792, "that monarchy and aristocracy will continue seven years longer in any of the enlightened countries in Europe."[32] The Irish revolutionary conspirator Theobald Wolfe Tone (1763–1798), who would lead the 1798 uprising in Ireland, observed in 1796 that for many centuries "every honest Irishman has mourned in secret over the misery and degradation of his native land, without daring to murmur a syllable in the way of complaint." But now everything had changed so that he saw "a new order of things commencing in Europe" and had become convinced that soon in all parts "the doctrine of republicanism will finally subvert that of Monarchy, and establish a system of just and rational Liberty, on the ruins of the thrones of the Despots of Europe."[33]

Meanwhile, from the 1760s onward the radical writers' discourse of equality was countered by an impressive new science that was simultaneously a potent ideological weapon, and recourse to which proved the strongest possible reply to talk of inequality: economics. Modern economics, as has often been noted, emerged specifically during the third quarter of the eighteenth century, especially the decade 1765–1775. Its foundations were laid by three pioneering works: Turgot's *Reflections on the Formation and Distribution of Wealth* (1766); Beccaria's *Elementi* (1771–1772); and Adam Smith's *Inquiry into the Nature and Causes of the Wealth of Nations* (1776).[34] What has not been generally noticed, however, is the wider intellectual context, the backcloth of disagreement between Radical and Moderate Enlightenment, against which the new science arose. Turgot, Beccaria, and Adam Smith were indisputably the key pioneers of this new science, but to study their economic ideas in isolation from their general philosophy, moral ideas, and social concepts— as is usual— risks reducing economics' emergence to something extraneous and detached from its age. To be properly grasped in its historical context, classical economics must be situated against the backdrop of struggle between Radical and Moderate Enlightenment thought.

The three foundational works of economics were almost wholly concerned with the production, expansion, and taxation of wealth, in demonstrating how economic development follows from the creation of an economic surplus, or net product, which then becomes the motor driving further generation of wealth by providing the means through which production can be raised, techniques refined, and commerce stimulated. The central proposition of these writers was that society will progress and improve if the laws of the market are set free and left untrammeled. Such improvement is attainable, they argued, without disturbing the principles of rank and aristocracy, or challenging monarchy and religious authority; the market suffices on its own to correct society's imbalances and difficulties. All three insisted on the broadly inhibiting effect of the obstacles to enterprise and production posed by tradition, mistaken policies, restrictions, privileges, monopolies, and wrongly conceived tariffs and taxes.[35] The question of the distribution of wealth in society, and issues of poverty and deprivation, meanwhile, remained not just secondary but largely outside the purview of eighteenth-century economics as conceived by Turgot and Smith.

In his *Reflections on the Formation and Distribution of Wealth*, as earlier in the *Encyclopédie*, Turgot envisaged economics as a pure science wholly subject to observable natural laws. He demonstrates with impressive precision the laws governing the performance and returns on capital in different economic contexts and different ways capital interacts with land, labor, and skills. Money put into land for renting out, he explains, always brings least because it involves the least risk and is the most predictable form of investment. Since investing in agriculture, industry, or commerce, on the other hand, involves more considerable trouble and risk, it would be in no one's interest to undertake such investments unless the likely returns on money invested in these sectors significantly exceeds the predictable return on capital lent out at interest or tied up in renting out land.[36] Obviously, different capital investments bring very different yields. "But this inequality," he showed, "does not prevent them influencing each other, and establishing between them a kind of equilibrium, just as two liquids of different specific gravity balance each other when separated in sections of an inverted siphoning system connected by a pipe running underneath them."[37] The liquids are not then level, but if the level of one rises the other must rise, too.

When many landowners wish to sell simultaneously, the price of land must drop precipitately and investors can then, for the same money, undertake larger-scale agricultural enterprises than before. This cannot happen, though, Turgot explains, without the rate of interest on money borrowed rising simultaneously because those with funds to invest would now rather use it to buy land for renting out than lend at rates no greater than the revenue from the land purchased with that money. If, therefore, capitalists investing in agriculture or rents when land prices drop borrow more capital, they must do so at higher rates of interest. But the more interest rates rise, the more attractive it becomes to invest in loans rather than riskier, less predictable sectors such as farming, industry, and commerce. "The rate of interest," he adds, "can be regarded as a kind of water level falling below which all labour, cultivation, industry, and commerce are engulfed and promptly cease."[38]

Turgot, like Adam Smith after him, was a true apostle of the pure, free-trade conception of capitalism. "It is this continual advancing and returning of capital that constitutes what ought to be called the circulation of money—this beneficial and fruitful circulation which animates all the work of society, maintains the activity and life of the body politic, and which there is good reason to compare with the circulation of the blood in the animal body."[39] Disdainful of virtually all medieval economic institutions and practices,[40] Turgot's theoretical and practical contributions in economics were designed to bolster efforts to remove such barriers to the unrestricted flow of capital, labor, and commodities as regional tariffs, guild regulations, provincial fairs, and royal and municipal controls on the internal movement and pricing of grain and wine. In his article "Foire," composed for the *Encyclopédie* before he withdrew from that enterprise in 1757, he argues that the great commercial fairs of Europe, when carefully examined, prove to be more detrimental than conducive to the advancement of trade.[41] He contended that a healthy society is one in which circulation of money and goods proceeds unobstructed by extraneous factors.

Turgot acknowledges the ubiquitous character of poverty as a characteristic problem of modern society, but sees it as one that could be eased by removing hindrances to the flow of capital and investment. Equally, for Smith poverty may sometimes constitute a chronic problem, but freeing up trade and especially injecting more dynamism into an economy will accomplish all that can be done to ensure that the "wages of labor" rise. This chiefly happens, he argues, as a by-product of enhancing economic dynamism and national wealth via free trade and market forces, not from tackling the problem of destitution as such, an issue he rarely addresses.[42] He held that economic stagnation, such as what was then typical of China, for instance, was much the greatest cause of poverty. China itself was not poor, but due to the stagnation of its economy "the poverty of the lower ranks of people in China," he observed, "far surpasses that of the most beggarly nations in Europe."[43]

The differences between Turgot and Smith are slight compared with their similarities. But their economic theories were tethered to their providential conception of human progress, opposition to the materialism of Diderot and d'Holbach, and vigorous defense in their other writings of the principles of rank and aristocracy. Like Turgot, Smith was not lacking in a robustly critical attitude toward many economic institutions and practices of his time. He was not oblivious to the "expensive and unnecessary wars" typical of his age.[44] But expressions of indignation at how the law and institutions are exploited by the rich and privileged for the oppression of the poor, while they do occur, are mostly found in his unpublished papers and at any rate remained marginal to his thought.[45] Smith, in fact, never seems to have departed far from the stance he adopts in his earlier *Theory of Moral Sentiments* (1759), where he asserts that success in business, like aristocratic birth, should be deemed a sign of divine favor and that men ought to consider "wealth and external honours" the proper recompense of a life of virtue "and the recompense which virtue can seldom fail of acquiring."[46]

Smith's rationale for inequality underpinned the quintessentially "moderate" stance of the Scottish Enlightenment and its providential conception of society, though it is true that such views were expressed more emphatically in the 1750s than subsequently. "It has pleased Providence, for wise purposes," argued Ferguson in an early text, "to place men in different stations and to bestow upon them different degrees of wealth." Such providential rhetoric softened later. But there is no sign that Smith or Ferguson ever really departed from their early view that "subordination" is the very basis of society and what makes government, industry, and the social order possible. "Every person does good," contended Ferguson in 1757, "and promotes the happiness of society, by living agreeable to the rank in which Providence has placed him."[47]

Turgot's attitude to poverty and distress was, if anything, still harsher. In his eyes, social inequality was not just inscribed in nature and integral to the way things are, but also not inherently an evil. Even more than Ferguson and Smith, Turgot viewed inequality as a positive good, indeed the driving force behind technological progress and increasing wealth, and assuredly ordained by the Creator.[48] From early on, he exhibited a particular attitude toward the peasantry and the poor, and, unlike his radical-minded young friend Condorcet, saw absolutely no need to lessen the disproportion in men's fortunes or check what the latter considered the prevailing excessive inequality.[49] Rather Turgot, like Smith and Ferguson, considered the whole debate about equality and inequality irrelevant and fundamentally misconceived.

Assuredly, he had no wish to make men insensitive to the distress and suffering of the destitute, or weaken the spirit of benevolence and charity, or substitute for these a base and selfish preoccupation exclusively with one's own affluence. But Turgot believed that when it came to providing basic subsistence for the poor, pious charitable foundations had proved an unmitigated failure. He severely criticized the way foundations lock up capital in static situations in contradiction to his own chief doctrine that the general good arises from the sum of efforts of each and every individual in his or her own interest.[50] Every healthy person should work to provide for himself, for if he or she is fed and accommodated without needing to work, it must then be at the expense of others. What the state owes to all its members, he maintained, is neither more nor less than the removal of all obstacles to individual effort and the unrestricted flow of goods, capital, and services.[51]

None of the founders of economics mentioned above—or, for that matter, the Dutch Sephardic Jewish *philosophe* Isaac de Pinto (1717–1787), another connoisseur of capital flows and one who went beyond the others in justifying empire on grounds of commercial interest— figured at all in the Enlightenment debate about how directly to mitigate deprivation and correct social problems stemming from unequal wealth distribution. A lifelong admirer of Voltaire, and, like him, an ardent admirer of Locke, Newton, and Condillac,[52] Turgot, scion of an old Norman family, remained not just an avowed providential Deist but also a staunch defender of nobility. His ambition to reform the French monarchy was wide-ranging but inspired by British and Dutch models of urban, commercial society grafted onto a French agricultural base. Thoroughly opposed to the new *philosophie*, he repeatedly disclaimed being an *encyclopédiste* and sought to distance himself as far as possible from Diderot.[53]

Turgot and Smith were unquestionably economic geniuses and the preeminent founders of classical economics, but they were also, and not unconnectedly, amongst the chief conservative social theorists of the mainstream Enlightenment. The most brilliant expositions of free-market thinking of the eighteenth century, their writings represented the foremost "enlightened" challenge to the radical thesis regarding inequality and poverty. To their view, their new science, cogent and rigorous, demonstrates that poverty increases and decreases essentially owing to market forces, rising most steeply when capitalists who invest in enterprises are forced, as Turgot expressed it, to "reduce their undertakings." Where investment significantly recedes, the "total of the labour, of the consumption of the fruits of the earth, of production and of revenue must be equally diminished, so that poverty will then succeed riches and the common workman, finding less or no employment, will fall into the deepest misery."[54]

Laissez-faire economics and radical egalitarianism first collided in the pamphlet controversy known as the "grain wars" that followed the onset of famine conditions in France in the years 1769–1770. This transpired five years after the French crown—humiliated by its recent defeats in the Seven Years' War (1756–1763), resulting in British triumph in Canada and India, and weighed down by debts—embraced *économiste* doctrines in a desperate attempt to escape its mounting financial predicament, declaring in 1764 that grain would be freely traded both internally and for export.[55] But free-market economics were at the same time vigorously countered by several publications, most notably the Abbé Ferdinando Galiani's (1728–1787) *Dialogues on the Grain Trade*, (Dialogues sur le commerce des blés) (1769), a text partly rewritten as well as edited and published by Diderot.

Louis XV's leading minister, the duke de Choiseul, irritated by Galiani's intervention in the controversy, arranged his recall to Naples. To Diderot, though, it seemed his Neapolitan friend was being unjustly vilified by influential adversaries motivated by political and self-seeking considerations that did not serve the true interest of the people. Galiani, secretary of the Neapolitan embassy in Paris since 1759, disciple of the great Neapolitan enlightener, Antonio Genovesi (1712–1769), and a famously witty conversationalist, had been on friendly terms with the *coterie d'Holbachique* for some time, though his general approach to social issues owed rather more to Genovesi and Montesquieu than to them.[56] Indeed, though friendly with d'Holbach, he seemingly disliked his books. Galiani, however, convinced Diderot and d'Holbach of the limited relevance of free market economics in the wider context of subsistence, social stratification, and fairness. The free market doctrines of Turgot and the *économistes* that Diderot had fully adopted when editing the *Encyclopédie*, he now modified.[57]

The *Dialogues*, much to Choiseul's irritation, had a considerable impact. Turgot (seemingly unaware of Diderot's contribution) granted the book was eloquent and surprisingly well written but totally rejected its argument.[58] Diderot and Galiani now argued that while Turgot's free-trade theories were not inherently wrong, when judged from a purely theoretical economic perspective, they concluded, that a dogmatic generalization from them could have gravely adverse social consequences in a hierarchical, agrarian country like France. The authors observed that the shortages and high bread prices that little affected a commercial society with a large pool of shipping, such as Holland, very differently in France led to an unacceptable degree of distress among the poor and disadvantaged. It is morally wrong, they held, to risk harming not only the neediest but also the majority, by permitting a free hand to speculation and the profit motive in a commodity so basic to human subsistence as grain.[59]

In this controversy, in which the Abbé André Morellet (1727–1819), a disciple of Turgot, acted as spokesman for the party of *laissez-faire* and the doctrine that proprietary rights are sacrosanct,[60] Galiani and Diderot chiefly stressed the discrepancy in practice between Turgot's theoretical equality of the individual, in offering and buying grain in the market, and the manipulative powers of a strongly entrenched social hierarchy built on massive inequality in ownership of land and that actually controlled most of the grain available for sale.[61] Here was a theoretical clash that tended to intensify over the years and that decisively polarized the surviving *philosophes* into sharply opposed radical and "moderate" blocs during the early stages of the Revolution. In 1789, despite having lived on friendly terms with some of them for decades, Morellet quarreled bitterly with practically all the disciples and heirs of Diderot, Helvétius, and d'Holbach, who were by then virtually without exception staunch supporters of what Morellet dismissively termed the *parti démocratique*.[62]

A controversy such as this, affecting vital interests of the entire nation, was exactly the kind that, in Diderot's view, should be judged in the open, without restriction, before the tribunal of public opinion.[63] Seeing the *Dialogues* under heavy attack, especially from Morellet, he penned his *Apologie de l'Abbé Galiani* (1771), a further contribution to the debate (which he toyed with publishing before putting it in a drawer), in which Diderot again pretends to be Galiani. Free-market exchange is again judged a valid principle up to a point. It is often right to remove internal barriers to enterprise. *Laissez-faire* economics becomes potentially harmful, though, when elevated to an overriding principle. Indeed, what Diderot calls *la liberté illimitée* entails great dangers for society, creating a constant need for government and municipalities to maintain strict vigilance and a reserve net of powers designed to combat speculation, collective anxieties, manipulation, hoarding, and all manner of "friponneries."[64] Though he questioned Morellet's motives, he did not charge Turgot and other advocates of free market economics with a lack of integrity. Their error, in his opinion, lay in taking too narrow a view. The *économistes* had simply forgotten about the social effects of cupidity. But honest or not, Diderot argues, no one has the right to sanction manipulation of price rises in grain while his fellows succumb to famine.[65]

From 1769, Diderot, Helvétius, and d'Holbach constructed a social theory in part antagonistic to the free-market economics of Turgot, Adam Smith, Morellet, and the *économistes*. Of the radical *philosophes* only Condorcet leaned toward Turgot's doctrine of entirely free domestic commerce in all commodities—at any rate until 1793.[66] The rest, including Brissot, later a leading figure in the Revolution, and Maréchal, who was to denounce *laissez-faire* economics during the Revolution, followed Diderot and d'Holbach in their economic ideas no less than in their materialism and hostility to "priestcraft."[67] Half of society languishes in complete poverty, observed Brissot in 1777, and a further quarter has a thoroughly mediocre standard of living. Of the final quarter, part lived in comfortable circumstances while a tiny percentage wallowed in wealth.[68] How could this be right?

The sight of three-quarters of humanity serving the re-maining quarter was so abominable, exclaimed the eru-dite librarian Sylvain Maréchal (1750–1803) in 1788, that it was enough to convince any atheist that he should em-brace the doctrine of divine Providence to avoid despair. Atheists, he suggested, dream of a world to come where it would be the turn of the abject three-quarters to be "served" by their former masters.[69] In May 1792, when press freedom under the Revolution was at its height, Morellet who had now broken with the circle of Madame Helvétius (1722–1800), above all because they refused to recognize the rights of noble and ecclesiastical property, published an article in the *Journal de Paris* denouncing those who pressed for greater equality, and Brissot in par-ticular, for turning the Revolution into a war against property.[70]

During the mid-1770s, Turgot was for a time a powerful figure in the French government, where he exemplified the rule that champions of enlightened ideas striving for the ear of the royal and princely courts must formulate reform proposals in terms of Moderate Enlightenment concepts. Should we gather from this that all the realistic, practical enlighteners of solid good sense belonged to the Moderate Enlightenment? Some historians seem inclined to think so. The moderate mainstream constantly vaunted their "moderation," respect for older institutions, willing-ness to compromise with religion, veneration for Locke and Newton, and general enthusiasm for the British model. And because, initially, in the 1760s and 1770s such men held the initiative, first having the opportunity to implement their proposals, it has often appeared that they represent the real Enlightenment, the sensible Enlightenment, the Enlightenment that counts. One recent historian even claims everything praiseworthy and still relevant in the Enlightenment was pragmatic along these lines and in inspiration, essentially "British."[71] But, on closer examination, such an analysis hardly seems plausible. For precisely the moderate reformers, *économistes*, and Turgot himself were soon seen to fail, and fail spectacularly.

Turgot's eventual fall from power and the furor over his attempts to introduce free trade in grain, like the capsizing of Joseph II's and Catherine the Great's "enlightened" reform programs in the 1780s, were paradigmatic of a wider failure of the moderate mainstream to achieve significant, or at least sufficient, reforms and improvements by means of free-market economics, legal reformism, and administrative rationalization within the existing framework of monarchy, aristocracy, ecclesiastical authority, and colonial empire. The moderate enlighteners did register some significant reforms in Italy, Germany, Scandinavia, and Russia in the three decades between 1760 and 1789. But not enough could be accomplished within existing structures of authority and society to correct the most harmful imbalances, difficulties, and consequences of privilege. By 1789 the schemes of the moderate enlighteners had not even managed to deliver a comprehensive toleration in respect to religion so that Dissenters, apostates, and Jews were still not freed from disabilities or accorded equality of status, let alone significantly curtail the privileges of the aristocracy, correct the one-sidedness of marriage, legalize divorce, or ameliorate poverty. For the most part, neither the serfs in Eastern Europe nor the slaves in the Western Hemisphere had been emancipated. Individual life-style remained under the shackles of theologically-motivated prohibitions on "fornication," adultery, homosexuality, and other forms of prohibited personal conduct, leaving harsh punishments and stigmas in place that often weighed particularly unfairly on unmarried, single mothers.

The social and political doctrines of Hume, Ferguson, Smith, Turgot, and Voltaire were simply inadequate and insufficient for tackling the major structural problems Europe faced at the time. Traditional forms of authority, law, tradition, and rank in *ancien régime* Europe were simply too strongly entrenched to be dealt with by free-market economics, legal reformism, or the other tools of the moderate mainstream. Moderate Enlightenment, in the 1770s and 1780s, consequently had comparatively little success when evaluated as a reform program, which meant that resentment and disaffection continued to grow.

Diderot and d'Holbach believed that institutionalized inequality undermines the political order and, by fomenting crime and misanthropy, the moral order as well.

The man discriminated against is aggrieved. The man who possesses nothing lacks any stake in society.[72] How can anyone expect destitute men unschooled in any principles or true morality to remain tranquil spectators of the luxury, opulence, and unjust exactions extorted by self-seeking, corrupt individuals who scorn the distress of the multitude and rarely attempt to ease their hardship? Here was reasoning—echoed subsequently by others, including Brissot, Mirabeau, and Maréchal in his fiercely anti-royalist, anti-aristocratic *Apologues modernes* (1788), which depicted *ancien régime* Paris as a society built on injustice—that seemed utterly perverse to the Dominican father Dom Charles-Louis Richard (d. 1794), who roundly rejected the impious implication that the only basis of aristocracy were the lands and other assets that a few, more ruthless than the rest, had once wrested by violent or fraudulent means, contrary to the common good.[73] Like other *anti-philosophes*, he vigorously championed loyalism and the hereditary principle against the *nouvelle philosophie*, reaffirming the legitimacy of separate orders and social hierarchy alongside religion and monarchy.[74]

In short, Moderate Enlightenment was simply unable to do the job that major portions of society required it to do and hence it eventually lost the initiative. By the 1780s control of events had passed to the radical enlighteners and, equally evident, to the out-and-out opponents of all Enlightenment, the ideologues of the Counter-Enlightenment. It was thus the moderate mainstream's comprehensive failure, more than anything else, that triggered both the "General Revolution" following in the wake of the Radical Enlightenment's "Revolution of the Mind" and the simultaneous upsurge throughout Europe of a powerful Counter-Enlightenment culture of faith, anti-intellectualism, and reactionary thought and politics based on unquestioning rejection of democracy, equality, and personal liberty.

CHAPTER IV

The Enlightenment's Critique
of War and the Quest
for "Perpetual Peace"

Only with more regard for others can there be fewer wars and what greater need, asked the radical thinkers, has humanity than that? What else is there so opposed to the general happiness, progress of reason, and to human civilization generally, demanded d'Holbach, than the vastly destructive wars everywhere ceaselessly waged by princes in pursuit of quarrels that have nothing to do with the interests of those they consider their subjects?[1] And without an equally vast fund of crass credulity, error, ignorance, and prejudice among men that nothing has so far managed to tackle, how else would it be possible that millions of men ceaselessly acquiesce in participating in conflicts detrimental to the common good, "l'utilité générale," and that are totally unconnected with their own personal interests?[2] The only kind of war Diderot deemed legitimate in his last, most militantly radical phase, in the *Histoire philosophique*, were the wars of liberation he foresaw on the horizon when the oppressed peoples of the world rise up against the monarchs, aristocrats, merchants, and priests who, in his view, relentlessly exploit them.[3]

Of course, the whole Enlightenment denounced the wars and militarism of the eighteenth century. So why, one might ask, distinguish between radical and moderate in this regard? The answer is that there were very different forms and intensities of anti-war sentiment in eighteenth-century Europe and America. In some thinkers the revulsion against the wars of the age was deep and systematic, in others much less so, and this divergence was directly linked to each thinker's wider philosophical stance. Much of the aversion to the public pretensions of the Moderate Enlightenment infusing the writings of Herder, for example, one of Voltaire's and Kant's foremost German critics, arose from disgust with Frederick the Great and his court, resentment against a monarch who boasted of Enlightenment and vaunted reason and rejection of superstition, but who actually did more than any other of his contemporaries to plunge Europe almost constantly into war and bloodshed. Herder judged it appalling, cynical hypocrisy, and a betrayal. Indeed, he thought the wrong kind of Enlightenment can be even more pernicious than obscurantism and plain barbarism. "The universal dress of philosophy and love of mankind," he wrote, "can be made to disguise persecutions—violations of the true, personal freedom of men and countries, citizens and peoples—such as Cesare Borgia himself could only dream of."[4]

So universal at a certain level was the Enlightenment's impact in the European courts that even so celebrated and widely eulogized a warrior-king as Frederick suffered some embarrassment under the growing blast of Enlightenment criticism of his wars, as we learn from his sarcastic comments in letters to Voltaire. Writing to Voltaire from Charlottenburg Palace in Berlin in May 1770, whilst composing his reply to d'Holbach's *Essai sur les Préjugés*, he complained that the Russian empress, Catherine, evidently had a special dispensation from Diderot, "bought with hard cash"—an allusion to the pension she had allocated, affording him financial security, in return for acquiring his books and papers after his death—"permitting" her to launch a vast war of aggression against the Turks. Meanwhile, he felt impeded by these "censeurs philosophiques" and, being unwilling to commit the crime of "lèse-philosophie" or undergo "l'excommunication encyclopédique," felt constrained to keep the peace.[5] A year later, he returned to this theme, mockingly to be sure, but yet in a manner proving the *encyclopédistes'* antimilitarist barbs had pricked the skin of even this hardened man of arms: *Messrs les encyclopédistes* had so vigorously rebuked "the mercenary executioners who transformed Europe into a theatre of gore and carnage," he wrote from

Potsdam, "that in future I shall take good care to avoid their censures."[6]

Frederick's sarcasm was directed at Diderot and d'Holbach, not Voltaire. Indeed, in the same missive he expresses confidence that his retort to d'Holbach would elicit Voltaire's approval, being full of the "moderation" favored by the *philosophe* of Ferney himself.[7] As Voltaire, Frederick, and the moderate mainstream saw it, war and standing armies, the culture of court militarism, were simply integral to a world of princes and aristocracy; to them, "perpetual peace" was a utopian dream concocted by unworldly men devoid of practical sense.[8] Certainly, Voltaire worried more than Frederick about the resulting carnage and not infrequently made cutting remarks about the role of royal vanity in fomenting the wars of the age, a criticism reflected in Paine's comment that Voltaire was "both the flatterer and satirist of despotism."[9] But Voltaire's philosophy discouraged anything beyond ironic, muted complaint. He knew well enough that neither kings nor their courts, the leading players in his Enlightenment, would desist from war or listen to anyone who asked them to.

The only "perpetual peace" obtainable among men, affirms Voltaire in his essay *De la paix perpétuelle* (1769), is "tolerance," the gains that ensue from curbing bigotry and weakening belief in religious authority. The more general peace "imagined" by the Abbé de Saint-Pierre, the early eighteenth-century French utopian who first urged the quest for an end to war, he dismissed as "a chimaera that could no more exist among princes than elephants and rhinoceroses, or between wolves and dogs."[10] Voltaire, a *philosophe* quite prepared to heap effusive praise on Catherine the Great for launching a blatantly offensive war against the Turks in 1769–1770—an outright aggression that would, he hoped, crush the Ottoman Empire completely and precipitate the rebirth of Greece—and to celebrate her expansionist ambitions in the most bombastic terms, could find nothing negative to say in the entire twenty-five pages of his essay against monarchs; indeed he there denounces only intolerance and religious dogmatism. For him curtailing "fanaticism" is the only way mankind can edge closer to a "perpetual peace."

Rousseau, too, with his commitment to pristine, "manly" virtues and national feeling, dismisses "perpetual peace" as an impossible dream. Immanuel Kant, by contrast, in his tract *Perpetual Peace* (1795), holds that the dream of "perpetual peace" is not "a chimaera," but truly the supreme goal of human progress, a goal realizable, however, only via a transition from arbitrary and despotic government—on whose shoulders he, much like the radical enlighteners, pinned the blame for the militarism and wars of his time—to legislative "republicanism."[11] Kant, too, however, manages to preserve the princes' executive authority by introducing, as we have

seen, a conception of "republicanism" that confines collective consultation to the legislative process while leaving
monarchical executive authority intact.[12] Hence, he opens
no political path by which man's progress toward "perpetual peace" can be accelerated. Against this half-way position, and Voltaire's still greater subservience to princes
and their courts, radical thinkers equated despotism and
arbitrary government with monarchy itself and republicanism with abrogating or emasculating monarchy and
substituting for it representative democracy, in both the
legislative and executive spheres.

Moderate Enlightenment, then, and Rousseauism
lacked any political strategy that could conceivably produce the kind of structural changes capable of transforming the existing order so as to diminish the likelihood
of war. Not only did Kant deliberately refrain from embracing democracy as a principle, but, even in his most
daring writings of the 1790s, continually reaffirms the legitimacy of princely authority, claiming subjects have no
defensible "rights" against the will of sovereigns. The only
justifiable way a "republican" mode of government can
be achieved, he urges, would be through the initiative of
the prince, or via debate and legislation sanctioned by an
enlightened prince. Where princes deny the moral superiority of republican principles, in legislation there is, according to Kant, no countervailing right of resistance or
rationale of justified revolution of the sort proclaimed by
Diderot, Raynal, and the "boutique d'Holbachique."

The Scottish enlighteners likewise refrain from any broad critique of war, standing armies, and the aristocratic military code (as well as empire and slavery). "War is justly avoided," agrees Ferguson, "and peace among mankind is admitted to be a supreme object of consideration and desire: but we must not therefore enjoin it as an article of wisdom for nations to discontinue their military policy, and to neglect preparations for their own defence." Maintaining a strong military force and defenses, he argues, is "often the surest preservative of peace, and, joined to a scrupulous attention to abstain from wrongs or unnecessary provocations, [is] all that the most pacific nation can do to avoid the mischiefs of war." Ferguson was not one to condone the inexorable growth of armies and navies so characteristic of the eighteenth century for its own sake. Nevertheless, his general system and tendency to sanction rank and the status quo led him to accommodate war and the growth of armies as part of the natural order of things and to extol the moral qualities he believed war elicits. "War may be necessary, although it be not desirable on its own account," he writes, and he pronounces it folly "to consider the time of necessary war among nations as a period of misery, or the time of peace as of course a season of happiness."[13]

"It is the will of providence," averred Ferguson," that men have occasion sometimes to maintain the cause of their country against its enemies; and, in so doing, the virtues of human nature are its happiness, no less than they are so in reaping the fruits of peace."[14] Here we see, once again, the great chasm between Radical Enlightenment and the moderate mainstream. If those championing divine Providence and the legitimacy of the existing order were justified, then war was an integral part of the divinely ordained nature of things. For Radical Enlightenment, on the other hand, vast conflicts such as the War of the Austrian Succession (1740–1748) and the Seven Years' War (1756–1763)—in which many tens of thousands of soldiers were killed or maimed fighting all across the world for reasons few had the slightest inkling of, and which bore no relation to the true interests either of the population or of the soldiers and their families—were horrendous, unacceptable, and potentially avoidable. These wars, fought purely in the interests of monarchs, courtiers, aristocratic cliques, financiers, and merchants, they considered an inherent part of tyranny, an injustice abominably destructive and irrational caused directly by the system of authority, nobility, and princely courts. Their critique focused not least on the extensive use of Hessian mercenaries by the British Crown during the war to suppress the rebels in North America; many never saw Germany again and knew no English or anything about the American struggle for Independence, but fought in exchange for British subsidies subsequently used exclusively for the princes' own benefit.[15]

For d'Holbach, "all error is damaging; it is through being deceived that the human race has rendered itself unhappy."[16] But the wars of the eighteenth century represented error, and not just error, but misery, irrationality, and devastation on such a gigantic scale that they seemed to radical thinkers altogether inconceivable without a vast reservoir of credulous veneration for princely authority and noble rank, a credulity so ingrained in society that an unending supply of young and not-so-young men, often married and with children, were ready to risk annihilation in distant places for reasons wholly unconnected with themselves. "What an inconceivable mass of slaughter," exclaimed Joel Barlow, is due to "dark, unequal government, to the magical powers possessed by a few men of blinding the eyes of the community, and leading the people to destruction by those who are called their fathers and their friends!"[17]

Barlow contended that nothing was clearer than that superstition is a "blemish of human nature, by no means confined to subjects connected with religion. Political superstition is almost as strong as religious; and it is quite as universally used as an instrument of tyranny."[18] In monarchies, "political superstition" induces men "to spill their blood for a particular family, or for a particular branch of that family, who happens to have been born first, or last," or for a strand of a royal dynasty that adheres to one confession rather than another. "With the superstitious respect for kings," Priestley rebuked Edmund Burke in 1790, "and the spirit of chivalry, which nothing but an age of extreme barbarism recommended, and which civilization has banished, you seem to think that every thing great and dignified has left us."[19] If aristocracy and church power are bad, monarchy, for the out-and-out republican Paine, was "the master-fraud, which shelters all others. By admitting a participation of the spoil, it makes friends; and when it ceases to do this, it will cease to be the idol of courtiers," and thus it must continually provoke new conflicts.[20]

From the radical perspective, it was logical to blame the contemporary curse of war and militarism on "superstition" rooted in basic cultural, social, and theological structures that urgently required elimination in everyone's interest. But the mountain of "error" causing such havoc—composed of national prejudices, religious zeal, and, above all, popular veneration for monarchy, aristocracy, and ecclesiastical authority—would, clearly, not be easily leveled. The notion of glory that in their day still attached to the officer's status, success in battle, conquest, and military bravery in most societies "is evidently a vestige," suggested d'Holbach, "of the savage outlook prevalent among all peoples before they became civilized: as yet, though, there were hardly any nations wholly freed from a prejudice so damaging to the peace of the world."[21] Indeed, the noble ethic had become integral to monarchical and courtly tyranny. To d'Holbach, the thesis that *la vraie politique* "is nothing but the art of rendering men happy" implied that everything in statecraft and military organization not directed to this end could now be justifiably labeled "tyranny" and categorically condemned. Not only arbitrary rule but also colonial expansion and ambition, as well as mercantilist schemes to wrest trade by oppressive or violent means from others, could now be included under this rubric, since these can never be morally justified under the new criteria. The varieties of "superstition" responsible for fostering war were therefore seen by Diderot, d'Holbach, and their disciples to extend far beyond just veneration for rank and monarchy and religious intolerance. Thus, Condorcet disparages not only the "respect superstitieux" of the English for what radical *philosophes* considered the blatant defects of their constitution and legal system, but also their "préjugés commerciaux," meaning the aggressively mercantilist attitude evinced by their spokesmen toward foreign nations.[22]

Although not pacifists, the radical *philosophes* viewed with horror wars waged for the sake of spoils, prestige, and territory rather than to evict tyrants or repel unjustified aggression. Whenever a people is at war for justifiable reasons, to repel an aggressor or throw off oppression, they should scrupulously undertake, in their own interest, as well as from considerations of justice, to avoid dealing unjustly. Men at war should neither use excessive force nor mistreat prisoners, harm non-combatants, perpetrate atrocities, or otherwise oppress or humiliate the defeated, and least of all despoil whole peoples of their lands and goods. But most wars were not justifiably initiated. Radical writers denounced glory-seeking hereditary rulers as the chief menace to their own subjects as well as their neighbors. Needing standing armies to prop up their despotic power internally and nurture their nobilities, rulers of even the most civilized peoples showed little sign of being cured yet "of the madness of war," their upbringing and court milieu encouraging them to adhere to attitudes detrimental to "the happiness of society for which peace will always be the greatest benefit."[23] Only exhaustion of their armies and exchequers, and the consequent impossibility of persevering with the unjust and useless wars they so lightly undertake, ever induces great monarchs to embrace peace.

Monarchy's propensity to parade military valor and armies was continually encouraged by courtly culture's aristocratic code of glory—a code extolling combat, dueling, and indifference to wounds, death, and especially the wholesale slaughter of underlings—for which Diderot and his colleagues evinced the utmost contempt.[24] No wonder those raised amid such lofty conceit thought nothing of perpetrating vast carnage and destruction on all sides. To Barlow, who considered all monarchy inherently tyrannical, tyrannies, "whatever be the appellation of the government under which they are exercised, are all aristocratical tyrannies" and as such had no alternative but to "vindicate war, not merely as an occurrence of fatality, and justifiable on the defensive; but as a thing of choice, as being the most nutritious aliment of that kind of government which requires privileged orders and an army: for it is no great figure of speech to say that the nobility of Europe are always fed upon human gore." Nobility, avowed Barlow, "originated in war" and lives by war. Were mankind to cease fighting and take up only the tranquil pursuits of agriculture and industry, "the titled orders would lose their distinctions, mingle with society, and become reasonable creatures."[25]

All war that it is not for self-defense lacks justification. This credo, in turn, had broad implications for high culture and education. Since men naturally emulate whatever they see praised and revered during their childhood, averred d'Holbach, there flourishes a long tradition of heroicizing the most overweening conquerors of the past without the least critical scrutiny, a deeply rooted prejudice operating directly counter to the core doctrines of the new enlightened social and political morality. Spartan militarism, routinely extolled in schools as sublime, was nothing in reality but savage and bloody ferocity. Alexander the Great, universally exalted as a supremely fine hero, but to Maréchal "le plus grand perturbateur du genre humain," was a compulsive conqueror whose "criminal temerity" desolated the empire of the Persians. He died, added d'Holbach, without leaving mankind the slightest token of wisdom, enlightenment, or virtue, qualities without which there can be no true honor or glory.[26] Nothing more corrupts the hearts of peoples and princes alike, he contended, than unreasoning reverence inculcated into "youth for the great men, warriors and conquerors of antiquity who mostly knew nothing of the true principles of morality."[27]

"Conquest creates tyrants," proclaims d'Holbach, "never has it rendered peoples happy."[28] Great leaders who vanquish vast regions and subjugate peoples, no matter how vaunted by self-seeking eulogists, in reality only despoil, kill, maim, and render men miserable. In such conquerors' blindness to "true morality," teachers should explain, there is something distinctly childlike. The natural moral blindness and cruelty of the ignorant, being like that of children, can be corrected only through the guidance of those with more experience and understanding. The materialist thinkers concurred with Hobbes' thesis that the wicked person is not intrinsically different from the virtuous person but rather an immature person, a kind of grown-up child, an ignoramus in the deepest sense, someone who lacks a proper grasp of social and physical reality.[29] The comparison with children, furthermore, helps us realize that royalty is especially corrupt, since child-princes are practically never seen having their natural infantile wishes and tantrums disciplined by those around them. No doubt that is why, conjectured d'Holbach, thrones are so often occupied by the cruelest tyrants, like Nero, Caligula, and Tiberius.

Republics, some earlier antimonarchical treatises (including Spinoza's *Tractatus Theologico-Politicus* of 1670) had proposed, are by their nature more inclined to peaceable co-existence than monarchies, the latter being inherently more prone to involvement in succession contests, quarrels over precedence, and clashes over disputed territory. Diderot, Helvétius, and d'Holbach, as well as Rousseau, continued this line of reasoning. Kant, too, endorsed the view that republics are quintessentially peaceable, whereas government "arbitrary and despotic" tends to be geared for war.[30] While agreeing with much of the radical analysis and on the need to see "standing armies" eventually abolished, however, Kant simultaneously holds that we should not "confound (as is frequently done) a republican constitution with democracy." Democracy he deemed "necessarily despotic" since it "renders the representative system impossible, everyone striving to be master."[31] For radical thinkers, it was precisely the democratic representative republic that alone effectively counters despotism and promotes peace.

That representative democracies would not fight wars with each other they deduced from their fundamental political principle, already clearly expounded by Spinoza, that no man willingly renounces his natural independence and consents to submit to the wishes of others except in the hope of gaining a greater good than he enjoys living only according to his own wishes. Society's authority is grounded "on the advantages which it secures for its members," wrote the Franco-Dutch journalist and political theorist Antoine-Marie Cerisier (1749–1828), author of the *Tableau de l'histoire générale des Provinces-Unies*, a multivolume work published in Utrecht between 1777 and 1784.[32] "Why are not republics plunged into war," asked Paine, "but because the nature of their government does not admit of an interest distinct from that of the nation?"[33] It was this that seemed to carry the argument and render perpetual peace a distinctly plausible, even realistic, concept rather than just an inconceivable utopian dream.

Denying as they did that kings and churchmen were responsible for the wars between the European states, defenders of the existing order indignantly rejected the imputation that the interests of princes, nobles, and clergy were what fed "the rivalry and hatred between nations which at every moment provokes new wars" and the notion that the real interest of peoples is to erase such harmful prejudices, respect everyone's rights, and "concourir au bien universel."[34] The examples of Sparta and republican Rome were useful reminders that not only monarchies but also republics had in the past revered glory, war, militarism, and conquest. This might perhaps have afforded the moderate mainstream an effective riposte. Frederick the Great, angrily rebuking d'Holbach, observed that neither the Dutch nor the Venetian republic had refrained from waging war. Had not the Roman republic, insisted Frederick, been the most bellicose and expansionist of all states?[35] As for England, generally considered a crowned "republic" since the Revolution of 1688, was she not still prouder and more bellicose than any other eighteenth-century power? Had not Britain, objected Frederick (who was no anglophile), hounded and tricked Louis XV into the Seven Years' War without the slightest compunction, launching a campaign of global conquest and territorial acquisition in Canada, India, Africa, and the Caribbean that, for sheer aggressiveness, arrogance, ambition, and greed eclipsed anything wrought by kings?[36]

The snag with these counterarguments was that the radical *philosophes* refused to acknowledge as genuine "republics" those that were aristocratic in character, like Venice and Genoa, or oligarchic like the United Provinces, or based on a combination of aristocracy and limited monarchy like Britain. "This history of ancient Rome," asserts Barlow, "from beginning to end, under all its kings, consuls and emperors, furnishes not a single instance, after the conquest of the Sabians, of what may properly be called a popular offensive war; I mean a war that would have been undertaken by the people, had they enjoyed a free government, so organized as to have enabled them to deliberate before they acted, and to suffer nothing to be carried into execution but the national will."[37] What radical thinkers insisted on were the advantages not of old-style republics or British-style mixed monarchy but specifically of democratic republics based on representation.

The other main counterargument was that the existing system of standing armies and navies, and calculated efforts to balance the power of rivals, was actually the fittest means of preventing wars. "This," commented Barlow "is what the people of Europe are commanded to believe." He declared the formula a total fallacy and adroitly reversed it, pronouncing the "present military system" the cause of the wars of modern times, and standing armies the "best, if not the only means of promoting wars."[38] Regarding modern war and its devastating consequences, averred Barlow in 1792 with fierce irony, there were now more and more "heretics in the world (Mr Burke calls them atheists) who affect to disbelieve that men are made expressly for the purpose of cutting each other's throats; and who say that it is not the highest honor that a man can arrive at, to sell himself to another man for life at a certain daily price, and hold himself in readiness, night and day, to kill individuals or nations, at home or abroad, without ever enquiring the cause." "It is no compliment to the judgment or humanity of a man" to lead such a life, felt these unbelievers, who could "not see why aristocrats should not learn both judgment and humanity "as well as other people."[39]

Of the moderate mainstream thinkers rebuked by name in the great intellectual controversies of the age, no other was so reviled by radical writers as Burke, an Anglo-Irish parliamentarian earlier associated with progressive causes, including support for the American Revolution and the British parliamentary campaign to reform East India Company misconduct in India. His shift to an anti-democratic perspective, from 1787, when he publicly supported Britain's and Prussia's quashing of the Dutch democratic movement, offering national interest as his overriding principle, and his subsequent emergence as Britain's leading conservative thinker disappointed and angered many of the radical-minded, as did his subsequent perseverance in countering democratic and egalitarian principles (even refusing to condemn black slavery until a remarkably late date). His public detractors included Mirabeau, Paine, Cerisier, Cloots, Wollstonecraft, and Barlow, while Joseph Priestley, more politely, regretted he could no longer class Burke "among the friends of what I deem to be the cause of liberty, civil or religious, after having, in a pleasing occasional intercourse of many years, considered him in this respectable light."[40]

To kings, radical writers alleged, the tranquility of their subjects seemed entirely undesirable, to do away with which they devise a thousand pretexts.[41] The result is a "misère continuelle," in which men and women enjoy nothing of the natural abundance around them, populous lands are devastated, and societies disrupted. But are peoples forever fated to decimate each other, pursuing quarrels that have nothing whatever to do with the true interests of the majority? Surely, enlightenment can cure such ills. What real motives, asked d'Holbach (followed by Kant), do nations have to continually behave as each other's rivals and opponents? "Is anything more contrary to equity, humanity, and reason than to foster those hereditary hatreds among peoples, absurd and irrational, which perpetually divide the unfortunate inhabitants of the earth?"[42]

Neither military elites nor standing armies nor war itself would be possible, argued the radical *philosophes*, if society became more "enlightened." The cure they offered—demolish people's "superstitious" veneration for rank—was inherent in and directly derived from their philosophy. D'Holbach's system, protested opponents, is just Spinoza regurgitated and simplified. This was true. Yet, d'Holbach, and Diderot in his late writings, also go beyond, or develop, Spinoza in one crucial respect—their commitment to the idea that men's equality in a just society directly leads to the principle that the same moral laws and rules of justice as apply within such a society apply also between nations and societies so that humanity as a whole forms "la societé universelle." Wars they considered not merely highly damaging but attributable to lack of a proper sense of equity amongst peoples. They held that a lack of enlightenment and true moral values was the fundamental reason why nations ceaselessly fight fratricidal wars oppressing and destroying each other, exactly as lack of equity and respect for others is the reason that within each society "the powerful oppress the weak and wish to enjoy to the exclusion of others" the citizens' rights that justice accords to all men equally.[43]

It was a logic that, if carried through, spelt the end of monarchy and aristocracy. Frederick, spurning the radical exhortation to disavow war and become "le bienfaiteur de tous les peuples," powerfully counterattacked in his two tracts of 1770, lambasting the author of the *Système de la nature* for his impudent scorn for kings and vehemently repudiating his complaints about the alleged barbarity, destructiveness, and superfluousness of the wars of the age.[44] His opponent's scarcely concealed design, charged Frederick, was to undermine monarchy and introduce popular sovereignty. This was why the *Essai sur les préjugés* so loudly declaims against "great armies, which might impede [its author's] purpose."[45] Princes and their standing armies stood accused; yet, objected Frederick, "if ever the crude notions of our philosopher should be capable of being realized," the consequent elimination of monarchy and the hereditary principle in favor of popular sovereignty would render all government "incessantly exposed to intestine wars, which are a thousand times more dangerous than foreign conflicts."[46]

What is "peace," asks Diderot at one point, amid his contributions to the *Histoire philosophique?* Humanity yearns for "peace" in the sense of absence of war. But how can there be peace when internal violence rules practically all known societies in the form of tyranny, oppression, intolerance, and persecution?[47] The ignorance and super-stition on which all of these rest are the root cause of endless conflict and suffering within societies but equally of conflict between peoples. Disdain for the vulnerability, misery, poverty, and weakness of others to Diderot, as also for d'Holbach and Helvétius, is a moral outrage, an of-fense against humanity and a defect that princes and great aristocrats are particularly prone to since they see them-selves as belonging to a different species from other men and hence "are little disposed to show them humanity."[48] Louis XIV's devastation of the Palatinate in 1673 during the Franco-Dutch war of 1672–1677, charged d'Holbach, reveals this monarch, "so much vaunted by poets, to have been merely a savage barbarian as cruel as Attila the Hun."[49] Frederick was outraged. How dare this author speak so irreverently of so glorious a monarch, a repri-mand Diderot in turn witheringly rebutted in his private notes on the king's tract. Frederick's answer was absurd, he insisted, adding that he would not wish to have been "the ferocious beast" (that is, Louis XIV) who ordered the ruthless pillaging of the Palatinate.[50]

If nations took up arms, contended d'Holbach, only for their own defense, to ensure their own security, on account of their true interests—in other words solely for legitimate reasons—there would, in consequence, be hardly any wars. Paine and Barlow (but also Kant) re-stated d'Holbach's thesis as a point that was no longer just theoretical but that, as they believed in the wake of

1789, "bids fair to be a practical one, that the way to prevent wars is not merely to change the prevailing military and diplomatic system; for that, like the Church," wrote Barlow, "is an integral and necessary part of the government as they now stand, and of society as now organized: but the principle of government must be completely changed; and the consequence of this will be such a total renovation of society, as to banish standing armies, overturn the military system, and exclude the possibility of war."[51]

But doing away with monarchs and nobles evidently would not of itself suffice to secure international peace. Even without monarchy, many nations have cultivated warlike preferences and overly stressed the value of prowess and military discipline. The laws of ancient Crete and Sparta, notes d'Holbach, take it for granted that peace is inappropriate for men, and many modern regimes "seem to have preserved the same attitude." One would suppose, from the way most men think, that peoples are only placed on earth to hate, torment, and destroy each other. Among the most destructive forms of "superstition" still pervasive, they averred, were national animosities like the popular antagonism then notoriously poisoning relations between the British and French. One way of discrediting popular chauvinism was to dismiss it as an integral part of the baggage of monarchy. "As war is the system of government on the old construction," held Paine, "the animosity which nations reciprocally entertain, is nothing more than what the policy of their governments excites, to keep up the spirit of the system." Kings, in other words, were accused of deliberately fanning national antipathies to further oppressive government and militarism. "Man is not the enemy of man," protested Paine, "but through the medium of a false system of government. Instead, therefore, of exclaiming against the ambition of kings, the exclamation should be directed against the principle of such governments; and instead of seeking to reform the individual, the wisdom of a nation should apply itself to reform the system."[52]

The "system of universal peace" among mankind, concluded Paine, is not just conceivable but also practicable if only peoples became "enlightened enough not to be made the dupes of courts." Removing kings and substituting democratic republics would, it was thought, of itself cure national animosities. "The people of America," he observed in 1791, "had been bred up in the same prejudices against France" that in the 1770s "characterized the people of England; but experience and an acquaintance with the French nation have most effectually shown to the Americans the falsehood of those prejudices; and I do not believe that a more cordial and confidential intercourse exists between any two countries [today] than between America and France."[53] America, argued the radical writers, serves mankind as a model also in another respect, proving that people of different extractions can live side by side in concord and harmony. In the state of New York, observed Paine, "about half" of the population were Dutch and the rest a mixture of English, Irish, and Scottish whilst in New Jersey again one found "a mixture of English and Dutch, with some Scottish and Irish," and in Pennsylvania, where fully one-third of the population were German, the English amounted to no more than another third.[54]

"When all the governments of Europe shall be established on the representative system," declared Paine, "nations will become acquainted, and the animosities and prejudices fomented by the intrigue and artifice of courts will cease."[55] Radical thought considered national animosities, like love of combat and prowess, vestiges of the savage state of man, crude blemishes remedied only by propagating the new morality of equality and equity internationally as well as nationally. As Cerisier expressed it, "it is not impossible that the leaders of nations should one day desire the good of humanity." Cerisier has been classified as a follower of Montesquieu,[56] but until the early 1790s actually adhered to radical positions and was a particularly ardent supporter of the American Revolution. It may even happen, he predicted, that those who direct affairs will finally grasp that the interests of peoples violently clash only to their mutual disadvantage. Every power that thinks it is in its own particular interest to disrupt the ordinary commerce and relations between peoples is by that fact alone "opposée au Bonheur général." There had never been a more favorable time, he urged in his journal *Le Politique Hollandois* in April 1781, for a general congress of maritime powers to examine all the possible ways by which humanity could prevent future conflicts at sea by drawing up a general treaty, to which all would subscribe, embodying the right of peoples on the seas. This would be a crucial step toward a "perpetual peace."[57]

To find the path to universal peace, Diderot, d'Holbach, and their disciples extended the Spinozist idea of the moral ties binding each individual to the next in a just society on the basis of reciprocity to international relations. Every nation has moral obligations to its neighbors, including those weaker than itself, a lesson mankind finds very difficult to adopt. It was essential that international relations no less than government, manners, and religion should be fundamentally reformed in accordance with natural laws.[58] The "general will" of a particular society, in Diderot and d'Holbach, obliges every citizen to allow the others security and tranquility and to fulfill his obligations toward them, punishing violators and tying the hands of those who behave in an antisocial manner. This concept of "general will," that of Diderot and d'Holbach extending (contrary to that of Rousseau) to the law of the "grand society" of the nations of the world, presupposed the universality of the new secular morality of citizenship and equality.

Rousseau's "general will," by contrast—infused by his proto-nationalist commitment, preference for small, self-sufficient republics, and positive dislike of cosmopolitanism and internationalism—was of little help in this regard.[59] It was only the "general will" of the Radical Enlightenment that urged all states to uphold justice, tranquility, and good faith in the interest of everyone. Of course, there existed as yet no authority capable of dissuading or preventing princes and peoples from carrying out aggression and behaving unjustly toward one another. Princes and nations formed a kind of super society but yet one, unfortunately, without any head, without any fixed principles, and without laws. Hence, it was unsurprising that men continue to suffer the atrocious consequences of war and anarchy. With the spread of democratic republics, though, the position would rapidly improve. By creating an international tribunal of the powers, these writers proposed, a court of the nations, true moral principles, genuine order, and law could replace the unrestricted rivalry and unchecked greed of overweening imperial monarchies and ambitious princes.[60] Kant agreed with this but not that it is necessary to eliminate monarchy and aristocracy and adopt representative democracy universally to achieve it.

Hence, to bring about world peace, held the radical *philosophes*, a double process is required—a shift toward democratic republicanism within nations, on the one hand, and, on the other, a convergence of the interest of peoples in the form of an international general assembly with agreed rules for resolving disputes. Just as aggression and warlike traditions inevitably feed the trend toward tyranny and hereditary monarchy, so conversely the shift toward representation, consultation, and formal democracy will feed the appetite for peace and stability, the things genuinely in the true interest of everyone. Warlike peoples exalt the need for swift, secret decision making, disciplined action, and absence of dissent from undertakings decided on.[61] Thus, bellicose and aggressive propensities predispose society to autocracy, tyranny, suppression of dissent, and loss of individual freedom. Conversely, a people injured by war and tyranny, they contended, will strive for the opposite.

Peace is so necessary to the happiness of the human race, urged Cerisier in 1783, that there exists a need for a new body on earth powerful and respected enough to oblige all the powers to accept this benefit for human kind and concert the terms on which they can jointly nominate an international "senate" authorized to arbitrate the differences that arise between countries. This body, after rigorous inspection of all the rival claims, rights, and statements, would pronounce their findings and resolutions that would then be binding on all peoples. Such a "senate" of the nations must be composed of men virtuous enough "to have no other fatherland than the universe, no other

friends than justice and truth" (pour n'avoir d'autre pa-
trie que l'univers, d'autres amis que la justice et la vérité).
Its "assemblée générale," as Cerisier termed his United
Nations, in what was perhaps the first ever exact formula-
tion of the concept, would need to have a president and
every year this international "presidency" would devolve
upon a fresh deputy elected by majority vote.[62]

Establishing a general assembly to regulate the international relations of the world's representative democracies
was the only logical path to "perpetual peace." But human
society cannot consist of democratic republics based on
the principle of representation and elections without a
"General Revolution" preparing the way first. In sharp
contrast to Voltaire and Kant, this was the perspective of
the Radical Enlightenment. Monarchy, aristocracy, and
religious authority were the vested interests that stood in
the way, maintaining the standing armies, recruiting
schedules, system of high taxation, and constant waging
of war. "Reason, like time, will make its own way," predicted Paine, "and prejudice will fall in a combat with
interest. If universal peace, civilization, and commerce,
are ever to be the happy lot of man, it cannot be accomplished but by a revolution in the system of governments."[63] It was a program that, once again, shows how
vast in reality was the chasm between Moderate and Radical Enlightenment. For in essence the eighteenth-century
"perpetual peace" debate was not a controversy about
war, standing armies, and militarism, or about how to

create a United Nations, at all, but rather an integral part of the wider battle between radical and moderate thought, between the vision of a time-honored, God-ordained providential order, on the one hand, and monistic, Spinozistic systems anchored in representative democracy and egalitarianism, on the other.

Chapter V
Two Kinds of Moral Philosophy in Conflict

Despite the great variety of the world's religions, affirms Diderot, all peoples have felt, more or less along the same lines, that it is necessary to be just. All nations have honored such virtues as goodness, friendship, loyalty, sincerity, and gratitude. Consequently, we should not look to any particular event or revelation for the source of what is so general and unalterable.[1] True morality, argues Diderot, is essentially reverence for, and obedience to, just laws and good institutions, so that societies have good or bad customs and morals depending on whether they have good or bad laws; and the happiness of the people is determined by whether the laws are good or bad.[2] For Radical Enlightenment in the tradition of Spinoza, Bayle, Fontenelle, Meslier, Du Marsais, Diderot, Helvétius, and d'Holbach, but also numerous writers in other countries besides Holland and France, morality is a universal, purely secular system based on a conception of justice wholly separate from, indeed best cultivated without, the influence of any particular religion. This was a view Rousseau in later life claimed to have shared with his former friend, Diderot, during the late 1740s and early 1750s, but later firmly rejected from the period of his *Letter to d'Alembert* (1758) onward.[3]

Ministers of religion disagree, suggested Diderot, only because "through their systems they became the masters of regulating all men's actions, and of disposing all that men owned and wanted. In the name of heaven they endorsed arbitrary government on earth."[4] In the religious camp, those that could align with this conception of morality were, once again, the philosophical Unitarians and quasi-Socinians, such as Richard Price and Joseph Priestley, figures influential in Holland and America as well as Britain, who were virtual materialists themselves. For these insisted on uncoupling church-based theology from morality and social policy, and church authority from the civil power, thus leaving human inquiry free and unfettered. Society, Price admonished, must ensure "an open field for discussion, by excluding from it the interposition of civil power, [. . .] by separating religion from civil policy, and emancipating the human mind from the chains of church-authority and church-establishments."[5]

Admittedly, the Unitarians and their friends believed in some sort of Heaven, whereas the radical *philosophes*, Paineites, and Benthamites did not. But what chiefly mat-

tered for forging the new radical revolutionary consciousness in moral and social theory, no less than in politics,
was that Unitarians and atheistic materialists both placed
great emphasis on the universality, separateness, and primacy of a reason-based moral order and a predominantly
secular conception of the "common good" against church
doctrine, tradition, and belief. Priestley entirely concurred that

> to make the public good the standard of right and
> wrong, in whatever relates to society and government,
> besides being the most natural and rational of all rules,
> has the further recommendation of being the easiest of
> application. Either what God has ordained, or what
> antiquity authorizes, may be very difficult to ascertain;
> but what regulation is most conducive to the public
> good, though not always without its difficulties, yet in
> general it is much more easy to determine.[6]

Equally, Price and Priestley were universalists, the latter
describing his Heaven as a place where "a government of
consummate order will be established and all the faithful
and worthy of all religions will be gathered into it."[7] What
one believes or does not believe cannot be the ground for
exclusion, having no bearing on the dictates of universal
morality. This moral universalism was a key common feature of British, American, and French radical thought
alike, for it was this that anchored their common rejection

of ecclesiastical authority in social and political matters in whatever shape or form, and all intrusion of theology into legislation and politics.

Diderot's and d'Holbach's moral philosophy reflected and summed up the work of the clandestine philosophical literature of the early Enlightenment as formulated by Fontenelle, Boulainvilliers, du Marsais, Meslier, Fréret, d'Argens, and Boulanger, and before them by Bayle and Spinoza. Bayle and Spinoza in particular assert the absolute separation of morality from theology that became fundamental to all Radical Enlightenment, as did their insistence (in sharp contrast to Hume) on the need to base institutions, politics, and legislation on pure reason alone. Rousseau, by contrast, after breaking with the *encyclopédistes* in 1757–1758, rejected his own former radical views (except in some aspects of politics) and opposed the radical project, especially in the sphere of moral theory. Morality, he insisted, while acknowledging that before his break with Diderot and d'Holbach he had not known how to answer their arguments, cannot be anchored in reason, as they pretended, or detached from religion; not reason but the "voice of Nature," as expressed in human sentiment, is our guide in moral matters. The *encyclopédistes'* morality he dismissed as heartless, pompous, "aggressive," and mechanical while admitting that his alternative moral vision—which, among other things, classified woman as essentially "weak and passive," for which he

was so severely taken to task by Mary Wollstonecraft[8]—
was essentially based on feeling, the yearnings of the heart
and tradition.[9]

For Rousseau as for Hume it is mainly tradition and
practice, people's sense of where moral and religious authority resides, not philosophical reason that establishes
true moral values.[10] Radical ideas and moderate Deistic
moral thought (including here Rousseauism) diametrically clashed also over past models: was the warlike outlook of the Romans, a moral culture totally repudiated by
la philosophie moderne, repugnant and barbaric, or had
there indeed been a general decline in virtue since ancient
times, as Rousseau maintained, and especially since the
republican culture of the Spartans and early Romans? The
worst features of contemporary society, Rousseau argued,
constituted an "impulse to contradict nature," an attack
on the highest sentiments, a disastrous process of soften-
ing and feminization vitiating the bodily integrity of men,
and still more their minds and morality, while simultaneously debasing what he saw as the natural demureness
and modesty of women.[11]

The quarrel between Rousseau and the *philosophes
modernes* reflected a profound clash over moral principles
and also over the relationship between morality and reason. Both disputes lent a sharper edge to the personal
animosity that these former friends subsequently evinced
for each other and that Rousseau vehemently expresses in
his final work, *Les Rêveries du promeneur solitaire* (1777).

There he calls Diderot, d'Holbach, and their disciples "ardent missionaries of atheism "et très impérieux dogmatiques," so intolerant in practice that they were incapable of not losing patience with anyone thinking differently from themselves.[12] Rousseau again admits, though, that not only before 1757, when one of their number and pulled along by them, but also afterwards, he could find no adequate arguments in terms of reason with which to oppose their contentions. It was his heart, his feelings, he emphasizes, not reasoning, that told him they were wrong. The late Rousseau positively gloried in his rejection of "pure reason." Where the radical *philosophes* vaunted their erudition and knowledge of science and the history of civilizations, he prided himself on his anti-intellectualism and reading practically nothing.[13]

By contrast, mainstream writers, Christian and Deist, far from charging the *philosophes modernes* with excessive intellectual erudition and intellectual cogency, charged them with too little. Most claimed Diderot's and d'Holbach's philosophical atheism had become a powerful force in society not through sound arguments but by proving useful to libertines as a pretext for unleashing the passions. And no other single work seemed more apt, in their view, to provide fresh justification for libertines and criminals (through fomenting atheism) than d'Holbach's *Système de la nature*, a work discussed all over Europe in the 1770s and 1780s that appeared also in English and likewise, in 1783, in a clandestine German version under the title *System der Natur*.[14] This book was everywhere vilified as philosophically ruinous and morally fatal, a charge answered by Weishaupt and Christian Ludwig Paalzow (1753–1824), who rendered the book into German, a Halle-trained jurist who supported Lessing in the latter's battles with the Lutheran theologians during the 1770s, with the retort that the *Système* breathes an intense, universal, and pure moral fervor. Its morality is of a kind Christians cannot simply ignore, an ethics uncommonly fired by zeal for what Paalzow calls "die Rechte der Menschheit" (the rights of mankind).[15]

Remarkably, Paalzow invokes Priestley, in his translator's preface, as exemplifying a pre-eminent Christian who acknowledges the *Système de la nature* as a work impressively grounded in moral principle and, hence, not really "atheistic."[16] Priestley, indeed, posed a rather formidable challenge to the "moderate" and traditionalist standpoints. The sincerity of his religious fervor was unquestionable. But so committed was he to "defend Christianity"—by freeing "it from those corruptions which prevent its reception with philosophical and thinking persons, whose influence with the vulgar and unthinking," he complained, "is very great"—that his ideas seemed barely distinguishable to many Protestant and Catholic theologians from "atheism."[17] An openly avowed Socinian from 1768, his rigorously "philosophical," scientific approach to Christianity later induced him (under d'Holbach's influence, he acknowledged) to embrace a systematic materialistic monism, denying spirit is a separate substance, rejecting immortality of the soul, and holding, like the Spinozists, that soul and body are just one substance, and mind, perception, and thought products of corporeal organization.[18]

This was from 1774 onward. Yet even in sermons delivered while pastor at the Mill Hill Chapel in Leeds (1767–1773), before he became an openly avowed materialist, years in which he strenuously advocated Socinianism but not yet determinism,[19] Priestley always heavily discounted faith. Indeed, so contemptuous was he of mere "belief and zeal" on their own, so hostile to "mysteries" and insistent on the primacy and universality of reason, on the need for men who love virtue to base their understanding of the world on philosophy and consistent reasoning, that it was exceedingly difficult to discern from his public discourse where the guiding force of theology and tradition, if there was any, lodged.

Of course, mainstream Christians flatly disavowed his exalting of "reason." But taking refuge in what most believers, devoutly embracing Protestant or Catholic teaching, term "faith" was, to his mind, in no way a cogent standpoint or viable option. Rather, "when Christians are thus degenerated and corrupted they become insignificant and useless so that it is exceedingly difficult to recover them." Since most so-called Christians are actually in this corrupted state and since the "final doom of such apostates," as he labels faith-based, unreasoning

Christians, was worse than that of non-Christians, to many he appeared to be reducing belief in doctrines, conformity and obedience to church authority, and worship of Christ to nothing while substituting for Christianity as generally understood his doctrine that virtue is the "only thing absolutely necessary" to man's acceptance by God and man's "final happiness."[20] His shift toward materialism in the wake of d'Holbach's *Système*, a book that convinced him that the age-old distinction between body and spirit was philosophically untenable, and that it was in the interest of Christians to abandon it, thus appreciably narrowed the gap between English radical Rational Dissent, as reconfigured by him and his allies, and *philosophisme*, as the *anti-philosophes* categorized non-Rousseauist, non-Voltairean radical French thought.[21]

Priestley's rule that when Christians merely believe, ignoring the rational principles on which all worthwhile belief must rest, they are contemptible "and as unlikely to be profitable to others as the man who is void of all religious principles whatever," made him the implacable opponent of practically all faith-based doctrine.[22] Like Diderot and d'Holbach, Priestley and Price charged that in organized Christianity, as manifested in history, "love of one's neighbour was never anything more than a charade," such religion being the age-old ally of tyranny and inequality and therefore, over the centuries, itself an agent of the moral corruption that tyranny, according to radical philosophy, always propagates in its wake.[23] Few other English Unitarians gravitated to quite such extreme philosophical, moral, and political positions. But Priestley remained the close ally of Price and, in building the Unitarian wing of the new English radical tradition, was joined by others, including, as we have seen, the outcast Cambridge don, John Jebb, likewise a declared materialist and proponent of sweeping reform and democracy.[24] Priestley's influence in England and Holland was formidable for a time, especially in the 1780s, and from the late 1780s spread also to America, becoming entrenched at Harvard.

Priestley and Jebb refused to charge the *philosophes modernes* with immorality. Most other churchmen did so effusively. Diderot answered the charge of nurturing immoral attitudes and behavior, among other places in his *Commentaire* on the Dutch philosopher Frans Hemsterhuis (1721–1790), composed a year or two after the appearance of the *Système*, where he vigorously reaffirms the Spinozistic monism of his general system, and asks what moral ills his individual liberty, rooted in liberty of the press and propagated by materialist writings, could reasonably be held to promote. Men were no more wicked now, he observed, than thirty years before (that is, prior to the *Encyclopédie* and the appearance of his own, Boulanger's, d'Holbach's, and La Mettrie's early writings). Changes in the moral condition of nations seemed to him to occur owing to very different causes than metaphysical debates. No consequent materialist, he urged, seeks to at-

tack the foundations of true morality or render the notions of "virtue" and "vice" ridiculous. If La Mettrie, unlike the others, had become the apologist of vice, he had
been scornfully dismissed as a charlatan by every reader
ever since. "*Matérialistes*," he added, citing the *Système de
la nature*, in the genesis of which he had played a part,
"reject the idea of God, founding their ideas of just and
unjust on the eternal relations of men to men."[25] If some
individuals try to legitimize immorality using imperfectly
grasped principles of philosophy, it is certain, he insisted,
that these would be equally depraved even without any
philosophical fig-leaf.

The principal split dividing thinkers in his day, observes d'Holbach, was between a majority believing body
and soul to be fundamentally distinct—and the laws governing the mind and moral action as separate from the
laws governing bodies—and those, the minority, con-
tending body and mind are one (that is, the *Spinosistes*
and Priestleyian Unitarians).[26] Catholic and Protestant
Christian apologists writing from a Moderate Enlightenment stance—in France, men like Hayer, Bergier, Richard,
Marin, Jamin, Crillon, Camuset, and Chaudon—accused
the *matérialistes* of severing theology from morality and
condemning popular religion as idolatry and fanaticism
and daring even to pronounce Christianity "the enemy
of society."[27] All mankind, replied Diderot, Helvétius,
d'Holbach, and their disciples, whether white, red, yellow,
or black, shares the same single set of ethical principles.

The happiness of humanity as a whole depends "on the progress of reason," and this morality of reason has no connection with, indeed is hampered by, the "unnatural duties" arising, as d'Holbach puts it, from imagined obligations between man "and beings of which he has no conception."[28]

Revealed religion, maintained the radical *philosophes*, fragments rather than consolidates society, undermining true morality by extolling credulity and ignorance and discouraging science (as Rousseau was also accused of doing). Equally, Christianity's supposedly divinely ordained abstinence, austerities, and submissiveness, far from helping men and nurturing genuine piety, invariably injure society, indeed if rigorously adopted would, they averred, infallibly entail the ruin of whole nations. Finally, revealed religion inevitably creates a harmful chasm between government and the source of moral authority, making it much harder to "direct the citizens" passions toward the common good, the true end, for d'Holbach, of good government and morality alike.[29]

All these "defenders of materialism," remarked the Abbé Camuset, conceived of justice as standing in opposition "like forces opposed one to the other," to the Christian principles of compassion and forgiveness, and, indeed, these opposed moral codes did collide at numerous points, not merely over questions of sexuality. For example, theological admonition to the *anti-philosophes* was the sole effective bar preventing those plunged in

misery or severe pain from seeking release through suicide. The utilitarian rationalism of Diderot, Helvétius,
and d'Holbach, on the other hand, explicitly justifies killing oneself (as the Italian radical enlightener Radicati had
in a famous text long before) wherever the balance of suffering outweighs all prospect of recovery, satisfaction, or
pleasure. Radical *philosophes*, therefore, were apt to be accused of fomenting suicide among the unhappy, poor,
sick, and betrayed. To the *anti-philosophes*, the *nouvelle
philosophie* was, in Camuset's words, the "mother of despair" and "despair the father of suicide."[30]

Human feelings, in *la philosophie moderne*, including
sexual desire, cannot be sinful or censured as wicked,
blameworthy, or subject to penance. Only pleasure-seek-
ing harmful to others, or oneself, is morally wrong. The
implication was that all pleasure not physically or emo-
tionally damaging to others, whether fornication, homosexuality, lesbianism, masturbation, adultery, and enjoying voluptuous art or fantasies, is morally neutral and
permissible. The Abbés Richard and Nicolas-Sylvestre
Bergier (1718–1790) combated such claims by insisting on
the obvious depravity of peoples who ignored or disavowed sexual self-denial and the passion-denying virtues.
All modesty, decency, and sexual propriety were banished
from Sparta, noted Bergier, so that the dissoluteness and
libertinage of Spartans became proverbial throughout
Greece. As for the Athenians, their young men, not content with living surrounded by willing courtesans and

female dancers, were "even more given to those passions [homosexual intercourse] that nature abhors."[31]

Hence, radical ideas spelt the end, protested the *anti-philosophes*—and also Rousseau—of all codes of austerity, celibacy, and the curbing of desire. *La philosophie moderne* appeared completely to overturn the cult of virginity, feminine modesty, and monastic rigor, as well as the vigorous repression of homosexuality.[32] Morals are only maintained, insisted Rousseau, where the sexes dwell separately for the most part and women are strictly confined to the home, with meetings and groups segregated into distinct male and female milieus. Nothing could be more degrading, he averred, than a society abounding in opportunities for extramarital sexual contact.[33] To the *anti-philosophes*, the entire moral order, built over millennia, seemed on the point of dissolution. "Adieu donc retraite, solitude, éloignement du monde, mortification, pénitence, célibat clérical. Adieu virginité!" lamented the Abbé Richard, would the countless eulogies of self-denial and virginity accumulated over the centuries henceforth count for nothing![34]

Diderot, objects the Abbé Michel-Ange Marin (1697–1767), exults in unbridling men's lusts while castigating the Church for condemning the passions.[35] The same charge was continually leveled at Helvétius, d'Holbach, Condorcet, Mirabeau, and Brissot, who all ground their utilitarian moral philosophy on the Spinozist principle that "the desire for happiness is common to all men," and that it is in all men "the strongest motive," so that to obtain this happiness, which all alike strive for, "everyone will always do everything that it is in their power to do."[36] Acquisition of all our ideas through the senses as physical, efficient causes meant that physical sensibility, and hence personal interest, is necessarily the exclusive source of all motivation, reason, justice, and morality. This principle became integral to the materialists' campaign to redefine virtue exclusively in terms of what is personally and socially useful. Men will be virtuous, avowed d'Holbach, when they find it "useful" to be virtuous.[37]

Marin, erudite head of the French "province" of the Minim Friars at Avignon, retorted that separating morality from religion can never work, for only religion establishes true morality.[38] Faith and religious devotion alone, he and the other the *anti-philosophes* held, can nurture a virtuous society. The doctrine that religion alone restrains men's impulses and curbs crime is not only unproven, averred Diderot and d'Holbach, but the moral goals urged by Christian tradition twist and distort moral striving in wrong directions. Society cannot bring men to virtue by identifying it with combating the natural inclinations.[39] Men need to be trained to be good citizens, not pious self-deniers. Otherwise, we would surely not daily hear of assassination, rapine, and brigandage in Europe's most devoutly religious lands, such as Spain and Italy. It is not religion that curbs human passions, he and Diderot insisted, but reason reinforced by education, together with fear of dishonor and punishment. Only thus do the people acquire notions of honesty and adopt an orderly lifestyle.

To the *anti-philosophes* this was just camouflage for profligacy. Perhaps Diderot himself was honest, genuinely in quest of virtue, though he could only be such, averred opponents, by inwardly abandoning "les principes de l'incrédulité."[40] More likely, he and his disciples were not proceeding in good faith, their "intolerance" and insufferable arrogance in any case scarcely according "avec leurs idées."[41] Their real goal, supposedly, was to debase morality and unsettle society out of libertine motives. Marin, adhering to his order's reputation for humility, by in 1758 declining a call to become "General" of the Minims in Rome, implored especially young people to "eschew Mr D . . .'s, and all other freethinkers' writings. In his long *anti-philosophique* novel, *Le Baron Van-Hesden, ou la République des Incrédules* (Toulouse, 1762), a lively, five-volume assault on the *encyclopédistes*, written in a style even the relatively uneducated could follow, Marin's undeviating aim was to vindicate Scripture, rescue Christian morality, and heap opprobrium on the now all-pervading philosophical construct forged by Spinoza, Bayle, and Diderot.

Set on a passenger river boat plying the Rhone from Lyon to Avignon, his novel features a wise Christian hermit, representing Marin, and the Baron van-Hesden, a confident young nobleman representing the *philosophique* outlook, which the hermit progressively demolishes. A fascinated audience listens, among them the boat captain, who, having heard everyone speak so much about "Spinosa et de son système," desires finally to hear the truth about the whole business of "Spinoza," philosophy, and reality.[42] The contemporary author chiefly under attack, however, is Diderot. What Diderot had done, alleges Marin, granting that he writes in a lively fashion, "avec esprit," was to revive a false philosophy forged by Spinoza and Bayle from vestiges of the most corrupt moral traditions of ancient Greece, mixed with the "systems of the Japanese and Siamese," to produce a virulent atheistic metaphysics permeated by libertinism.[43]

An especially pernicious feature of radical thought, held Marin and other *anti-philosophes,* was precisely its moral universalism: the *philosophes* seemed always eager to allege the high moral caliber of oriental and other non-Christian moral traditions. Not least resented was admiration of the Japanese, a nation since the early seventeenth century openly antagonistic to Christianity, whom Diderot accounts ethically equal to Europeans, indeed closely akin to them in their moral thinking. Certainly, in his article on Japanese philosophy in the *Encyclopédie* and again, in 1770, in the *Histoire philosophique,* he dismisses Japanese popular religion as contemptible. But Diderot calls the latter "le fanatisme le plus affreux" only because this is the creed of ordinary people.[44] He saw Japan, like Europe, as the age-old arena of perpetual conflict between credulity, ignorance, and priestly ambition and science, scholarship, and reason. In this eternal battle, what was admirable were "the true principles of the morality of Confucius" and of Confucius's Japanese disciple, "Moosi," whose books, remarks Diderot, enjoyed great authority in Japan.[45] Refined by Confucianism, the Japanese "way of philosophy" is accounted a philosophical cult "sans religion" that absorbs what is best in Shintoist tradition and offers as its core principle, both the *Encyclopédie* and the *Histoire philosophique* assert, that men should practice virtue because virtue alone can render men as happy as our nature permits us to be. There is no need to threaten men with retribution in the next life; man can and should be virtuous, hold the sages of Japan, because man is rational. The ethics of the "Sendosivistes ou philosophes Japonais" reduce to several principal points, Diderot reports, the first two being the requirement to conform one's conduct to virtue and the principle of *gi*, the requirement to render justice to all men. The Japanese sages postulated a universal world soul animating everything, from which everything emanates, and to which everything returns.[46] Of course the Spinozistic reverberations of this account were not lost on Diderot's readers.

In Marin's novel, his hermit adheres to the Catholic Moderate Enlightenment and deems Lockean and Newtonian concepts perfectly attuned to the Christian faith. Bacon, Boyle, Locke, and Newton had never adopted reason as man's sole guide as Spinoza, Bayle, Diderot, and his Baron van-Hesden had. Neither do Locke and Newton question miracles or deny divine Providence. Is reason such a reliable guide that we can trust in her alone?[47] "Certainly not," answers Marin, but he gladly applies Diderot's chief criterion to evaluating the *philosophe*'s own writings, mainly attacking such early texts as the *Pensées philosophiques* (1746), *Lettre sur les aveugles* (1749) and *De l'interprétation de la nature* (1753). Diderot, avers Marin, does not try to present his thought as an integral, coherent whole but plainly sought a looser format, hoping this would mask his "contradictions," cunning pieces of deception, and "absurdities."[48]

To prove its "inconsistencies," Marin assails Diderot's thought using philosophical arguments alone, seeing his basic propositions as all deriving from Spinoza's system. In Diderot, there is no sense in which things can be absolutely or intrinsically evil. For in his state of nature, like that of Hobbes and Spinoza, there exists no right or wrong outside society. Like Bergier, Marin holds that Hobbes's and Spinoza's contention that right and wrong are not absolute values but acquire moral significance only relative to society destroys the foundations of the moral order and ultimately condones lawlessness, lies, theft, murder, adultery, arson, and all the brigands of the world.[49] In the eyes of *la philosophie moderne*, concubinage, fornication, marriage, and adultery, as Brissot later observed, were all mere synonyms for wholly indifferent acts, all equally virtuous or not virtuous depending on social circumstances.[50]

The validity of a morality wholly independent of religion, suggested Bergier, is not hard to evaluate. Put two "atheists" together and ask them whether they prefer to deal with *incrédules* like themselves or devout Christians. Those aspiring to the title of *philosophes*, and openly affecting irreligion, would be shocked, indeed, if their own wives, children, and domestics adopted their principles, and yet they want us to praise their philosophy! Wretched physicians who themselves eschew the remedies they peddle! Any morality "purement naturelle, civile, politique, philosophique" should undoubtedly condemn lying, imposture, and calumny. Yet the books of "our *philosophes*" are crammed with all of these. So what does "la morale philosophique" really amount to?[51]

According to Bergier, where Diderot impugns Christian teaching by allusion and insinuation, the author of *Le Christianisme dévoilé* (d'Holbach), was the first to attack Christian morality outright. He denounces it as useless, false, and wrongly grounded and the source of much harm to humans, a creed that, "far from enlightening man and making him a reasonable creature," keeps him in an eternal infancy.[52] Religion, argues d'Holbach, much like Spinoza before him, stems from the fears and anxiety of primitive man in the savage state, and harms society by turning man into an *automate* afraid to consult his reason, someone who lets himself naively and passively be supervised and directed by those with power and author-ity. Appealing to history and experience, Bergier, Marin, Richard, Crillon, Chaudon, Jamin, and the other *anti-philosophes* strove to prove Christianity's sacred character and superiority over all other systems through the work-ings of divine Providence. Compare, Bergier urged his readers, Asia's development since ancient times with that of Europe. Once the home of science and civilized conduct, Asia, devastated by the Scythians and Arabs, lapsed into barbarism and unending decay due princi-pally, he maintains, to its conquerors embracing Islam instead of Christianity. Europe by contrast, equally rav-aged by barbarians after the fall of Rome, recovered and flourished, primarily because her conquerors embraced Christianity.[53]

A much-cultivated philosophical strategy of the *anti-philosophes* was to invoke the great Moderate Enlighten-ment thinkers—Montesquieu, Voltaire, and Hume (and also Rousseau)—against "nos philosophes modernes." In this way, they aspired to demonstrate that the views of one set of *philosophes* was entirely incompatible with those of another and, consequently, that the nonreligious Enlight-enment was irretrievably divided against itself. By high-lighting in this manner the deep chasm between Radical Enlightenment and the Deist mainstream while at the same time also sharply criticizing the latter, Christian Moderate Enlightenment refined a powerful rhetoric ef-

fective for disparaging and discrediting all the philosophical authors it condemned.

Father Nicolas Jamin (1711–1782), prior of the royal
abbey of Saint-Germain-des-Prés, in Paris, for example,
in his *Pensées théologiques* (1768) repeatedly cites Montesquieu, Voltaire, and Rousseau as writers whom "les nouveaux philosophes" respect and yet who, even if defective
in some respects, affirm categorically that religion is the
most powerful brake men possess for disciplining the
common people's behavior and enforcing what Jamin
calls "just subordination" to monarchy.[54] He enthusiasti-
cally endorsed Montesquieu's defense of Christianity as
the best basis for *gouvernements modérés,* Voltaire's repu-
diation of the materialists' social and political goals,
Hume's demolition of their conceptions of reason and
morality, and Rousseau's antagonism to their atheism,
materialism, and *tolérantisme.* In this way, French *anti-
philosophie* could present itself as a philosophically and
scientifically up-to-date Christian standpoint, assailing
radical thought from an essentially "enlightened" and rational, if not fully tolerationist, stance.

Rousseau proved particularly useful to *anti-philosophie.*
Where Diderot, Helvétius, and d'Holbach envisaged a
new secular morality based on reason alone, Rousseau,
whose novel *Émile* (1762) Bergier and Jamin cite *in extenso*
in this connection, insists that virtue stems from feeling
and faith in God.[55] Rousseau not only champions immor-

tality of the soul and the majesty of Scripture, observes
Jamin, but argues more adamantly than anyone that the
encyclopédistes were dogmatic, intolerant, arrogant, and
dangerous.[56] With equal glee, Bergier cites Rousseau's re-
mark that the only lesson Diderot and the *philosophes
modernes* had taught him was the erroneousness of his
own earlier admiration for and naïve trust in them and
their motives. Their actual proceedings showed their ideals were worthless illusions from which, in his *Confessions*,
Rousseau professes inwardly to have emancipated himself
by the mid-1750s.[57]

Of course, *anti-philosophie* eyed Rousseau less favorably in other respects, even if no *anti-philosophe* ever ap-
proached the hostility of Diderot's disparagement of the
Genevan in his essay on Seneca (1782) as a perverse, tor-
mented mind lacking the slightest shred of philosophical
consistency.[58] The Abbé Bergier, ever courteous in combat, and with a nod in particular to Diderot (whom he
privately somewhat admired), considered the personal
morals of the leading *encyclopédistes* above reproach,
which, he regretted, was considerably more than he could
say for Rousseau. As for the latter's reverence for the "virtue," austerity, and physical prowess of the Spartans and
pristine Romans, this Bergier considered just as ridiculous
as did Diderot and d'Holbach. The Romans, a bellicose
and ferocious nation eyeing the whole universe as their
prey, were relentless foes of the liberty of all other peoples.[59] Unlike Diderot and d'Holbach, though, he did not

forget to add that the early Romans were uncompromising republicans contemptuous of kings and monarchy.[60]

Professional theologians, the *anti-philosophes* mostly
relied on philosophical objections supplied by others. A
philosophically more formidable adversary of Radical Enlightenment moral thought was the Scottish Enlightenment. Modern historians and philosophers are unused to
locating the Scottish Enlightenment within its wider international context, or the framework of two warring and
wholly incompatible enlightenments, Moderate and Radical. The Scottish Enlightenment is habitually treated in
isolation, as a separate tradition largely unconnected with
continental developments. But the Scottish thinkers
viewed themselves rather differently and not least as general opponents of atheism and materialist ideas. And since
the conflict between the two rival enlightenments remained relentless in the moral sphere and proved extremely wide-ranging, there is a need briefly to examine
Scottish thought in this wider connection.

Powerfully felt in British moral philosophy generally
was the influence of Shaftesbury's, Hutcheson's, Smith's,
and Hume's "moral sense." There were certainly many
differences between the moral philosophies of Hume and
the Scottish "Common Sense" thinkers, the most acute of
whom was the Glasgow philosopher Thomas Reid (1710–
1796), a writer highly critical of Hume. But a more fundamental divide separated all those who, on the one hand,
ascribed moral ideas among men to an "original power

or faculty in man," as Reid puts it, which some thinkers call "the Moral Sense, the Moral Faculty, Conscience," and, on the other, philosophers, like Spinoza, Bayle, and the materialists who "think that our moral sentiments may be accounted for without supposing any original sense or faculty appropriated to that purpose."[61] Only in Spinoza and Bayle, and later in Diderot, Helvétius, and d'Holbach, do we encounter that absolute, uncompromising linkage of reason, knowledge, and philosophy with morality (and politics) that reached back in its earliest form to Socrates and was so roundly rejected by Hume.

Shaftesbury's, Smith's, Reid's—and despite his reservations about Shaftesbury's moral sense philosophy, Rousseau's—conception of "moral sense" as a natural sentiment growing in every person at a certain point in their development was generally rejected by *la nouvelle philosophie* owing to its lack of any identifiable physical foundation. Radical thinkers, unlike Rousseau, rejected "moral sense" theory especially because of its assumption that the soul exists as a separate substance, sensibility, or entity from the body and because moral sense philosophy was always coupled with efforts to restrict the scope of reason. For the mature Diderot, Helvétius, and d'Holbach, like Spinoza, every "sense" must inhere in something physical. Consequently, they dismissed "les Shaftesburistes," as Helvétius calls the British "moral sense" philosophers, as "theologians"—that is, confused thinkers illegitimately mixing philosophy with theology. The

Anglo-Scottish conception of ethics was rejected outright by Helvétius in his *De l'homme* (1771), d'Holbach in his *Système social* (1773), and Diderot's disciple, Delisle de Sales, in his *De la Philosophie de la nature* (1770) as resting on wrong foundations, amounting in Hutcheson's case to a quite useless "galimatias," neither a "system" nor "philosophy," just an endless assertion of the idea of moral instinct.[62]

Scottish Common Sense, a philosophy long dominant at Princeton from the 1770s onward, seemed an effective way to block the sway of both reason and Hume's skepticism in the determination of moral theory and men's awareness of right and wrong. According to Reid, author of the *Inquiry into the Human Mind* (1764) and the *Essay on the Intellectual Powers of Man* (1785), human rationality and that which makes rational men fundamentally different from the insane and from animals, is not the ability of the mind's faculties to abstract from sense-impressions, as Locke and Hume supposed. Rather, it is the guidance provided by Common Sense in determining the true relations between qualities and powers; a knowledge of truth prior to sense is the real touchstone of human rationality. In other words, men are distinguished from animals by a prior store of awareness and ideas, acquired, ingrained, or bestowed quite independently of sense-impressions. The most important example, for Reid, is our knowledge of the being and attributes of God that we know with certainty from Common Sense but that cannot be demonstrated by either reason or the senses. Similarly, from Common Sense we know of our future life in the hereafter though this, too, is not fully susceptible to rational demonstration. A third key instance is our knowledge of our moral duty in relation to our fellows, our country, and to God.

In effect, Scottish Common Sense adjusted and further reinforced a powerful existing tendency. Locke's empiricist epistemology and Hume's skepticism had served to narrow the scope of reason in British philosophy in ways that tended to prioritize sentiment and tradition as the true basis of the moral order. This was now taken further. To Adam Smith, in his *Theory of Moral Sentiments* (1759), it seemed clear that morality's general rules are "ultimately founded upon experience of what in particular instances, our moral faculties, our natural sense of merit and propriety, approve or disapprove of." Building on the doctrines especially of Hutcheson, whom he warmly admired but whose moral thought seemed to him to require adjustments, Smith rejects any notion that we consider particular actions praiseworthy or blamable because they conform to, or are inconsistent with, our general principles of morality. "The general rule, on the contrary, is formed," argued Smith, "by finding from experience that all actions of a certain kind, or circumstanced in a certain manner, are approved or disapproved of." Feeling, sentiment, and social reaction and pressure, accordingly, are the prime factors in the forming "of the general rules of morality."[63]

The upright person of integrity is someone who shows a "sacred regard" for society's rules. There was little risk of error, ignorance, or prejudice, it seemed to the Scots thinkers, interfering with this process or debasing the moral content of society's rules. That we are not misled in relying on moral sense was assured by the way these thinkers ground their moral thought in what is ultimately a theological and socially deferential stance. Since "no other end seems worthy of that supreme wisdom and divine benignity which we necessarily ascribe [to God]," philosophers linking belief and reason in the manner the Scots prescribe felt justified in trusting that the "happiness of mankind, as well as of other rational creatures, seems to have been the original purpose intended by the Author of Nature when he brought them into existence."[64] The inextricable entwining of Smith's moral philosophy and, later, economics, with notions of divine providence and his (and Hume's) defense of existing social norms, is well expressed by his contention that "when the general rules which determine the merit and demerit of actions come thus to be regarded, as the laws of an All-Powerful Being, who watches over our conduct and who, in a life to come, will reward the observance and punish the breach of them; they necessarily acquire a new sacredness from this consideration."[65]

It was only a short step from this to pronouncing those who defy or oppose established moral rules—these being "the scheme which the Author of Nature has established for the happiness and perfection of the world"—to be "in some measure the enemies of God."[66] But precisely the social conservatism implicit in Scottish moral thought and its emphatic restricting of philosophical reason by means of faith and theology lay at the root of its immense appeal at the time (and subsequently). By the 1770s the prime philosophical alternative to radical moral philosophy was now the British, and particularly the Scottish, moral sense tradition, or what Helvétius called "ce sens moral tant vanté par les Anglois." To the radical thinkers, though, it was intellectually no formidable opponent, since "cette philosophie théologique de Shaftesbury," appeared to them unsustainable when detached from its theological (or in Shaftesbury's case, Platonic) base.[67] But "absurd" or not, British and especially Scottish moral sense and, most of all, Scottish Common Sense, were destined for a long and glorious career, remaining for decades highly influential in Germany and Scandinavia as well as Britain and North America.

Scottish Common Sense, in the eyes of many, satisfyingly resolved the difficult problem of how to relate faith to reason and separate philosophy from theology while convincingly grounding moral philosophy. It was a style of thought that seemed simultaneously to block Hume's skepticism and Priestley's determinism and materialism, of which Reid was also fiercely critical. The new president at Princeton, appointed in 1766, John Witherspoon (1723–1794), a recently emigrated Scottish clergyman, was a great enthusiast for this new type of philosophy, especially as expounded by Hutcheson and Reid. His suspicion of Locke, Berkeley, and Hume, as well as old-style Calvinist dogmatism, came to dominate the Princeton philosophical arena. Witherspoon's influential *Lectures on Moral Philosophy*, the first significant American philosophical textbook, though not published until 1800, was already circulating among Princeton students in manuscript in the 1770s. Defining the moral sense as the same as conscience, "the law which our Maker has written upon our hearts" that "both intimates and enforces duty, previous to all reasoning," it was a philosophy widely viewed in America as a surer and better resource than Locke's epistemology for defending Protestant principles against the idiosyncratic and threatening novelties of Berkeley's idealism, Hume's skepticism, and radical ideas.[68]

But the weaknesses of Common Sense were not easily hidden from view. There was also sharp and plentiful criticism. Priestley, especially, had little time for Scottish Common Sense. Among the unsatisfactory consequences of this philosophy, he stressed, were its practical political and social implications. Since, for Reid and its other exponents, the vital issues in human life concerning God, our afterlife, and right and wrong are so definitely known from Common Sense, and these are securely grounded in what the people believe and uphold, "those occasional persons who, to scandalize the public by choosing to dissent from these basic convictions [. . .] publicly combat basic principles that derive from them," Priestley pointed out, might according to Scottish Common Sense justifiably be suppressed or constrained to silence with the aid of the magistracy.[69] This notably illiberal result follows directly from their principle that the most vital truths we "know with a quick, clear and indubitable certainty given and assured to us by our Maker to serve as an almost infallible direction in the whole conduct of life and especially in matters of religion."[70] Priestley uncompromisingly rejected Reid and was even more dismissive of James Oswald, who, in his hugely popular work *An Appeal to Common Sense in Behalf of Religion* (1766), states that "by the discernment peculiar to rational beings called common sense, we perceive all primary truths in the same manner as we perceive objects of sense by our bodily organs," claiming this doctrine wholly circumvents Locke as well as disables Hume's skepticism.[71] "The disgust his writings gave me," commented Priestley, "was so great that I could not possibly show him more respect."[72]

Scottish moral sense philosophy and Radical Enlightenment clashed also in that for the former, where tradition and theology rather than reason are man's chief guide, the deep differences among religions and traditions made it difficult to conceive of mankind as a true moral universal, a unity sharing in the same problems and difficulties. "The first principles of morals," held Reid, "are the immediate dictates of the moral faculty."[73] But it is hard to be sure that what is traditionally judged just by one group is essentially the same as what is called "just" by another. The only way to ground a true universal morality, according to the radical thinkers, is by discarding all existing moral systems. Only they, in any case, could unequivocally affirm that all humanity forms a single "vast society whose diverse parts are the members spread across the face of the earth," that all men are warmed by the same sun, subject to the same needs, and prone to the same desires, all alike seeking "well-being to avoid pain" and that it is this that grounds the single universal true morality.[74]

Radical enlighteners repudiated British moral sense philosophies and, no less forcefully, moral relativism, especially that of Montesquieu. Hume, too, thought Montesquieu assigns excessive weight to climate and geography as influences on moral systems.[75] However, Helvétius's attack on Montesquieu's moral relativism, in both his *De l'Esprit* (1758) and *De l'homme* (1773), applies to Hume's no less than Montesquieu's relativism. For any thinker prioritizing in his moral thought custom and tradition, as Hume does, blocks the universality of moral values. Since the radical *philosophes* considered practically all the world's moral and legal systems unenlightened, barbaric, and morally wrong, fit only to make men pusillanimous and credulous, the effect of Helvétius's critique was to make both Montesquieu's and Hume's moral philosophies resemble apologies for everything in human life restrictive, oppressive, and detrimental.[76] To place morality on a sound basis, contended Diderot, Helvétius, d'Holbach, and Condorcet, one must cease assigning responsibility to tradition, popular sensibility, and climate.[77] Rather, each nation should observe the same duties and rules regarding other nations that social life prescribes for each individual toward other individuals within a particular society.[78] Equality and reciprocity are the golden rules.

To the *anti-philosophes*, the post-1750 resurgence of Spinozistic principles seemed the ultimate catastrophe for morality, faith, and humanity alike. The notion that when emerging from the state of nature each individual cedes to society part of his or her "natural right," as Spinoza calls it, for the sake of the advantages of collaboration and mutual protection seemed to mean that only fear of reprisal by society or the state deters individuals from unbridling their basest appetites and passions and perpetrating the most atrocious crimes. To the Radical Enlightenment, by contrast, the new natural morality anchored in reason alone seemed a triumph of human progress and a landmark in human history.

At the same time, the *nouveaux philosophes* by no means wholly abandoned Spinoza's contention that "religion" is not identical to "superstition" and that the term "religion" can be meaningfully redefined to denote those ingredients of conventional religion philosophers consider not harmful or actually beneficial to society in terms of the new, purely secular moral standpoint of radical thought. For Spinoza, the basis of a sound morality and "religion" in this sense is found in the moral instruction in the Old Testament books and especially in Christ's purely ethical teaching. Diderot and d'Holbach are more hostile to Christianity than Spinoza. But they, too, agree there are "two religions in civilized societies," one scheme of "religion" forbidding man to think independently, the other encouraging him to do so, one exclusively busy, according to d'Holbach, with propagating fantasies and phantoms, plunging its adherents into "l'aveuglement," the other acknowledging nature, embracing true morality, and purging minds of the vapors of priestcraft and false religion.[79] The latter, potentially a force for good, should be fostered among those incapable of "philosophy."

The priests of "true," as opposed to conventional, traditional, and false religion, as Delisle de Sales put it, are all the good and well-meaning folk, "tous les gens de bien."[80] What the radical *philosophes* deemed the wrong kind of religion—that is, religion dealing in supernatural entities ravaging the world of men—inevitably injects terror into men's minds and trouble and discord into society while the beneficial kind encourages serenity, stability, "la concorde et la paix."[81] The one, concludes d'Holbach, is "surnaturelle, mystique, obscure, contradictoire," and impossible to practice, whilst the other preaches "une morale humaine." This way of distinguishing between true and false religion was of course also a bridge between atheist radicals and the Unitarians. These could all insist on the universal character of "true religion."

The right kind of religion can help, but the most effective way to transform ideas about right and wrong, eradicating the false moral consciousness pervading society, urged Diderot, Helvétius, and d'Holbach, is to reform education, institutions, and the law with the support of government.[82] A key element in changing society's accepted norms was ending the clergy's control over education: "either no priests or no true morality."[83] Any moral science worthy of being taken seriously must be closely linked to proposals for the reform of both education and legislation. The ultimate goal, in Helvétius's view, dismissed as crass immoralism by Rousseau, is the equal repartition of happiness among the citizenry, a goal that simultaneously requires a purely secular, socially orientated moral code and a less unequal repartition of wealth in society.[84] This for Helvétius was the meaning of the ancient maxim, "salus populi suprema lex esto," which he revived as the lynch-pin of the new morality and social theory.[85]

Pain and pleasure are, for Helvétius, "les seuls moteurs de l'univers moral" and love of oneself, and self-interest, the only realistic basis for constructing a meaningful and useful moral science that is truly universal.[86] "Le désir du bonheur," as Helvétius expressed it, "est commun à tous les hommes."[87] Thus, the whole art of legislation consists in prodding men through "their feeling of love for themselves to be always just towards one another."[88] With persuasive examples of his key distinction between "virtues of prejudice" and "true virtue," Helvétius demonstrates how such a universal standard of moral rationality can be rendered plausible and effectively applied to reform the law, penal code, marriage, and every area subject to moral considerations.[89] "Virtues of prejudice" he defines as those that are either damaging or irrelevant to general well-being and the *bonheur public*, ranging from human sacrifice, cannibalism, genital mutilation, and self-immolation to fasting and sacred prostitution, along with repression of homosexual and other forms of sexual activity deemed shameful or criminal.[90] Hardly any land exists where some such "virtues" are not more revered by ordinary folk than true virtues and, conversely, their violation, *crimes de préjugé* (no matter how senseless to persons from other cultures, or when dispassionately assessed in terms of reason) are not regarded with greater horror than even the worst real offenses against the public good.

The only answer to the Church's nurturing *vertus de préjugé* is to unmask hypocrisy, deride ignorance, and show who are the real and "les plus cruels ennemis de l'humanité." Everywhere society embraces false virtue, obfuscating even the most basic rules of "true morality" and hampering access to knowledge and enlightenment. If the pagan priests of Athens persecuted and executed Socrates and menaced his followers, that was because their own particular interest, held Helvétius, was wholly opposed "au bien public." All those trained for priest-hood are by definition priests of false religion since they preach "virtues of prejudice" and have a vested interest in keeping men as ignorant as possible. Ignorance underpins their authority. What, for instance, is more ridiculous than the ban on Montesquieu's *L'Esprit des Loix* imposed by ecclesiastical authority in "certain countries" (that is, in Italy, Spain, Portugal, and Austria)?[91]

Elements of Helvétius's moral thought, however, ap-peared simplistic to Diderot and d'Holbach. What dis-turbed Diderot about Helvétius's system was not its general orientation but its excessively streamlined, deduc-tive character, its mechanical simplicity and, as he saw it, consequent superficiality. Helvétius is too glib in consid-ering physical sensibility "la cause unique de nos actions" and deriving morality exclusively from pursuit of physical "pleasure" and avoiding pain, contentions that led him to rely excessively on the power of education.[92] Helvétius's insistence on *l'intérêt public* as the sole basis of morality seemed to imply, as he admitted himself, that practically everything, even murder and cannibalism, can under ex-ceptional circumstances become legitimate "et même vertueux pour le salut public."[93] Helvétius's discussions with Diderot and d'Holbach, regular during the early 1760s, resumed during the last years of his life, Diderot closely examining his second major work, *De l'Homme* (1771), in manuscript, and subjecting it to searching queries and criticism in the months prior to his friend's death in 1771. During 1773–1774 Diderot elaborated on his criticisms in his *Réfutation de l'ouvrage d'Helvétius intitulé* De l'Homme (1774), one of his longest and most detailed works.

Diderot and d'Holbach sought a wider definition of self-interest than Helvétius allows and one less rigidly physical. They aspired to explore the relationship between self-interest and the general will in a nuanced, thorough, and multifaceted way. Is not the distinction between "the physical" and "the moral" just as solid, asked Diderot, as that between the animal that feels and the animal that is capable of reasoning?[94] It is imperative for the philosopher, urged Diderot, to keep abreast of developments in biological science and engage fully with the numerous difficulties raised by empirical research into physiology, animal reproduction, sexuality, untypical behavior, mental instability, moral quandaries, and the mechanics of the mind generally. It seemed to Diderot still an open question whether he, Helvétius, and d'Holbach were justified in attributing sensibility, and hence thought, to matter as such. To his mind this remained just a working hypothesis, the most plausible explanation, not a truth conclusively demonstrated.

A point Diderot was especially dissatisfied with was Helvétius's account of intelligence, which provided no way of accommodating the vastly different levels and types of intellectual attainment among humans, merely attributing these to environment and education alone.[95]

What about stupidity, insanity, and unstable behavior, asked Diderot, or, for that matter, genius? Surely these were not simply consequences of adverse or especially favorable environment and education? Nor did it seem likely that, having established its educational priorities, the state could simply proceed to mould society's youth after the image it deemed best in the general interest. As for Helvétius's proposition that it is relatively easy, through education, to change a people's religious opinions, this seemed totally implausible to Diderot.[96] The notions of particular peoples, like those of individuals, are usually "très fausses" but this does not make them easy to change.

Diderot and d'Holbach anchored their moral mechanics, following Spinoza, in their axiom that all men's emotions and desires are subject to the same laws as all bodies in nature and that these are regular and determined but complex. Hence, mental movements—"mobiles," d'Holbach calls them, prompting men to moral or immoral decisions—are mechanistically caused in diverse ways, so that there is no grand schema or teleology, theological or utilitarian, governing human behavior but rather a complex array of drives, inclinations, and motives. This approach enables Diderot and d'Holbach to develop a conception of temperament, personality differences, and intelligence considerably more nuanced and variegated than that of Helvétius. Awareness of self-interest broadens and deepens with the growth of awareness more generally. While their approach, in the end, is akin to the utilitarianism of Helvétius or, later, Bentham—happiness for Diderot and d'Holbach, too, being a smooth, uninterrupted feeling of pleasure, serenity, and satisfaction filling one's days—their analysis expands the range of motive forces, personality drives, and moral categories and assigns a more pivotal role to justice.[97]

The correct way to determine morality's content is first to fix the universal and eternal collective interest of men, the permanent interest or "l'utilité constante de la société."[98] No one can really abandon sight of what is in his or her interest. But pursuit of one's "interest" is morally praiseworthy only where the individual grasps that his true interest requires being useful and agreeable to others, nature having placed him in society among others with the same basic motives as himself. By acting morally, on the basis of equity, equality, and reciprocity, the individual ultimately advances his or her own happiness along with that of others.[99] Where it is thus grounded in experience and reason and has for its object "des objets vraiment utiles pour la société," pursuit of self-interest becomes "grand, noble, sublime"—indeed, virtue itself. Pursuit of self-interest is abject and base, on the other hand, when blindly self-absorbed, inconsiderate, and unenlightened.

Virtue conducive to individual happiness, in *la nouvelle philosophie*, consists in contributing to "la felicité générale et particulière," assisting others to win esteem, affection, and cooperation.[100] To secure others' collaboration, one must treat them as one wishes to be treated oneself, on a basis of reciprocity and equality. Justice and benevolence anchored in equality, therefore, as in Spinoza's *Ethics* and *Tractatus Theologico-Politicus*, became for the *philosophes modernes* the exclusive ground of morality itself. For those whom the *anti-philosophes* labeled *Spinosistes*—Boulainvilliers, Fréret, Du Marsais, Boulanger, Diderot, and the *côterie d'Holbachique*—justice and injustice, charity and lack of charity, as Marin complained, are effectively the sole moral categories. Only behaving justly—upholding equity, refraining from injuring others with regard to their rights, security, and possessions—is judged "moral" by these writers. It was a concept of justice that pivots on acknowledging individuals' and nations' natural equality of rights, a justice of equality and reciprocity now proclaimed, as d'Holbach puts it, "la vraie base de toutes les vertus sociales."[101] It is here that we discern the essential link between Radical Enlightenment's moral values and its constant stress on the principles of equality and democracy.

While some modern historians have felt the Enlightenment savors of excessive optimism, was naïve in imagining that man is naturally good and perfectible, actually Diderot and d'Holbach, as the Abbé Richard observes, consider man neither good nor bad by nature but rather a being acquiring moral characteristics only through society and education.[102] Envisaging the clash between Christianity and *philosophisme* as a war of two irreconcilably opposed moral systems, Richard, attacking d'Holbach in 1775, locates the *nouvelle philosophie*'s most fundamental error in claiming the moral corruption of society arises from ignorance, prejudice, fashion, wrong education, unjust government, and laziness. Men's vices and immorality, to them, stem from wrong ideas and "institutions déraisonnables."[103] It is through not grasping the necessary relations existing between him and others that man undervalues his responsibilities toward others of his species and fails to see these are necessary to his own happiness.[104] Wrong, retorted Richard, and utterly perverse! It is pride, avarice, ambition, lust, and appetite for sensual pleasure generally that drive man's moral corruption, just as the Church teaches, and also these shortcomings that inspire *philosophisme*, which renders man's corruption still worse. Evil is innate in men and philosophy powerless to combat evil, as we see from the abominable Nero's having had Seneca as his teacher. Religion alone can fight immorality, depravity, and sin.

For the radical *philosophes*, what is morally good is simply that which is directed toward the common good, or "l'utilité générale," understood in terms of what Paine later called "the unity of man," construing men as "being all of one degree."[105] All men being basically the same, "they vary only in outward form."[106] Once one has the correct starting-point, philosophy can, despite the infinite variety of men, establish a morality that is truly universal and meaningfully applies to all.[107] Intended for everyone, the rules of this morality must be simple, clearly demonstrable, and intellectually accessible to everyone. For Diderot and d'Holbach, the essence is simple and straightforward: "love, if you wish to be loved" (Aimez, pour être aimé), intoned d'Holbach, citing Seneca's maxim: "si vis amari, ama"—there is the simple precept to which "the universal morality boils down."[108]

Politics on these criteria is just morality applied to the conservation of states, legislation morality consecrated into law, Natural Law—the assemblage of moral rules drawn from the nature of man, and education, our need to inculcate and nurture moral awareness based on reasoning in men. D'Holbach, like Helvétius, saw education as an especially potent tool, but, like Diderot, also considered it something far broader than merely what individuals learn in school. To this, Richard answered that education, even in the most enlightened countries of Europe—and he did not deny that Enlightenment had everywhere had a deep impact—had thus far done nothing to improve behavior as far as anyone could tell. "Our century is that of Enlightenment, reason and philosophy," exactly as the *philosophes* assert, but has this brought any improvement in moral standards: "en sommes-nous meilleurs et plus virtueux?"[109] There was little sign of that.

Resting on the study of human nature and human relations, morality is the science of how to manage human needs, desires, and aspirations, the "science of happiness," "le bonheur," consisting in "desiring only that which one can obtain."[110] Consequently, study and cultivation of morality are eminently useful to everyone on earth—to nations, rulers, and individuals alike, rich and poor, powerful and powerless, parents and children: without it, society comprises only rivals, "des ennemis toujours prêts à se nuire."[111] Governments not built on justice, however—that is, practically all actual governments—have always feared true morality. Rulers regularly disdain ethics as a purely speculative science, useless for governing empires, ignoring the fact that morality is the exclusive basis of what *la philosophie moderne* termed "happiness both general and particular." They disdain it, because princes and aristocrats are not interested in the happiness of their subjects and because few of those whose lives are blighted in consequence grasp this. After 1770 Diderot and d'Holbach increasingly lamented that men have so often confused opulence and power with justice, blindly preferring impressive sway to their own "happiness." Since ignorance and servitude buttress the interests of princes and churchmen and have the inevitable side-effect of rendering men base, "méchants et malheureux," the happiness of the human race crucially depends, proclaimed (the post-1770) Diderot and d'Holbach, on overturning the despotic alliance of kings with priests and priestcraft. Moral progress is conceivable but, for d'Holbach as for Diderot, men must have just government and laws before there can be any real prospect that they can be "justes, moderés, sociables."[112] True enlightenment, then, enlight-

enment of society as a whole, necessarily requires comprehensive revolution: first a revolution in ideas and then
a revolution of action, whether peaceful or violent. The
inevitable first step in the "General Revolution" aimed at
emancipating mankind must be utterly to condemn ignorance, prejudice, and credulity: "it is only by showing
[men] the truth," wrote d'Holbach in 1772, "that they will
come to know their most vital interests and the true motives which should incline them towards what is good."[113]

CHAPTER VI

Voltaire versus Spinoza: The Enlightenment as a Basic Duality of Philosophical Systems

D'Holbach argued that no people can feel true loyalty and love for its government without being aware of the advantages just and equitable government brings. "Hence, we must enlighten the people" if we want them to behave reasonably and understand the drawbacks that arise from being misled by hypocrites, ambitious men, and religious leaders. "It is through general education," he declares, that the "people can be rendered reasonable," be led to understand their true interests, and become convinced of the loyalty they owe to government, of their duties, of the advantages of peace and tranquility.[1]

Under then-existing conditions, with most educational establishments being run by the churches or provided solely for the nobility, everything in eighteenth-century culture and education seemed to the *philosophes modernes* wrongly grounded and self-contradictory. Everyone "who wishes to know something," states d'Holbach, as things presently stand "is obliged to educate himself."[2] To become an enlightened and reasonable person, one must erase from one's mind the entire complex of "false principles" parents, teachers, and preachers had striven to "infect" everyone with. "My faith is in reasoning," declared Matthew Turner, foremost figure of the Radical Enlightenment in eighteenth-century Liverpool—surgeon, chemist, and self-declared atheist and admirer of Helvétius and other "modern philosophers"—and "though I have formerly believed many things without reason, and even many against it, as is very common, I hope I shall never more."[3]

To reorientate in this way is neither easy nor quick, since nothing is harder than to divest oneself of notions imbibed during childhood. The progress of the human spirit, agreed Herder, is impossible without great effort, without encountering strong resistance and without revolution.[4] Yet this painful procedure must be undergone for the sake of oneself and others. The less reason is developed in a society, the greater the resistance and upheaval will be. For the less people know, the more obdurate they are in upholding what they think they know. It is the totally ignorant person, admonished d'Holbach, who, being entirely credulous, has no doubt about anything and becomes violent and ferocious when challenged.

As the climb is arduous and even the greatest genius can easily take a wrong turn, the progress of human reason should always be deemed a collective effort: it is for the combined enlightened resources of all thinking beings, proposed d'Holbach and his German disciple Weishaupt, to refine and perfect ideas presented to the public. This became a favorite theme: true Enlightenment arises from the collective efforts of all the enquirers and *philosophes* who lead the way, as they themselves had done in compiling the *Encyclopédie* in the face of mounting opposition, while no less vital is the critical, adjudicating role of the readership—of debate, controversy, the participating wider intellectual public. If it is each individual writer's responsibility to be clear, sincere, and truthful, that of the reading public is to evaluate and judge the outcome. Since enlightened men should, by definition, know their true interests better than others, it is incumbent on philosophers and men of learning, intrinsic to their proceedings, to eschew all petty feuding, rivalry, and discord. The most enlightened should be distinguished by their sociability, their humanity toward everyone, "and their harmony among themselves." Brotherly concord, amiability, and group effort were proclaimed core values by the *coterie d'Holbachique.*

Rousseau was deemed outrageously to have fallen short in all these respects.[5] Admittedly, philosophy had been marred from the outset by longstanding antipathies and personality clashes. Radical *philosophes* deplored the spirit of zealous competition and faction among the ancient Greek philosophical schools and sects. Collaboration between all honest searchers after truth and a genuinely tolerant, eclectic spirit are essential, they thought, for all genuine human progress, and not least their clandestine subversion of *ancien régime* society. Where necessary, philosophers must collaborate against the rest. The true philosophical spirit, "la saine philosophie," frowned on excessive zeal and all impulse merely to eclipse and contradict: "those who cultivate philosophy" must be always "completely honest among themselves, always calm, and must not defer to anything except reason illumined by experience which alone can show us things as they really are; philosophy must accept truth from whoever's hands it comes and reject error and prejudice no matter whose authority it rests upon."[6]

Diderot and d'Holbach, through their historical researches and editing work as chief compilers of the radical thought of the past, and prime theorists of prerevolutionary *philosophie moderne*, summed up the entire radical tradition of thought, acknowledging their considerable debt to past writers such as Boulainvilliers, Boulanger, Fréret, Meslier, Mirabaud, and Du Marsais, as well as Helvétius, Bayle, Hobbes, and Spinoza. Both also recognized that the early initial insights and breakthroughs, first steps on the long road to Radical Enlightenment, had indeed been taken by the ancient Greek thinkers. But at the same time, they contended, there had been no true antecedent to late seventeenth- and eighteenth-century radical ideas morally, politically, educationally, or philosophically, either in ancient or medieval times, or in Machiavelli's Italy.[7]

Ancient Stoicism struck Du Marsais and d'Holbach, as Spinoza earlier, as austere, wrong-headed, and fanatical, a system that rejects the passions and fails to characterize "virtue" correctly or realistically or render it appealing to well-balanced humans.[8] Asceticism has always been cultivated by some, commented d'Holbach, but also always been considered a form of piety of which only a few are capable. The cult of abstinence, revered by Catholic authors, was thus dismissed by them as a method of deprecating the majority and lowering them to subordinate status. Epicureanism they rated higher; Epicurus who, in d'Holbach's opinion, had been unjustly maligned by Christian writers, was regularly lauded. Yet, the Epicureans, too, were judged as being far from "universalist" under the new *esprit philosophique*'s criteria, being a sect that had managed neither to explain themselves clearly on many basic issues nor resolutely combat their foes. As for Aristotelianism, this school was dismissed as a heap of obsolete distinctions and empty definitions that, however dominant over the centuries, had contributed nothing useful to elucidating "true" philosophy, science, politics, or morality.

While the Greeks deserved high praise for their special role in the history of science and philosophy, radical thinkers denied their achievement derived from any innate ethnic characteristics, or from Greek Europeanness, or even, originally, from the Greek world. The great honor of having introduced men to philosophy simply did not belong exclusively to them. It was from Egypt and Phoenicia, according to d'Holbach, that the Greeks received their cults and first notions about nature and "morality, in a word their philosophy."[9] Pythagoras and Plato, especially, allegedly drew on Egyptian sources. Diderot and d'Holbach considered the deep reverence of most contemporaries for classical antiquity generally misplaced and blameworthy, mankind's "respect stupide et scrupuleux pour l'antiquité" being judged by them as absurd as any other pious veneration for ancient precedent.[10] Especially objectionable was the Greek philosophers' failure to censure their society's worst failings. If Greek and Roman treatment of their slaves was revolting, if individual Helots were left miserably stripped of all protection and rights, sunk in the most abject servility under Spartan law, what did the ancient thinkers and moralists say or do to counter such oppression?[11]

Radical ideas stressed the oneness of humanity, moral equality of all men, and the universal character of the human condition. Consequently, the "modern philosophy" disagreed with Voltaire and other conservative Deists as to whether any particular branch of humanity possessed a special gift or genius to enlighten and instruct others that the rest of humanity lacks. If a Eurocentric superiority complex infused much of the Moderate Enlightenment (as postcolonialist critics stress), such notions were rejected by radical thinkers and also Voltaire, who, like them, regularly eulogized the Chinese, Persians, and Indians, as well as the Greeks. But only the former refused to draw up any hierarchy of superior and less-gifted peoples of the sort Voltaire adhered to. For the radical thinkers philosophy is a task for all and, like the benefits accruing from the universal lessons of experience-based reason, belongs to all equally and this, to their way of thinking, requires considering all peoples as each other's equals.

Enlightenment in this sense entailed full freedom of thought, expression, and the press on an equal basis for everyone, a key aspect of the "revolution of the mind" the *philosophes modernes* aspired to engineer. For a movement urging an end to ancient rivalries, personality clashes, and unnecessary scholastic feuds in philosophy, education, and legislation, unbridled freedom of expression and of the press posed obvious risks. But while the *philosophes modernes* acknowledged that "liberty of the press results in some inconveniences"—as Diderot more than once experienced to his cost, malicious attacks in the press can be exceedingly distressing for individuals—they considered these "trivial and ephemeral compared with the advantages" they expected from giving full scope to the power of reason, critical inquiry, and persuasion.[12] Unrestricted freedom to publish may facilitate rumor-mongering and calumny motivated by envy or hatred, but they hoped that chiefly lies and imposture would suffer from being publicly exposed and that the truth would generally gain from being publicly aired and discussed. Every author who is deceitful or unjust soon receives his just deserts, suggested d'Holbach, "every author of an unjust publication will quickly be punished" by the disapproval he elicits from society.[13] Public indignation, he expected, would avenge malicious affronts and, if it failed to do so, then it was still better to suffer that "inconvenience" than in any way restrict the citizenry's freedom to write and speak "sur des objets importans à leur felicité."[14] This remained not just a brave and noble but a necessary part of a campaign first initiated in European thought by Spinoza in 1670 in his *Tractatus Theologico-Politicus*.[15] Radical thinkers understood that the inherent links between freedom of the press, freedom of expression, individual liberty, and the advancement of knowledge universally were too close and direct to be qualified in any way. Freedom of expression and publication, "la liberté dans les écrits," was rightly recognized by them to be an essential precondition for advancing their social, moral, and political revolution.

The more enlightened man becomes, and aware of his own true interests, the more he comprehends his ties and relationships with others. In *la philosophie nouvelle* men are wicked only insofar as they are irrational or lose sight of the proper way to conduct themselves in relation to their fellow men. Princes, nobles, and the very wealthy, being unenlightened, routinely cheat them and trample on other men's happiness. Some nations are altogether wretched, plunged in misery, and without virtue. But this is never because they are excessively wise or know too much, but rather because they are deprived of the fruits of reason, and those who should help render them wiser do not wish them to become more aware, preferring to cheat them and lead them to their ruin. If men are to be happier in the future this can only occur through Enlightenment overthrowing ignorance, prejudice, privilege, and credulity.[16] Only by enlightening all of humanity can men finally topple the vast and gloomy prison of faith, "mysteries," damaging rites and institutions, archaic law, senseless usages, vicious fanaticism, callous rapacity, and absurd forms of vanity that everywhere blights mankind.

Diderot and d'Holbach, like Rush or Priestley, strove to "enlighten" the whole body of society. Allies and disciples—such as Raynal, Mirabeau, Cloots, Naigeon, Condorcet, Volney, Cerisier, Maréchal, Paine, and Brissot, and, in Germany, Lessing, Herder, Weishaupt, Knigge, Bahrdt, and Forster—emulated them, aiming well beyond society's elites, seeking eventually to institute systems of universal education that the clergy would possess no leverage over and kings be powerless to suborn. Frederick the Great and the aged Voltaire generally scorned such efforts to enlighten the common people, though this did not prevent the former from becoming incensed at d'Holbach's accusation that kings were the "cause of the ill education of their subjects."[17] Voltaire's arguments for not enlightening the majority, however, seemed weak and unconvincing. Only Rousseau, deeply ambiguous regarding the social as opposed to individual role of education, combated his former friends' efforts to eradicate traditional ideas from men's minds—and still more those of women—with real passion and vigor.

The full sweep and significance of the "revolution of the mind" preceding the Revolution of fact was already clear to philosophical readers by the early 1770s, in the wake of d'Holbach's principal works and the *Histoire philosophique*. The considerable impact of these writings left majority opinion in Western Europe disturbed, perplexed, and usually appalled. One need only consider the profoundly unsettling impact of the *nouvelle philosophie*'s "revolution of the mind" on Voltaire in his last years to appreciate the shock administered to European thought, politics, and culture. D'Holbach's *Système de la nature* in particular moved Voltaire to reconsider his entire philosophical stance and reorganize his polemical strategy, leading him, in his last decade, to shift his attention from nearly everything else, decelerate his attack on Christianity, and concentrate on attacking Spinozism, atheism, and materialism.[18]

In all Voltaire's late writings, from 1769, most notably in his *Questions sur l'Encyclopédie* (1770–1771; his last large-scale work), his reply to d'Holbach's *Système* (1770), the *Lettres de Memmius* (1771), and *Il faut prendre un parti, ou le principe d'action* (1772), the ideas of Diderot and d'Holbach, and the latter's *Système de la nature* in particular, constituted his main target. He assailed these together with Spinoza's system, which he more and more recognized as the philosophical underpinning of Diderot's and d'Holbach's atheistic materialism. Likewise, in the *Histoire de Jenni* (1775), his last major *conte philosophique*, his mouthpiece, Dr "Friend," a paragon of English good sense and Lockean premises, is chiefly concerned with combating atheism and materialism.

Voltaire reacted forcefully and often indignantly to d'Holbach and Diderot's *philosophisme* ideology, insisting time and again, in his letters as well as in his extended texts of the period, that they were mistaken in their conclusions, indeed disastrously wrong, and were undermining the entire cause of the Enlightenment with their errors. Already in his anonymously published *Tout en Dieu* (1769), supposedly a "commentaire sur Malebranche," Voltaire had begun to deepen and refine his critique of one-substance solutions to the metaphysical problems he had wrestled with almost continuously since the 1730s.[19] He now admitted that there were serious problems with the "argument from design," the core element in the Newtonianism he had embraced in the 1730s.

In his last great philosophical encounter, Voltaire notably retrenched, conceding now in a way he had been un-

willing to previously, that the divine power must be located in nature itself and that there is, after all, no
contradiction between the necessity of the divine will and
its freedom. Differently from in the past, he now also
abandoned man's freedom of will, thereby lessening the
scope of his natural theology: man is free when he does
what he wants; but he is not free, Voltaire now granted,
to will or not will what he desires.[20] Like all other creatures
and bodies produced by the divine power, men are entirely subject to the unalterable and eternal laws of nature.
But the aging *philosophe* held the line there. He continued
to adhere to Creation, fixity of species, and the Newtonian
doctrine that the regularity and organization of the plane-
tary system reveals a combination of mutually interactive
laws that must have been concerted by a single intelligence
and it was with this that he still chiefly fought Spinoza's—
and hence Diderot's and d'Holbach's—rejection of final
causes and all teleology in nature.

We see most evidently in nature, held Voltaire, that
"dans le grand tout" there is "une grande intelligence"
and therefore also will; this must be the basis of any viable
metaphysics, he alleged, whereas Spinozism denies this.[21]
Equally, and not unconnectedly, there remained a crucial
clash between Spinoza's moral order rooted exclusively in
society's needs and Voltaire's unshakable conviction that
all the religions known in history deliver roughly the same
code of right and wrong, a single system that therefore
must have been bequeathed to man by "l'intelligence

suprême" and be inherent in the providential order, something man discovers through experience.[22]

Philosophically, the basic split remained irresolvable and there was little real movement by either side, nor indeed could there have been. But openly acknowledging it meant accepting that the schism in the Western Enlightenment was now public and irreparable. At the root of the disaster, for Voltaire, was the one-substance doctrine put forth by Spinoza and embraced by Voltaire's opponents. To his mind, their fundamental error had been to adopt the basic ideas of Spinoza, for Spinoza had not only provided the main philosophical grounding on which the new atheistic materialism had arisen, but throughout been the most incisive, systematic, and seductive teacher of what Voltaire termed *l'athéisme philosophique*.[23] Meanwhile, he denied Hobbes had openly professed atheism or rejected all final causes,[24] a position not uncommon in the eighteenth century. Yet Spinoza, no matter how pivotal to the rise of philosophical materialism, had his philosophy wrong. Diderot, Helvétius, and d'Holbach, rather like Bayle earlier, had neither read Spinoza carefully enough nor understood him correctly. Voltaire would show that it was indeed possible to breach "les remparts du Spinosisme," vowing to do so on a side that Bayle, consciously or unconsciously, had neglected to attack.[25]

Again and again in his *Questions sur l'Encyclopédie*, his *Dieu. Réponse de Mr. de Voltaire au* Système de la Nature (1770), and the thirty-seven-page *Il faut prendre un parti*

(1772), Voltaire probes Spinoza's equating of God with nature, observing that Spinoza, unlike the crowd "de ceux qui crient Spinosa, Spinosa"—a reference to Diderot, Helvétius, and d'Holbach—acknowledges the need to recognize in nature a power both necessary and "intelligent."[26] With the realization that Spinoza's "universal substance" is not a fully cogent concept, as his mistake in denying the existence of void illustrates, his entire system begins to unravel. For if nature possesses "intelligence," the power to think, how can this infinite, universal Being lack the power to make designs? If it has designs, how then can Spinoza's God or nature not have a will? If this *grand tout* has a will, how can Spinoza continually deny and even mock the notion of "final causes"? An intelligence destitute of will would be "something absurd, because this intelligence would have no purpose." The great necessary Being, concludes Voltaire, has thus willed everything he has created and Spinoza had trapped himself in a fatal fallacy in denying divine Providence.[27]

This was Voltaire's last throw and he repeated it, including in letters to d'Alembert, Frederick the Great, and high courtiers at both Versailles and in Berlin, a dozen times. Only by cutting at the root of Spinozist metaphysics could he undercut the rapid advance of French philosophical materialism. But if God had really created the cosmos, answered Diderot and d'Holbach and their growing body of disciples, not only would the order of the universe be the result of divine Providence, so, too, would all the disorder, violence, malignity, and oppression that renders all worldly existence precarious and human life generally wretched and miserable.[28] If the order of the universe proves the omnipotence and intelligence of the divine Creator, then the disorder, and all the perverse and incompetent regimes that blight men's lives, should prove that Creator's feebleness, inconstancy, and unreasonableness. Whilst traversing Germany on his way to Russia in the late summer of 1773, Diderot, sarcastically described as "le Spinosiste de Langres" by Frederick the Great, stopped at Düsseldorf and Leipzig but circumvented Berlin so as to avoid the detested Prussian monarch (who felt grievously insulted, he complained to Voltaire). On the way, Diderot not only openly proclaimed his materialism and atheistic morality "avec la ferveur d'un visionnaire," reported a Swiss pastor who met him in Leipzig, but assured all who would listen that Voltaire the man might still amaze but that his philosophy is "absurde."[29]

Spinoza had gone wrong, contended Voltaire, in envisaging nature as creating itself, which, by implication at least, forced him toward evolutionary tendencies in biology, a tendency still more marked in Diderot's writings but directly contradicted by Voltaire's doctrine of divine Creation and fixity of species. God, joked Voltaire in a letter to Frederick the Great of 20 August 1770—a month before the appearance of the first of his public refutations of materialism, *Dieu. Réponse de Mr. de Voltaire au* Système de la Nature—in any case now had "the two least superstitious men in Europe" on his side, "which ought to please him a lot." His rebuttal, he explained to Frederick, involved discrediting the entire scientific grounding on which the author of the *Système de la nature* had tried to build, especially his borrowing the "transformist" naturalism of de Maillet and Buffon, which had been adopted into *la philosophie nouvelle* by Diderot as early as the late 1740s.

Both de Maillet and Buffon were materialists and claimed, ridiculously in Voltaire's opinion, that the world's geology had evolved over millions of years, and that the Pyrenees and the Alps were created by the sea, a notion endorsed among others by the recent French translator of Lucretius (d'Holbach's assistant, Lagrange), a commentator who had indeed embraced all the modern materialists' "transformism" and evolutionism. Evolutionary ideas had always been anathema to Voltaire. The materialists wish us to believe, he commented scornfully, that all living creatures once lived in the sea and men were originally "porpoises whose divided tail-fins evolved in the course of time into buttocks and legs." Even more preposterous in his (and Frederick the Great's) opinion was the thesis about the spontaneous production of eels advanced by the English Jesuit biologist John Turberville Needham (1713–1781), and adopted by the French materialists, a stance negated, Voltaire alleged, by the experiments of the Italian naturalist Lazzaro Spallanzani (1729–1799).[30]

Voltaire believed he had the better arguments and scientific evidence but, disastrously, was failing to win the battle. The author of the *Système*, Voltaire noted in late September 1770, had thrown all European thought into chaos, rendering the *philosophes* hateful, and making philosophy itself ridiculous, especially at Versailles and in Berlin. Writing to the comte de Schomberg on 5 October, he observed that the *Système* was turning many heads in Paris, and indeed was dividing "tous les esprits" down the middle as neatly as any minuet at Versailles, repeating his condemnation of it as a dangerous and incoherent work grounded on defective science.[31] In a letter to Grimm a few days later, in which he also asked him to extend his greetings to "Frère Platon" (Diderot) even if the latter does not concede "intelligence," as Spinoza does, he repeated that "ce maudit *Système de la nature*" had done irreparable damage.[32]

In a letter of 11 October, Voltaire assured Condorcet that he agreed with the claim of the veteran Benedictine Spinoza fighter Dom Deschamps (1716–1774) in the latter's just-finished manuscript refutation of the *Système de la nature* that "la nouvelle philosophie" if not strenuously resisted would assuredly conjure up "une revolution horrible."[33] Voltaire considered the direction *la philosophie* had now taken extremely dangerous and was especially distressed that "all" the other *philosophes,* as he put it with considerable exaggeration, were siding with d'Holbach and Diderot and disdaining or ignoring his own *Réponse.*

Among those known to have spoken out in favor of the *Système de la nature*, besides Diderot and his disciples and the rest of the inner circles of the salons of d'Holbach and Madame Helvétius, was the leading astronomer in Paris, Jérome Lalande.

Voltaire's complaints concerning the direction taken by the leading men of the mind in Paris reflects his growing frustration, wounded pride, and bitterness. He was conceding, in effect, his increasingly obvious inability any longer to dominate the *parti philosophique* intellectually or morally.[34] Deploring the harm done to *la philosophie*'s reputation at court, he assured a warm admirer of his, Choiseul's friend Madame Du Deffand, a long-standing foe of Diderot, that in its general effect the *Système* resembled the financial schemes of John Law (1673–1729), the much reviled Scottish adventurer whose issue of banknotes in France had catastrophically crashed in 1720, causing considerable loss, recrimination, and scandal. By this he meant that while the materialists were enjoying a fleeting huge success and sweeping along everyone who counted intellectually, behind the scenes they were actually inflicting colossal damage material and moral on France's rich and powerful elites and destroying what he saw as the right kind of Enlightenment.[35] In any case, he added jocularly, he expected to die shortly and would soon find out who was right concerning immortality of the soul—Plato or Spinoza, Saint Paul or Epictetus, Christianity or Confucianism.

As Voltaire envisaged it, the unrelenting war between Moderate and Radical Enlightenment after 1770 was philosophical in the first place but far from being only philosophical. Voltaire's life-long fight for more toleration and to discredit the Church among the higher echelons of society was an attempt to change the world in alliance with Europe's nobility and courts, weakening only ecclesiastical power and theology while leaving the faith of the common people intact. The battle Diderot and d'Holbach were fighting against accepted values had become a social, political, and intellectual struggle, and even as he edged closer to them philosophically, Voltaire could no longer afford, politically and culturally, to be in any way associated with them. The "revolution of the mind" they sought to engineer was a universal re-evaluation of all values and thus one of a fundamentally different kind from the "revolution" to which he had for so long been committed. Their philosophy may have been more coherent, more of a piece, more closely tied to their philosophical core doctrines than his, and better connected to the more daring recent developments in biology and geology, but it was also altogether more sweeping, dangerous, and difficult, and bound, as Deschamps and many other *antiphilosophes* predicted, to have a vast and far-reaching revolutionary effect.

Voltaire remained as convinced as ever that the common people required a strong "brake" on their unruly passions and that this could only come from traditional

religion and especially the promises and threats of retribution of a God who rewards and punishes in the
hereafter—hence his insistence that ordinary folk neither
could nor should be "enlightened."[36] Deriding his long-
dead rival for European fame, Montesquieu, for what he
considered the latter's feeble rebuttal of Bayle's argument
that a society of true Christians could not survive in a
world of non-Christians,[37] Voltaire also thought Bayle
gravely mistaken in supposing a society of atheists could
thrive: had Bayle been allocated five or six hundred
peasants to govern, he commented, he would assuredly
not have failed to proclaim "un Dieu rémunérateur et
vengeur."[38]

The split between Radical Enlightenment and court-
sponsored Moderate Enlightenment was now obvious
and the logic of court politics and ecclesiastical reactions
constantly worked to polarize further these points of view.
Admittedly, there are examples of collaboration and long
friendships between writers who belong on one side of
the divide with writers on the other, such as the well-
known collaboration between Turgot and Condorcet.
Condorcet has recently been described by one scholar as
a "close ally of Turgot."[39] But while there were, indeed,
many practical issues, including questions of fiscal, judi-
cial and naval improvements, toleration, and widening
freedom of expression where the two men agreed,[40] their
friendship was plainly based on the fact that both were
accomplished mathematicians and during the 1770s en-

joyed exploring new refinements of algebra together. Whenever it came to basic philosophical questions, however, the two were entirely at odds and repeatedly, if always politely, returned to the same, unbridgeable points of disagreement that were, in essence, exactly those differentiating Moderate from Radical Enlightenment.

Turgot adhered to a basically Newtonian and Lockean vision of the universe. He detested the ideas of Diderot, Helvétius, and d'Holbach and, even if somewhat reluctantly, was an accessory to the temporary banishment from France in 1775 of Raynal, a radical *philosophe* and close colleague of Diderot.[41] Touching on his basic disagreement with Condorcet in a letter of May 1774, he invoked the principle of universal gravitation. Like Newton, but entirely contrary to Spinoza, Diderot, and d'Holbach, Turgot held that nature requires an outside force to put it into movement, maintaining that an external mover must exist, indeed that all movement in the universe is initiated by a higher cause working outside and independently of all known mechanical causes.[42] This "first cause," responsible, in his view, for all movement, must be both free and "intelligent" like the soul of humans, and since "freedom of the will" seemed to him equally undeniable, he totally rejected the arguments by which "les philosophes irréligieux"—that is Diderot, Helvétius, and d'Holbach—sought to show its "impossibility." Minds, as Turgot formulated his metaphysical dualism and Lockean psychology, are determined not by "des moteurs" but by motives, not by mechanical causes but in pursuit of final causes. Beings that feel, think, and desire, he contended, have goals and choose means, and hence constitute a realm of things "at least as real and as certain" as that of beings deemed purely material and moved by purely mechanical causes.[43]

To this Condorcet replied that he had examined his friend's "reflections" on metaphysical questions with much pleasure but disliked his sliding from clear facts of physics to "mythologie."[44] His contention that the principle of an intelligent first cause and the existence of minds that are free is at least as consonant with what we know from physics, and from experience, as is mechanistic determinism, struck Condorcet as being altogether unproven and improbable, and actually at odds with what we know, indeed completely "de mythologiques." He assured Turgot—who, incidentally, possessed an immense personal library abounding in bibles and works of theology but containing relatively little philosophy—that he, too, was as certain of the existence of his own mind as of his body but that he had no "certitude" about its composition, taking other minds to exist only as a probability. Particularly implausible, he thought, was Turgot's trust in the existence of a general, or first, cause.[45]

CHAPTER VII
Conclusion

By the mid-1770s the split in the French, German, Dutch, American, Italian, and British enlightenments had become open, clear, and irreparable. It was impossible to bridge the gap between Moderate and Radical Enlightenment in philosophy, science, moral thought, or politics, and many could see that this was the case. It was a vast conflict—political, social, and intellectual—that had to be fought out and one that in the 1770s, 1780s, and 1790s, looked dangerously unresolved. What is more, despite Voltaire's last great throw and Turgot's adamant stance against materialism, it was clear, even to the former, that he had lost the fight in the philosophical arena, at least for the time being, and that it was the radical thinkers who had gained the upper hand.

By the 1770s the radical *philosophes* were diffusing an entirely new form of revolutionary consciousness that in their minds applied not to France alone, or any particular country or Europe specifically, but to the whole world.

All the world suffered under the sway of tyranny, oppression, and misery, buttressed by ignorance and credulity, and all humanity required a revolution—intellectual to begin with, practical later—through which to emancipate itself. The last and most radical version of the *Histoire philosophique*, that of 1780, generalized the radical analysis of what was wrong with Europe, taking in the colonial empires spanning the world, announcing with unprecedented force the need for a general revolution, in India and Africa no less than in Europe and the Americas.

Different radical writers began applying the same basic formula introduced by Diderot and d'Holbach to all the world's regions and civilizations. Thus, the young Volney who later, in 1789, was to be one of the leaders of the democratic movement in the revolutionary French National Assembly, a thinker highly critical of Montesquieu, applied it with considerable cogency to the Middle East, where he spent three years learning Arabic in the mid-1780s. Apart from a few nomadic groups such as the Bedouin, Druze, and Mesopotamian Turkmen, practically all the societies of the region, and especially the sedentary population of the main cities and agricultural tracts, according to Volney, had for many centuries languished under a relentlessly oppressive alliance of religious and political despotism firmly grounded in "superstition." Only a "grande révolution" or general "révolution" could rescue the inhabitants of Syria and Egypt from the oppression, destitution, and misery in which most of them–

the nomadic peoples excepted—dwelt. In Western Asia, he thought, this "grande révolution" would begin via an armed revolt among the fiercely independent nomadic tribes of the Arabian desert.[1]

But however it began, the first step had to be the spreading of awareness of the havoc wrought upon human life by despotism, religious authority, ignorance, and superstition. Radical Enlightenment, unlike Voltaire's enlightenment, could not hope to advance by winning over influential court advocates. It had no other recourse but to turn philosophy into effective ideology and inundate the reading public with its new revolutionary awareness via a torrent of clandestine publications, and to do so to such an extent as to set in motion a general process rendering society more "enlightened." Ultimately, their aim was to transform the political and social framework of modern life. Only by eradicating the reading public's former attitudes could Radical Enlightenment hope in the end to raise the general level of education, undermine privilege and special interests, and, at some future point, redirect the levers of government toward reforming the law and institutions and making society more secure and protective, and more equal for all.

Consequently, the rise, growth, and diffusion of Radical Enlightenment from the 1660s down to the 1780s is not merely relevant to the advent of the French Revolution, and indeed the entire revolutionary wave of the late eighteenth century, but arguably much the most important factor in any proper understanding of how and why the Revolution developed as it did—that is, how and why it became a conscious and systematic effort to erase completely the institutions and consciousness of the past and replace these across the board with the principles of liberty, equality, and fraternity. Over many decades a majority of historians have been famously loath to concede that ideas played a formatively crucial part in the Revolution. But if one looks at the great public intellectual controversies of the 1770s and 1780s it becomes obvious that there is no place for such an attitude. The prevailing view about the French Revolution not being caused by books and ideas in the first place may be very widely influential but it is also, on the basis of the detailed evidence, totally indefensible. Indeed, without referring to Radical Enlightenment nothing about the French Revolution makes the slightest sense or can even begin to be provisionally explained.

Since, however, the Radical Enlightenment in the later eighteenth century has only recently come to be studied as an international intellectual, cultural, and social phenomenon, today's student, inevitably, is presented with a highly perplexing problem of historiography. For although historians have now for some years been more aware of a huge and striking gap persisting in the historiography of the French Revolution, becoming conscious of the astounding failure dragging on over the decades to look seriously at the intellectual background to the Revolution, efforts to fill the gap remain rather sparse. Keith Michael Baker, in his *Inventing the French Revolution* (1990), stresses that "there has been relatively little explicit or systematic attention in recent years to the question of the ideological origins of the French Revolution."[2]

So incomplete and sketchy is current historiography's understanding of the intellectual origins of the French Revolution, and such the continuing tendency to focus excessively on the great constitutional conflicts of the mid- and later eighteenth century in France prior to 1789 (which for the most part have little to do with the intellectual origins of the Revolution), that Baker's complaint can perhaps usefully be reiterated in much stronger terms. For the fact that a massive torrent of democratic, egalitarian, radical literature and journalism welled up before 1789, infused with Radical Enlightenment ideas propagated by works like the *Système de la nature*, the *Système Social*, and the *Histoire philosophique*, had a profoundly unsettling effect on the best minds—as the reactions of Voltaire, d'Alembert, Deschamps, Bergier, Richard, and many others show—is both undeniable and massively important. The evidence of book-history demonstrates that these books achieved a far greater penetration in the 1770s and 1780s than did Rousseau's political and social theoretical works, or indeed any other political and social ideology. This has been known for some time.

Yet thus far these crucial developments have failed almost entirely to penetrate the consciousness of historians of the revolutionary era, a strange state of affairs indeed.

The result is a vast corpus of literature on the Revolution, and the revolutionary era more generally, extending right down to the last few years that is absurdly inadequate in its account of the relationship between Enlightenment and Revolution. Thus, in François Furet's widely read and admired *Revolutionary France, 1770–1880*, for example, a 600-page synthesis that appeared in 1988, Diderot and d'Holbach are not even mentioned in the index; no mention is made of Brissot's, Mirabeau's, Volney's, Maréchal's, or Cloots's pre-1789 philosophical writings; there is no reference to Cerisier, Paape, or any of the Dutch radical democrats who worked in France before 1789; the radical character of Condorcet's pre-1789 thought is not developed, even briefly; no reference is made to Tom Paine, Weishaupt, or Georg Forster; and nothing is said about Volney's pre-1789 publicity campaign in Rennes to turn the local population against the Breton nobility and local *noblesse de robe*. In a few lines, on one page, Furet acknowledges that the Enlightenment in France was a factor in the Revolution owing to "the scale and the forcefulness of the condemnation it brought to bear on contemporary life—including the Church and religion," conceding that the Enlightenment presided over a "tremendous reshaping of ideas and values."[3] But he says the Enlightenment did this "unwittingly," which is perfectly absurd and, in any case, makes no attempt to build on these insights in developing his analysis.

Even Keith Michael Baker, who expressly set out to redress this highly distorting imbalance, arguably does not really do so. An important contribution in many respects, his study very usefully distinguishes the discourse of institutional and parliamentary constitutionalism in the French Revolution from what he calls the discourse of Enlightenment reason, on the one hand, and the Rousseauist discourse of will, on the other. Identifying these three intellectual impulses as core elements, each fundamentally different and in many ways incompatible with the other, is a valuable advance.[4] Yet when it comes to the intellectual roots of the French Revolution's ideology as such, again we find practically nothing. Diderot is almost entirely missing (except for one highly relevant quote); d'Holbach goes virtually unmentioned; Volney, Cloots, Maréchal, Cerisier, Priestley, Price, Paape, Barlow, Weishaupt, Forster, and except for one brief mention, Tom Paine, are all missing from the index. Not a word is said about the *anti-philosophes* and their analysis of the "revolution of the mind," one of the most important factors in diffusing radical ideas, especially outside France, since their literature was very widely disseminated in Italian, German, and Spanish, as well as in French. The *Histoire philosophique*—the culminating literary blow to the *ancien régime*, the single most devastating intellectual assault on existing structures of authority and conventional thinking of the eighteenth century, a work furiously debated throughout the 1770s and 1780s, appearing in nearly fifty editions in French by the early 1790s, with more than twenty in English and several also in German, Dutch, and Danish—rates only one brief reference.

What intellectual history based on the "controversialist" method (studying public controversies) identifies as much the most important factor in the making of the French Revolution before Robespierre and the Terror— the "revolution of the mind" before the revolution of fact, engineered by the spread of the "modern philosophy"— is largely omitted from the picture, even in Baker, never mind the rest. This is dismaying to anyone who researches the intellectual content of the debates of the Revolution. It is a state of affairs bound seriously to mislead every student reader as to what was really happening in French culture and society in the 1770s and 1780s. Generations of historiography, consciously or unconsciously, give students and the general reader the totally false impression that in the months before the calling of the Estates General in 1789, everyone was busily discussing the national political crisis in terms of traditional and conventional ideas—in terms of precedent, existing institutions, and what the populace was used to, just as in other major early modern events—when in reality this was absolutely not the case.

On the contrary, in France, Germany, Britain, Holland, and elsewhere, there was by 1788 already an acute and widespread consciousness in influential circles of the need to abolish privilege and rank because "philosophy" had for two decades been teaching men that this is what a rational society needed to do. One cannot begin to grasp the revolutionary position in 1789 rightly without acknowledging that *philosophisme* was seen to have engineered a vast "revolution of the mind." And this phenomenon is in turn inexplicable without looking at the long, and in part self-conscious, build-up to its climax in the 1770s and 1780s of a radical tradition reaching all the way back to the 1660s. "They are sapping the foundations of society," protested Father Jamin, by representing loyal "subordination" as a set of barbaric ancient rights, obedience as mere weakness, and authority as tyranny.[5] All belief in supernatural beings and spirits, and therefore all supernatural authority, is eliminated by these *philosophes modernes.* "Tout est matière," they affirm, "avec Spinosa."[6] The principal agent of this (to the *antiphilosophes* obvious) coming revolution was, beyond any question, *la nouvelle philosophie,* and here Jamin, Deschamps, Bergier, Marin, Maleville, and the rest were assuredly right.

It was a claim clearly echoed in 1789 in the *cahiers,* or collective reports, submitted by all the localities and different orders of society, in each locality throughout France, to the meetings of the Estates General convened in that year. These were the meetings that triggered the French Revolution, and the reports provide detailed information as to what different social groups thought was wrong with French society at the time. Many *cahiers* of the clergy testify to this sense of a "revolution of the mind" being already far advanced. The Angoulème clergy, for instance, reporting in March 1789, cited the fatal effects of incredulity, the whole of France, they complained, being inundated in less than a century with impious and scandalous books that, to the prejudice of religion, had become the only "code d'instruction d'une jeunesse insensée."[7] Among their main points the clergy of Armagnac urged forceful measures to halt the withering of all religious, moral, and civil principles caused by this scandalous multitude of books "où règne l'esprit de libertinage, d'incrédulité et d'indépendance," books subverting with impunity and great temerity faith, sexual modesty, throne, and altar.[8]

The Revolution came and went. It proclaimed liberty, equality, and fraternity but failed to establish a viable democratic republic. Robespierre, and the Terror of 1793–1794, wholly or partially discredited the Revolution in the minds of contemporaries in France and abroad just as they have in the minds of modern readers and students ever since. "Moderate" *philosophes* in France during the Revolution, such as the Abbé Morellet, who quarreled definitively with the circle of Madame Helvétius and the Radical Enlightenment in 1789–1790, blamed the catastrophe on what he saw as the perversion of *la philosophie* by radical ideas, and the Terror and the atrocities to which this perversion gave rise, on the *parti démocratique* and the democratic tendency itself. Morellet, citing Volney as one of those most responsible, argues that the radical intellectual tendency in the Revolution was unjust and criminal from the outset in not wanting to respect property rights, including the property and special right to representation of the nobility and clergy.[9] But if radical ideas dominated the opening stages of the Revolution down to early 1793, and then the post-1794 phase, it is arguable that the darker side of the French Revolution, the Revolution of 1793–1794, was chiefly inspired by the Rousseauist tendency. The crass demagoguery and murderous violence directed by Robespierre and the Jacobins did not hesitate publicly to condemn all the *philosophes* and the whole Enlightenment.

Historians generally have given nowhere near sufficient emphasis either to the distinction between Radical Enlightenment and Rousseauism or to the intensity of the clash over democratic Enlightenment ideas within the Revolution. *Assemblée nationale* deputies and their supporters—such as Condorcet (who, along with Paine, had called for a republic as early as 1791, months before Robespierre had dared to),[10] Cloots, Cabanis, Garat, and Volney—were horrified when Robespierre and other Montagnards initiated a program of systematic denunciation and harassment of the Enlightenment heritage and the key principles that it had introduced, and that the early and post-1794 phases of the revolution fully embraced.

The battle between the two impulses was evident at many points before the onset of the Terror. In December 1792, the Jacobin Club ordered the destruction of the busts of Mirabeau and of Helvétius, a *philosophe* at that juncture particularly identified as an opponent of Rousseau. In April 1793 Robespierre publicly denounced the *philosophes* for their alleged servility to court and nobility. But the anti-Enlightenment purge hugely intensified once the Terror began. In July 1793 the Jacobin-dominated National Convention ordered the arrest of Condorcet, who had already gone into hiding. He died, shortly after finally being caught by the Robespierriste authorities, in March 1794.

Nor was it by any means only in relation to ideas and philosophy, or their rival conceptions of the state and of democratic organization that the two revolutionary impulses sharply diverged. They were opposite also in many other areas. Full freedom of thought, expression, and the press, for example, was adopted in 1789 and remained in force, indeed was further broadened, down to August 1792;[11] it was then systematically suppressed by the Jacobins, and replaced by a stifling censorship, but reinstated with a flourish after Robespierre's downfall in the mid-1790s.

In May 1794, by which time nearly all the chief Radical Enlightenment spokesmen, Tom Paine among them, were either in hiding or in prison, or else, as in Cloots's case, had been guillotined, Robespierre delivered a keynote speech to the assembly condemning what he called the arid materialism of the *encyclopédistes* (Diderot and d'Holbach in particular), *philosophes*, who waged war not just on the great Rousseau but on sentiment, common opinion, and the simple virtue and beliefs of ordinary people.[12] Robespierre's and the Jacobins's most powerful and effective argument against the Radical Enlightenment was their constant complaint that the "modern philosophy" opposes "feeling," and especially the sentiments of the ordinary person. Here, ironically, Robespierre's Jacobinism closely converged with royalist Counter-Enlightenment ideology, both propagating the myth of the Enlightenment as a coldly clinical, unfeeling machine of rational ideas, brutalizing natural sentiment and destroying instead of furthering what is best in human life. This allegation was taken up internationally and became a stock theme of British attacks on the "modern philosophers" in the 1790s.

An Enquiry concerning Political Justice by William Godwin, a thinker who turned radical after reading d'Holbach, as he himself stated in 1793 in the preface, was vehemently attacked soon afterwards by an author denouncing "the modern philosophy" as inhumanly mechanistic, a "very harsh principle," almost a "savage barbarism" utterly demolishing "marriage, friendship and filial piety." "The ruthless sacrifice of individuals," he asserts, is easily justified by "modern philosophy," a form of brutality that decimates everything and "with unabating rigour and unfeeling cruelty, sacrifices thousands and tens of thousands to the ideal and imaginary principle of public utility."[13] The menace was universal and "appears under the disguise of enlightened philosophy, whilst gloomy superstition and organized barbarism lurk beneath, and soon display themselves in all their horrors."[14]

Radical Enlightenment writers who survived the Terror subsequently denounced Robespierre, not just as an abominable and bloody dictator but also, as Cloots had before his execution, as a crassly anti-intellectual demagogue and Rousseauist fanatic. After Robespierre's downfall and execution, the Revolution of reason again had the upper hand, through the mid- and later 1790s, and the so-called *ideologues*—Volney, Cabanis, Garat, and the former officer, Destutt de Tracy—heirs to the legacy of Diderot, Helvétius, d'Holbach, and Condorcet—again set the intellectual tone down to the consolidation of Napoleon's dictatorship. Condorcet's public rehabilitation and the National Convention's commissioning three thousand copies of his *Tableau historique de l'esprit humain* in April 1795 typified the Radical Enlightenment's brief restoration to the status of chief guide of the Revolution by looking back to the "revolution of the mind" of the 1770s and 1780s as the decisive turning-point in the history of modernity and all humanity.

Of course, these *ideologues* failed too, but they did not fail entirely. Something of their legacy survived the royalist-aristocratic reaction following Napoleon's fall in

1815, and since theirs was the intellectual tradition that kept the radical agenda alive—and not only survived the nineteenth and early twentieth centuries but gradually gained ground under the surface—it is important to acknowledge their achievement far more than historians generally do. In the end, their principles emerged as the official values of a major part of the world after 1945.

It is especially vital for the modern historian and philosopher to explore the "revolution of the mind" of the 1770s and 1780s in all its aspects and richness and to trace it back to its origins that, we have seen, lie in the late seventeenth century. For it was a revolution that was a century in the making. Radical Enlightenment, plainly, began partly in France and England but especially in the Holland of Spinoza and Bayle.[15] From around 1720 onward, its main focus shifted decisively toward France. Yet it is vital to remember that the tradition developed vigorously also in late eighteenth-century Britain and Germany and that most major works of the Radical Enlightenment (as well as those of Rousseau) were originally published in and distributed from Holland. In this respect, as also with the democratic *Patriottenbeweging* of 1780–1787, the Dutch Republic remained pivotal.

Throughout the eighteenth and nineteenth centuries, mainstream thought in Britain, Ireland, and America, following Locke and Newton and supplemented by Scottish Common Sense, remained always implacably hostile to this tradition of radical thought. This in turn may have been a factor behind the traditional neglect of the radical philosophical tradition in English-speaking countries. But, as we have argued elsewhere, it is vital not to adopt a "national" or "confessional" view of this phenomenon, or to associate Britishness, or "American values" as such, as they developed later, with eighteenth-century Moderate Enlightenment attitudes. For the moderate mainstream, whether we consider Hume, Ferguson, Adam Smith, Frederick the Great, Benjamin Franklin, Montesquieu, Turgot, or Voltaire, was inherently antidemocratic, anti-egalitarian, and reluctant to concede a full toleration. In Britain, Moderate Enlightenment, culminating in the ideas of Edmund Burke, eventually developed a remarkably dogmatic and intolerant social and political conservatism, stubbornly intent on defending virtually all existing institutional, ecclesiastical, and legal forms. Much the same unbridgeable dichotomy between a dominant Moderate and oppositional Radical enlightenment infused the Enlightenment controversy in Ireland. Mainstream publicists in the Irish debate of the 1780s and 1790s routinely distinguished between "True Enlightenment," as they designated Enlightenment based on Locke and Montesquieu, and "pernicious" Enlightenment, meaning Enlightenment rooted in "modern philosophy," which they deplored as materialist, atheistic, and subversive of the British Empire. These publicists were, however, defending social and ecclesiastical hierarchies, privileges, discrimination, and disabilities that scarcely anyone today would attempt to justify.[16]

In any case, there was an impressive revival of indigenous radical thought in the English speaking-world from the 1770s onward, a resurgence that crucially contributed to the many partial triumphs of the Radical Enlightenment in the transatlantic context in the 1780s and 1790s, despite the derailment of the "General Revolution" by Robespierre and the Terror. Tom Paine, dubbed by Joel Barlow "a luminary of the age, and one of the greatest benefactors of mankind,"[17] emerged as one of the most successful publicists of his time, one who propagated the radical cause with unprecedented impact in Britain, America, and France and who resonated also in Ireland. A key exponent of radical thought, Paine broke with all the time-honored conventions of traditional British radical Whiggism, with his cosmopolitan universalism and reaching out to French philosophy effecting what one scholar has aptly called "a striking departure from the conventions of English political writing."[18]

Paine spoke in terms of universal human rights, not the liberties of Englishmen, grounding these universal rights in the freedom carried over from the state of nature into the state of society, loudly echoing Spinoza and the French radical *philosophes*. His was perhaps not an instance of direct influence: no one knows exactly, as Paine rarely cited his intellectual sources. But the affinities and rhetoric of natural rights are, in any case, striking. "Man did not enter into society," as Paine put it, "to become worse than he was before, nor to have fewer rights than he had before, but to have those rights better secured."[19] He was arguably the foremost spokesman of radical ideas in the later Enlightenment English-speaking world down to the 1790s, certainly in the political sphere. But there were numerous others, and these included outstanding and influential representatives of a variant of English Rational Dissent that developed powerful philosophical and universalist tendencies: in particular, Richard Price, Joseph Priestley, John Jebb, and, in America, at any rate before his later life, Benjamin Rush. Meanwhile, the *Aufklärung*, and for that matter, the Italian Enlightenment, and that in the Spanish-speaking world, were no less profoundly divided.

The irreconcilability of the two enlightenments, the impossibility of forging any compromise between, or synthesizing, moderate and radical thought patterns, was rooted, on the one hand, in the intellectual chasm separating the two, but no less importantly in social forces that exerted, as we have seen, a continuously polarizing effect. This state of affairs obviously impacted very variously on different Enlightenment thinkers but overall ensured a lasting duality that shaped the entire history of the Enlightenment.

In the voluminous pre-1789 eighteenth-century literature attacking the thought of the radical *philosophes*,

Bayle is almost always allocated a prominent place as a key inspirer, father-figure, and progenitor of radical ideas and was often considered the most insidious figure of the radical tradition. Recognized by both sides as among the first and most effective to urge a full toleration, separate morality from theology, and base morality on reason alone, as well as propose that a society of atheists would be more viable than a strictly ordered Christian community, Bayle stands as one of the two great formative minds of the tradition.[20] Equally, in later eighteenth-century discussions of the origins of Enlightenment, atheism, naturalism, and materialism, and not least in the famous *Encyclopédie* of Diderot and d'Alembert, Spinoza is assigned a key position. Bayle who devoted the longest single article of his most famous work, the *Dictionnaire historique et critique* (1697), to Spinoza, thought that the Dutch philosopher's most important contribution had been to integrate all the previous strands of materialist, libertarian, and anti-theological thought reaching back to ancient Greek times into the most coherent, integrated, and incisive form they had thus far been given, and in this he was surely right. Spinoza in fact forged a system that was destined to exert an unparalleled impact on all aspects of eighteenth and early nineteenth-century intellectual debate.

Compared to Spinoza and Bayle, no other writer had an even remotely comparable importance as a perceived originator and author of radical ideas. Some historians deny this, but the proof lies in the controversies. If one compiles a list, for instance, of the dozen or so foremost *anti-philosophes* attacking French radical ideas in the later eighteenth century—men such as Bergier, Richard, Jamin, Marin, Hayer, Gauchat, Griffet, Chaudon, Nonnotte, Crillon, Deschamps, and Feller—those who indict earlier philosophers as originators of the "contagion" allegedly destroying *ancien régime* society, and especially thrones and altars, invariably cast Spinoza or Bayle, and frequently both, in this role. Nobody gives comparable coverage to Machiavelli, Bruno, or Hobbes, though the latter is sometimes mentioned in passing as a contributor to the "contagion," albeit in the same breath as Spinoza and Bayle. Locke, by contrast, is generally regarded by the *anti-philosophes* as their ally rather than foe. They revered him as the most prestigious and useful modern philosopher for restricting the scope of reason, providing only a rather limited toleration, and for his defense of spirits, miracles, faith, and divine Revelation, as well as for separating civil and spiritual status, and hence potentially for defending nobility and even slavery.

In the longer perspective, Spinoza's role as a key progenitor of the Radical Enlightenment was unparalleled. He was the only seventeenth-century philosopher to remain a prominent and constant presence in the philosophical debates of the later eighteenth and nineteenth centuries. After 1750 Bayle receded gradually into the background. Spinoza, by contrast, remained at the forefront and was regarded throughout the later Enlightenment era by many intellectuals—and later by nineteenth-century freethinkers and creative minds, ranging from Heine to George Eliot—as the philosopher who, more than any other, forged the basic metaphysical ground-plan, exclusively secular moral values, and culture of individual liberty, democratic politics, and freedom of thought and the press that embody today the defining core values of modern secular egalitarianism: that is to say, of Radical Enlightenment.

Notes

PREFACE

1. Richard Bourke, "Enlightenment, Revolution and Democracy," in *Constellations: An International Journal of Critical and Democratic Theory* 15 (2008): 11.

2. Jeremy Waldron, *God, Locke and Equality: Christian Foundations in Locke's Political Thought* (Cambridge, 2002), 2.

CHAPTER I
PROGRESS AND THE ENLIGHTENMENT'S TWO CONFLICTING
WAYS OF IMPROVING THE WORLD

1. [Robert Bage], *Man as he is. A Novel in Four Volumes.* 4 vols. (London, 1792), 3:125.

2. Jonathan Israel, *Radical Enlightenment* (Oxford, 2001), 159–74.

3. Richard Price, *Observations on the Importance of the American Revolution* (1784; new ed. London, 1785), 3.

4. G. Spence, "Mary Wollstonecraft's Theodicy and Theory of Progress," *Enlightenment and Dissent* 14 (1995): 105, 108–9.

5. Voltaire to d'Alembert, 5 April 1766, in François-Marie Arouet de Voltaire, *Correspondence and Related Documents*, ed. Th. Besterman. 51 vols. (Toronto, Geneva, and Oxford, 1968–77), 30:159.

6. Voltaire to Damilaville, 28 April 1766, in Voltaire, *Correspondence*, 30:194.

7. Immanuel Kant, *Project for a Perpetual Peace* (London, 1796), 4, 20–21, 25–27; J. M. Knippenberg, "The Politics of Kant's Philosophy," in R. Beiner and W. J. Booth, eds., *Kant and Political Philosophy* (New Haven, 1993) 161–62.

8. Jonathan Israel, *Enlightenment Contested* (Oxford, 2006), 548, 681, 788; Jean-Pierre Poirier, *Turgot. Laissez-faire et progrès social* (Paris, 1999), 149–50.

9. F. E. Manuel and F. P. Manuel, *Utopian Thought in the Western World* (Oxford, 1982), 461; L. Dupré, *The Enlightenment and the Intellectual Foundations of Modern Culture* (New Haven, 2004), 208.

10. Adam Ferguson, *Principles of Moral and Political Science*. 2 vols. (Edinburgh, 1792; repr. New York, 1978), 1:165–66, 251.

11. Ibid., 1:173.

12. Ibid., 2:416–17.

13. Ibid., 2:418–19; J. Livesey, *Making Democracy in the French Revolution* (Cambridge, Mass., 2001), 39–40.

14. Ferguson, *Principles*, 2:499.

15. Tom Paine, *Rights of Man*, ed. E. Foner (1790; repr. New York, 1985), 75–76.

16. Ibid., 268.

17. Kant, *Project*, 32–33, 37.

18. John Jebb, *The Works, Theological, Medical, Political and Miscellaneous*. 3 vols (London, 1787), 2:203–24.

19. Jebb, *The Works*, 3:306–7.

20. Ferguson, *Principles*, 1:317; J. B. Stewart, *Opinion and Reform in Hume's Political Philosophy* (Princeton, 1992), 194–95, 208, 213, 225.

21. "Candidus" [William Smith], *Plain Truth: Addressed to the Inhabitants of America, containing Remarks on a late Pamphlet intitled* Common Sense [i.e., by Tom Paine] (Philadelphia, 1776), 2–3, 37.

22. Ferguson, *Principles*, 2:496–97.

23. Ibid., 497.

24. [Nicolas-Antoine Boulanger, rev. by d'Holbach], *Recherches sur l'origine du despotisme oriental, ouvrage posthume de Mr B.I.D.P.E.C.* 2 vols. ("Londres" [Amsterdam], 1762), 1:xii.

25. Jean-Jacques Rousseau, *Les rêveries du promeneur solitaire*, ed. H. Roddier (Paris, 1960), 31–33.

26. For a contrary view, see Margaret C. Jacob, *Living the Enlightenment: Freemasonry in Eighteenth-Century Europe* (New York, 1991), 219–20.

27. Benedict de Spinoza, *Theological-Political Treatise*, ed. Jonathan Israel (Cambridge, 2007), 161.

28. Ibid., 161–62.

29. [J. F. Bernard and B. Picart], *The Ceremonies and Religious Customs of the Various Nations of the Known World*. 7 vols. (London, 1733–1777), 6:208–9.

30. Ibid.

31. Ibid., 6:208.

32. [Micaiah Towgood], *Serious and Free Thoughts on the Present State of the Church and Religion* (1755; 4th ed., London, 1774), 5, 9, 32, 36.

33. Ibid., 43–44.

34. G. A. Koch, *Religion of the American Enlightenment* (1933; repr. New York, 1968), 57–95.

35. E. M. Wilbur, *A History of Unitarianism in Transylvania, England and America* (Cambridge, Mass., 1952), 393–97.

36. Cited in R. K. Webb, "Price among the Unitarians," *Enlightenment and Dissent* 19 (2000): 162.

37. Richard Price, *A Discourse on the Love of Our Country Delivered on Nov. 4, 1789* (2nd ed., London, 1789), 16.

38. H. T. Dickinson, "Counter-Revolution in Britain in the 1790s," *Tijdschrift voor Geschiedenis* 102 (1989): 358–60.

39. Anthony Page, *John Jebb and the Enlightenment Origins of British Radicalism* (Westport, Conn., 2003), 191–94, 200–201.

40. G. Gallop, "Ideology and the English Jacobins," *Enlightenment and Dissent* 5 (1986): 3–20; here 4, 7–8, 15.

41. J.G.A. Pocock, *Virtue, Commerce, and History* (Cambridge, 1985; repr. 1995), 155.

42. M. Canovan, "Paternalistic Liberalism: Joseph Priestley on Rank and Inequality," *Enlightenment and Dissent* 2 (1983): 25–26.

43. M. Fitzpatrick, "'The View from Mount Pleasant: Enlightenment in late-eighteenth-century Liverpool," in R. Butterwick, S. Davies, and G. Sanchez Espinosa, eds., *Peripheries of the Enlightenment* (Oxford, 2008), 119–44; here 130–36.

44. *Le vrai sens du* Système de la Nature, *ouvrage posthume de M. Helvétius* ("Londres" [Amsterdam], 1774), 25.

45. Paine, *Rights of Man*, 69–70, 83.

46. Dickinson, "Counter-Revolution," 361–63.

47. Paul Henri Thiry, baron d'Holbach, *Essai sur les Prejugés* ("Londres" [Amsterdam], 1770), 92; Paul Henri Thiry, baron d'Holbach, *Système social, ou principes naturels de la morale et de la politique* (1773; repr. Paris, 1994), 558–59.

Chapter II
Democracy or Social Hierarchy?
The Political Rift

1. Paine, *Rights of Man*, 143, 172–73.

2. Jacques-Pierre Brissot de Warville, *Correspondance universelle sur ce qui interésse le Bonheur de l'Homme et de la Société* ("Londres" [Neuchâtel], 1783), 5:295–97.

3. Antoine-Nicolas, marquis de Condorcet, "Réflexions sur l'escalavage des nègres" (1781), in Condorcet, *Oeuvres complètes*, ed. L. S. Caritat et al. 21 vols. (Brunswick and Paris, 1804), 11:83–198; here 249–50.

4. Hugh Thomas, *The Slave Trade* (New York, 1997), 480, 501.

5. Ibid.; Condorcet, "Réflexions," 308.

6. John Witherspoon, *Lectures in Moral Philosophy*, ed. V. L. Collins (Princeton, 1912), 73–74.

7. Fritz Hirshfeld, *George Washington and Slavery* (Columbia, Mo., 1997), 5–6, 190–92.

8. D. J. D'Elia, *Benjamin Rush: Philosopher of the American Revolution* (Philadelphia, 1974), 32–33, 66–67.

9. Ibid., 88–90.

10. Turgot to Price, 22 March 1778, printed in Honoré Gabriel, marquis de Mirabeau, *Considérations sur l'Ordre de Cincinnatus* ("Londres," 1784), 197.

11. D'Elia, *Benjamin Rush*, 70–71, 75, 81; Henry F. May, *The Enlightenment in America* (New York, 1976), 235–36.

12. D'Elia, *Benjamin Rush*, 91–92, 101.

13. Denis Diderot, *Oeuvres complètes*, ed. R. Lewinter. 15 vols. (Paris, 1969–1973), 15:547.

14. [Mirabeau], *Considérations*, 2–3, 14; Gordon S. Wood, *The Radicalism of the American Revolution* (1992; repr. New York, 1993), 205–7, 241, 263, 280; Livesey, *Making Democracy*, 26.

15. [Mirabeau], *Considérations*, 19, 50–51.

16. Ibid., 19.

17. See, for instance, Condorcet, "Réflexions," 251–55.

18. Sir William Jones, *A Discourse on the Institution of a Society for Enquiring into the History,* [. . .] *Arts, Sciences and Literature of Asia, delivered at Calcutta, 15 January 1784* (Calcutta, 1784), 20.

19. Claude-Adrien Helvétius, *De l'homme.* 2 vols. (1773; repr. Paris, 1989), 2:917.

20. Mary Wollstonecraft, *Political Writings*, ed. J. Todd (Toronto, 1993), 78.

21. Ibid., 239.

22. Voltaire, *Questions sur l'*Encyclopédie, *par des amateurs.* 9 vols. n.p. ([Geneva?], 1770–1772), 5:83–89.

23. d'Holbach, *Système social*, 551–52; Paul Thiery, baron d'Holbach, *Système de la nature, ou Des Loix du monde physique et du monde moral.* 2 vols. ("Londres" [Amsterdam], 1770), 2:61–66.

24. Helvétius, *De l'homme*, 2:774.

25. Ibid., 2:767–68.

26. Rousseau, *Rêveries du promeneur*, 31.

27. d'Holbach, *Système social*, 554–55; Helvétius *De l'homme*, 2:777.

28. *Esprit de Guillaume-Thomas Raynal, Recueil également nécessaire à ceux qui commandent et à ceux qui obéissent.* 2 vols. ("Londres" [Paris?], 1782), 1:112.

29. d'Holbach, *Système social*, 19.

30. Paul Henri Thiry, baron d'Holbach, *Représentans*, in Diderot and d'Alembert, eds., *Encyclopédie*, 14:143–46; J. Proust, *Diderot et l'Encyclopédie* (1962; new ed. Paris, 1995), 120, 432, 538.

31. John Lough, *Essays on the* Encyclopédie *of Diderot and d'Alembert* (London, 1968), 121, 135–37, 226; Proust, *Diderot*, 120; F. A. Kafker and S. L. Kafker, *The Encyclopedists as Individuals* (Oxford, 2006), 172; Edoardo Tortarolo, *L'Illuminismo* (Rome, 1999), 137.

32. Voltaire, *Questions sur l'*Encyclopédie, 4:285; R. Darnton, *The Literary Underground of the Old Regime* (Cambridge, Mass., 1982), 141, 199.

33. Alan Charles Kors, "Les résonances des débats du XVIIe siècle dans la pensée du baron d'Holbach," in *Matérialistes français du XVIIIe siècle*, ed. S. Audidière et al. (Paris, 2006), 296, 297.

34. See the ms. note before the title page of the copy of the *Système de la nature* (1770) at Corpus Christi College, Oxford.

35. d'Holbach, *Essai*, 26–28, 53; d'Holbach, *Système social*, 210, 221–22; Tortarolo, *L'Illuminismo*, 146.

36. d'Holbach, *Système social*, 222.

37. Ibid., 69–70; *Esprit de Guillaume-Thomas Raynal*, 1:25–28.

38. d'Holbach, *Système social*, 232–33.

39. Paul Henri Thiry, Baron d'Holbach, *La politique naturelle* (1773; repr. Paris, 1998), 119–21.

40. Ibid., 80–81; d'Holbach, *Système social*, 276.

41. Adam Ferguson, *Remarks on a pamphlet lately published by Dr Price* (London, 1776), 13.

42. Ibid., 11–12.

43. Jebb, *The Works*, 3:396.

44. Israel, *Enlightenment Contested*, 292.

45. [Boulanger, rev. by d'Holbach], *Recherches sur l'origine*, 1:248, 251–52, 255, 258.

46. d'Holbach, *Système social*, 268–69, 276; d'Holbach, *Politique naturelle*, 65–67, 172, 430–31; Kant, *Project*, 171–79.

47. Pieter Paulus, *Verhandeling over de Vraag: in Welken Zin kunnen de Menschen Gezegd worden Gelyk te zyn?* (1793; 4th ed. Haarlem, 1794), 68.

48. Ibid., 90–96; I. L. Leeb, *The Ideological Origins of the Batavian Revolution* (The Hague, 1973), 226.

49. J. Miller, *Rousseau: Dreamer of Democracy* (New Haven, 1984), 64, 80, 116–18,120; J. K. Wright, *A Classical Republican in Eighteenth-Century France* (Stanford, 1997), 123; Christopher Kelly, "Rousseau and the Case for (and against) censorship," *Journal of Politics* 59 (1997): 1232–51, esp. 1232, 1238–39.

50. Keith M. Baker, "'Reason and Revolution: Political Consciousness and Ideological Invention at the End of the Old Regime," in R. T. Bienvenu and M. Feingold, eds., *In the Presence of the Past. Essays in Honor of Frank Manuel* (Dordrecht, 1991), 79–91; here 85–86, 90.

51. Keith Michael Baker, *Inventing the French Revolution* (Cambridge, 1990), 26.

52. Kelly, "Rousseau and the Case," 1238–39; for a different view, see Ian Hampsher-Monk, "Rousseau and totalitarianism—with hind-

sight?" in Robert Wokler, ed., *Rousseau and Liberty* (Manchester, 1995), 272–73, 277.

53. d'Holbach, *Politique naturelle*, 275.

54. Ibid., 109–10, 166–67, 169; d'Holbach, *Système social*, 276–80.

55. Ibid., 285; d'Holbach, *Politique naturelle*, 112–14.

56. Ibid., 167–68; D. Locke, *A Fantasy of Reason. The Life and Thought of William Godwin* (London, 1980), 57.

57. d'Holbach, *Politique naturelle*, 169.

58. Rutger Jan Schimmelpenninck, *Verhandeling over eene wel ingerigte volksregeering* (Leiden, 1785), 35–36, 50–51.

59. Montesquieu, *Esprit des Loix*, 9, chap. 5; Ferguson, *Remarks*, 9.

60. W.R.E. Velema, "Elie Luzac and The Two Dutch Revolutions," in M. Jacob and W. Mijnhardt, eds., *The Dutch Republic in the Eighteenth Century* (Ithaca, 1992), 143–44.

61. Schimmelpenninck, *Verhandeling*, 4–5; Paine, *Rights of Man*, 180–81; Jonathan Israel, *The Dutch Republic. Its Rise, Greatness and Fall, 1477–1806* (Oxford, 1995), 1104, 1128–29.

62. Leeb, *Ideological Origins*, 182n.; S.R.E. Klein, *Patriots republikanisme. Politieke cultuur in Nederland (1766–1787)* (Amsterdam, 1995), 193.

63. Paine, *Rights of Man*, 180; John Dunn, *Setting the People Free. The Story of Democracy* (London, 2005), 112–13.

64. Willi Goetschel, *Spinoza's Modernity: Mendelssohn, Lessing and Heine* (Madison, 2004), 183–250.

65. Gérard Vallée, *The Spinoza Conversations between Lessing and Jacobi* (Lanham, Md., 1988), 9–11; Jan Rohls, "Herders Gott," in M. Kessler and V. Leppin, eds., *Johann Gottfried Herder. Aspekte seines Lebenswerkes* (Berlin, 2005), 273.

66. Ibid., 272.

67. Gotthold Ephraim Lessing, *Ernst und Falk: Dialogues for Freemasons* (1778–80), in H. B. Nisbet, ed., *G. E. Lessing. Philosophical and Theological Writings* (Cambridge, 2005), 184–216.

68. [Ludwig Adolf Christian von Grolman], *Die neuesten Arbeiten des Spartacus und Philo in dem Illuminaten-orden jetzt zum erstenmal gedruckt*. n.p. (Frankfurt-am-Main, 1793), 7:4–5, 34, 40, 46; [Ludwig Adolf Christian von Grolman], *Kritische Geschichte der Illuminaten-Grade*. n.p. (Frankfurt-am-Main, 1793), 27–28, 53, 64, 74–75, 80, 82.

69. David Sorkin, *The Religious Enlightenment* (Princeton, 2008), 162.

70. Martin Mulsow "Adam Weishaupt als Philosoph," in W. Müller-Seidel and W. Riedel, eds., *Die Weimarer Klassik und ihre Geheimbünde* (Würzburg, 2003), 27–66; here 30; W. Riedel, "Aufklärung und Macht. Schiller, Abel und die *Illuminaten*," in Müller-Seidel and Riedel, *Weimarer Klassik*, 107–25; here 112–13.

71. Ibid., 113; Weishaupt (Spartacus) to Zwack (Cato), 5 March 1778, in Richard Van Dülmen, *Der Geheimbund der Illuminaten* (Stuttgart, 1975), 220; *Die Korrespondenz des Illuminatenordens* (1776–1781), ed. R. Markner, M. Neugebauer-Wölk, and H. Schüttler (Tübingen, 2005), 1:32; Hans-Jürgen Schings, *Die Brüder des Marquis Posa. Schiller und der Geheimbud der Illuminaten* (Tübingen, 1996), 145n.

72. Stefan Winkle, *Struensee und die Publizistik* (Hamburg, 1982), 81–82; John Christian Laursen, "Spinoza in Denmark and the Fall of Struensee, 1770–1772," *Journal of the History of Ideas* 61 (2000): 194–98.

73. Balthasar Münter, *Bekehrungsgeschichte des vormaligen Grafen und Königlichen Dänischen Geheimen Cabinetsministers Johann Friedrich Struensee* (Copenhagen, 1772), 10.

74. *Alvorliger Betragtninger over den almindelige Tilstand* (Copenhagen, 1771), 16; Laursen, "Spinoza in Denmark," 196.

75. Adam Weishaupt, *Anrede an die neu aufzunehmenden* Illuminatos dirigentes (1782), in Van Dülmen, *Der Geheimbund*, 166–94; here 174–76, 183.

76. Weishaupt, *Anrede*, 178–79.

77. [Grolman] *Neuesten Arbeiten des Spartacus*, 49; Schings, *Brüder*, 167; Weishaupt, *Anrede*, 179.

78. Weishaupt, *Anrede*, 179, 192–93.

79. [Grolman] *Neuesten Arbeiten des Spartacus*, 40–41, 46.

80. Ibid., 37–38, 47, 69.

81. Ibid., 46–47, 50–51.

82. Ibid., 183.

83. Adam Weishaupt, *Apologie der Illuminaten* (Frankfurt and Leipzig, 1786), 105–6, 120–21, 127–28.

84. Ibid., 119–20.

85. Ibid., 46; Weishaupt, *Anrede*, 183.

86. Bahrdt, *Würdigung der natürlichen Religion* (Halle, 1791), 329.

87. Ibid., 328–29, 355; Carl Friedrich Bahrdt, *Geschichte seines Lebens, seiner Meinungen und Schicksale*. 4 vols. (Frankfurt, 1790), 2:43.

88. Bahrdt, *Würdigung*, 70–83.

89. Ibid., 96–97, 167–68.

90. d'Holbach, *Système social*, 281–82.

91. Wilbur, *History of Unitarianism*, 115; Derek Beales, "Philosophical Kingship and Enlightened Despotism," in M. Goldie and R. Wokler, eds., *The Cambridge History of Eighteenth-Century Political Thought* (Cambridge, 2006), 509.

92. d'Holbach, *Système social*, 282; Ernst Cassirer, *The Philosophy of the Enlightenment* (1951; repr. Princeton, 1979), 134.

93. d'Holbach, *Système social*, 428–30.

94. Ferguson, *Remarks*, 27.

95. d'Holbach, *Politique naturelle*, 85; Paine, *Rights of Man*, 220–21.

96. d'Holbach, *Essai*, 26.

97. Ibid.

98. T.C.W. Blanning, *Frederick the Great and Enlightened Absolutism*, in H. M. Scott, ed., *Enlightened Absolutism* (Basingstoke, 1990), 270–72.

99. Frederick the Great, "A Critical Examination of the *System of Nature*," in the *Posthumous Works of Frederic II, King of Prussia*, trans. Th. Holcroft (London, 1789), 5:147–75; here, 171–72; Cassirer, *Philosophy*, 71.

100. Denis Diderot, "Refutation du livre «De l'Homme» d'Helvétius," in Yves Benot, ed., *Diderot. Textes politiques* (Paris, 1960), 178–79.

101. d'Holbach, *Politique naturelle*, 156–60.

102. Denis Diderot, *Essai sur les règnes de Claude et de Néron et sur les moeurs et les écrits de Senèque.* 2 vols. ("Londres" [Amsterdam], 1782), 1:120.

103. d'Holbach, *Essai*, 53; d'Holbach, *Politique naturelle*, 158–59.

104. *Esprit de Guillaume-Thomas Raynal*, 129.

105. Kant, *Project*, 67–68.

106. Ibid., 13, 17–18, 20.

107. Frederick the Great, *Examen de l'Essai sur les préjugés* [of d'Holbach] ("Londres" [Berlin], 1770), 26–28, 46, 64.

108. Ibid., 52.

109. Vittorio Alfieri, *Memoirs*, ed. E. R. Vincent (London, 1961), 97.

110. d'Holbach, *Système social*, 283.

111. Jebb, *The Works*, 3:306–7, 387–90, 392–94.

112. Ferguson, *Remarks*, 32.

113. d'Holbach, *Système Social*, 246–47.

114. Ibid., 240–47; Paul Henri Thiry, baron d'Holbach, *La morale universelle, ou, Les devoirs de l'homme fondés sur sa nature*. 3 vols. (Amsterdam, 1776), 2:24, 44.

115. Ibid., 1:146–52.

116. Ibid., 2:40–43; d'Holbach, *Système social*, 42–50.

117. *Esprit de Guillaume-Thomas Raynal*, 1:121–22.

118. Paine, *Rights of Man*, 171.

Chapter III
The Problem of Equality and Inequality:
The Rise of Economics

1. Waldron, *God, Locke and Equality*, 11, 116–17, 137, 226–27; Israel, *Enlightenment Contested*, 546, 553–55, 560, 592, 603–5.

2. d'Holbach, *Essai*, 130–31, 136.

3. d'Holbach, *Politique naturelle*, 190.

4. d'Holbach, *La morale universelle*, 2:185.

5. Ibid.; Mirabeau, *Considérations*, 19, 25.

6. Ibid., 14.

7. d'Holbach, *La morale universelle*, 2:276.

8. M. F. Plattner, "Rousseau and the Origins of Nationalism," in C. Orwin and N. Tarcov, eds., *The Legacy of Rousseau* (Chicago and London, 1997), 193.

9. Denis Diderot, "Fragments echappés du portefeuille d'un philosophe" (1772), in J. Assézat, ed., *Oeuvres complètes de Diderot*, 6:447; d'Holbach, *La morale universelle*, 2:276–77.

10. d'Holbach, *Politique naturelle*, 70–71.

11. Helvétius, *De l'homme*, 2:44; d'Holbach, *Système social*, 153.

12. d'Holbach, *La morale universelle*, 3:94.

13. Helvétius, *De l'homme*, 2:565, 729, 732–33; Abbé Morellet, *Mémoires sur le dix-huitième siècle et sur la Révolution française*. 2 vols. (Paris, 1822), 1:141–42.

14. d'Holbach, *Politique naturelle*, 173–74.

15. Diderot, "Fragments échappés," 444; d'Holbach, *Système social*, 381–91; d'Holbach, *La morale universelle*, 2:188.

16. Claude-Adrien Helvétius, *De l'Esprit* (Paris, 1758; repr. 1988), 31–36, 39–40; d'Holbach, *Système social*, 204, 208, 258–59; David Wootton,

"Helvétius: From Radical Enlightenment to Revolution," *Political Theory* 28 (2000): 307–36; here 324, 326.

17. Paine, *Rights of Man*, 82.

18. Ibid., 81, 83–84, 106.

19. Mirabeau, *Considérations*, 22.

20. Paine, *Rights of Man*, 146.

21. d'Holbach, *Système social*, 232–36.

22. Nicolas-Sylvestre Bergier, *Examen du Matérialisme ou Réfutation du* Système de la Nature. 2 vols. (Paris, 1771), 102.

23. Jeroom Vercruysse, *Bibliographie descriptive des écrits du Baron d'Holbach* (Paris, 1971), 7; and entries for 1773, A2 and 3.

24. d'Holbach, *Politique naturelle* 32, 383–85; Paine, *Rights of Man*, 68–69.

25. D. M. McMahon, *Enemies of the Enlightenment* (New York, 2001), 21–22.

26. [Antoine-Louis Séguier], *Réquisitoire sur lequel est intervenué l'Arrêt du Parlement du 18 Août 1770 qui condamne à être brûles différens livres ou brochures* (Paris, 1770), 2–3.

27. Ibid.

28. Ibid., 6.

29. d'Holbach, *Morale universelle*, 2:252.

30. Ibid., 2:253.

31. Ibid., 2:191.

32. Paine, *Rights of Man*, 156; Eric Foner, *The Story of American Freedom* (New York, 1999), 16.

33. Wolfe Tone, *An Address to the People of Ireland* (Belfast, 1796), 1–3.

34. P. Groenewegen, *Eighteenth-century Economics. Turgot, Beccaria and Smith and their Contemporaries* (London, 2002), 20.

35. Ibid., 30–32.

36. Anne-Robert-Jacques Turgot, *Reflections on the Formation and Distribution of Wealth*, trans. K. Jupp (London, 1999), 44–45.

37. Ibid., 45–46; Poirier, *Turgot*, 174–76, 362–63.

38. Turgot, *Formation and Distribution*, 46–47.

39. Ibid., 35.

40. Turgot, art.: "Foire," in Diderot and d'Alembert, eds., *Encyclopédie*, 7:39–41.

41. Ibid., 41; Poirier, *Turgot*, 69–70.

42. Adam Smith, *An Inquiry into the Nature and Causes of the Wealth of Nations*, ed. R. H. Campbell and A. S. Skinner. 2 vols. (Oxford, 1976), 1:89–90, 98, 208–9; Poirier, *Turgot*, 149–50, 182–83.

43. Smith, *An Inquiry*, 1:89–90.

44. E. Rothschild, *Economic Sentiments: Adam Smith, Condorcet, and the Enlightenment* (Cambridge, Mass., 2001), 68–69.

45. Ibid., 69–70.

46. Adam Smith, *Theory of Moral Sentiments*, 50–54, 61–64.

47. Quoted in Jen-Guo S. Chen, "Providence and Progress," in E. Heath and V. Merolle, eds., *Adam Ferguson: History, Progress and Human Nature* (London, 2008), 181.

48. Robert Mauzi, *L'idée du Bonheur au XVIIIe siècle* (Paris, 1969), 153–54.

49. Ibid.; Jean-Antoine-Nicolas de Caritat, marquis de Condorcet, *Esquisse d'un tableau historique du progrès de l'esprit humain* (Paris, Year 3 [1795]), 340.

50. Condorcet, *Esquisse*, 74; H. C. Clark, *Compass of Society* (Lanham, Md., 2007), 238–39.

51. Clark, *Compass of Society*, 235, 237–38; F. A. Manuel, *The Prophets of Paris* (Cambridge, Mass., 1962), 23–24.

52. Ibid., 30–34, 37, 39.

53. Kafker, *Encyclopedists*, 376.

54. Turgot, *Reflections*, 76.

55. J. Hochstrasser, "Physiocracy and the Politics of *Laissez-faire*," in M. Goldie and R. Wokler, eds., *The Cambridge History of Eighteenth-Century Political Thought* (Cambridge, 2006), 426–27.

56. Clark, *Compass of Society*, 181–85.

57. Denis Diderot, *Apologie de l'abbé Galiani* (1771), in M. Barrillon, ed., Diderot, *Apologies* (Marseille, 1998), 63–133; here 89, 92–93.

58. Morellet, *Mémoires*, 1:194, 196.

59. Ibid., 89, 92; Paolo Quintili, *La pensée critique de Diderot* (Paris, 2001), 480–84.

60. Morellet, *Mémoires*, 1:37, 192, 196–97.

61. Clark, *Compass of Society*, 427; Colas Duflo, *Diderot philosophe* (Paris, 2003), 158.

62. Morellet, *Mémoires*, 1:380–90.

63. Diderot, *Apologie de l'Abbé Galiani*, 71–73; Duflo, *Diderot philosophe*, 475.

64. Diderot, *Apologie de l'Abbé Galiani*, 93, 97, 102.

65. John Hope Mason and R. Wokler, "Introduction," in Diderot, *Political Writings* (Cambridge, 1992), xxv–xxvi; Quintili, *Pensée critique*, 482–83; Rothschild, *Economic Sentiments*, 20.

66. Quintili, *Pensée critique*, 60.

67. M. Dommanget, *Sylvain Maréchal. L'égalitaire, «l'homme sans Dieu»* (Paris, 1950), 244.

68. Jacques-Pierre Brissot de Warville, *Lettres philosophiques sur Saint Paul* (Neuchâtel, 1783), 112.

69. Sylvain Maréchal, *Apologues modernes* ("Bruxelles" [Paris?], 1788), 96–97.

70. Morellet, *Mémoires*, 1:400.

71. G. Himmelfarb, *The Roads to Modernity: The British, French, and American Enlightenments* (New York, 2004), 5–6, 19 , 21–22, 229, 233–34.

72. d'Holbach, *Système social*, 441.

73. Maréchal, *Apologues modernes*, 90–91.

74. Abbé Charles-Louis Richard, *La défense de la religion, de la morale* [. . .] *et de la société* (Paris, 1775), 135, 206.

Chapter IV

The Enlightenment's Critique of War and the Quest for "Perpetual Peace"

1. D'Holbach, *La morale universelle*, 3:240; d'Holbach, *Système social*, 341–42.

2. Ibid., 396; d'Holbach, *Politique naturelle*, 34–35.

3. R. Niklaus, "The Pursuit of Peace in the Enlightenment," in John Pappas, ed., *Essays on Diderot and the Enlightenment in Honour of Otis Fellows* (Geneva, 1974), 242–45.

4. Johann Gottfried Herder, *Another Philosophy of History* (1774), ed. I. D. Evrigenis and D. Pellerin (Indianapolis, 2004), 89.

5. Frederick the Great to Voltaire, 24 May 1770, in Voltaire, *Correspondance*, 37:213.

6. Ibid.

7. Ibid.

8. Voltaire, *De la Paix perpétuelle* (1769), in *Oeuvres complètes de Voltaire*, ed. M. Auguis et al. 97 vols. (Paris, 1828–1834), 38:403–28; here 403, 405, 428.

9. Paine, *Rights of Man*, 93–94.

10. Voltaire, *De la Paix perpétuelle*, 403.

11. Kant, *Project*, 75; R. B. Louden, *The World We Want: How and Why the Ideals of the Enlightenment Still Elude Us* (New York, 2007), 101–6.

12. Kant, *Project*, 17–19; Knud Haakonssen, "German natural law," in Goldie and Wokler, eds., *Cambridge History of Eighteenth-Century Political Thought*, 288.

13. Ferguson, *Principles*, 2:502.

14. Ibid.

15. Ibid., 2:264.

16. d'Holbach, *Système de la nature*, 1:6.

17. Joel Barlow, *Advice to the Privileged Orders in the Several States of Europe* (2 vols., New York, 1792–1794), 1:66.

18. Ibid., 1:74.

19. Joseph Priestley, *Letters to the Right Honourable Edmund Burke* (2d ed. Birmingham, 1791), 29.

20. Paine, *Rights of Man*, 204.

21. d'Holbach, *La morale universelle*, 2:6.

22. Condorcet, *Esquisse*, 267.

23. Paul Henri Thiry, baron d'Holbach, *Le Bon-Sens ou Idées naturelles opposées aux idées surnaturelles* ("Londres" [Amsterdam], 1772), 164; d'Holbach, *Système social*, 341.

24. Diderot, *Essai*, 1:72.

25. Barlow, *Advice*, 1:61.

26. d'Holbach, *La morale universelle*, 1:162, 208, and 3:167n.

27. Ibid., 2:18; d'Holbach, *Politique naturelle*, 62; Maréchal, *Apologues modernes*, 28.

28. d'Holbach, *La morale universelle*, 2:20; d'Holbach, *Système social*, 348–49.

29. d'Holbach, *Le Bon-Sens*, 247; d'Holbach, *Système social*, 34.

30. Kant, *Project*, 4, 20, 59.

31. Ibid., 17–19.

32. Antoine-Marie Cerisier, *Le Politique Hollandois* (1783), 6:181–84.

33. Paine, *Rights of Man*, 145.

34. d'Holbach, *Essai*, 77; *Esprit de Guillaume-Thomas Raynal*, 1:83.

35. Frederick the Great, *Examen de l'*Essai, 40; *Esprit de Guillaume-Thomas Raynal*, 2:207.

36. Frederick the Great, *Examen de l'*Essai, 35–37, 41–42; Paine, *Rights of Man*, 262–63.

37. Barlow, *Advice*, 1:66.

38. Ibid., 1:63.

39. Ibid., 1:61–62.

40. Priestley, *Letters*, iii–iv.

41. d'Holbach, *Système social*, 341–42.

42. Ibid., 346.

43. d'Holbach, *Politique naturelle*, 389–91; d'Holbach, *La morale universelle*, 1:91 and 3:136.

44. Frederick the Great, *A Critical Examination*, 170–71, 174.

45. Ibid., 171.

46. Ibid., 171–72.

47. A. Strugnell, "La voix du sage dans *l'Histoire des Deux Indes*," in P. France and A. Strugnell, eds., *Diderot. Les dernières années, 1770–1784* (Edinburgh, 1985), 38.

48. d'Holbach, *La morale universelle*, 1:93–94; d'Holbach, *Politique naturelle*, 34–36.

49. d'Holbach, *La morale universelle*, 2:115n.

50. Denis Diderot, *Pages inédites contre un tyran*, ed. Franco Venturi. n.p. (1937), 2–3.

51. Barlow, *Advice*, 1:69; Waltz, "Kant, Liberalism and War," 335.

52. Paine, *Rights of Man*, 146.

53. Ibid., 35–36.

54. Ibid., 166n.

55. Ibid., 268.

56. Jeremy Popkin, "From Dutch republican to French monarchist," *Tijdschrift voor Geschiedenis* 102 (1989): 543–44.

57. Ibid., 534–44; Cerisier, *Le Politique Hollandois* (1781), 1:175.

58. d'Holbach, *Politique naturelle*, 383–84.

59. Louden, *World We Want*, 99–100.

60. d'Holbach, *Politique naturelle*, 411–12.

61. Ibid., 94.

62. Cerisier, *Le politique Hollandois* (1783), 5:56–58.

63. Paine, *Rights of Man*, 161.

Chapter V
Two Kinds of Moral Philosophy in Conflict

1. Diderot, *Fragments échappés*, 444; Denis Diderot, *Political Writings*, trans. and ed. J. H. Mason and Robert Wokler (Cambridge, 1992), 210–11.

2. P. Jimack, "Obéissance à la loi et révolution dans les dernières oeuvres de Diderot," in P. France and A. Strugnell, eds., *Diderot. Les dernières années, 1770–1784* (Edinburgh, 1985), 153–68; here 153–54.

3. Jean-Jacques Rousseau, *Lettre à M. d'Alembert sur son article* "Genève" (1758), ed. M. Launay (Paris, 1967), 190n.

4. Diderot, *Political Writings*, 210–11.

5. Richard Price, "The Evidence for a Future Period of Improvement in the State of Mankind," in Price, *Political Writings*, ed. D. O. Thomas (Cambridge, 1991), 165.

6. Priestley, *Letters*, 23.

7. Price, "The Evidence," 175.

8. Wollstonecraft, *Political Writings*, 157–63.

9. Rousseau, *Rêveries du promeneur*, 33–35, 38–40.

10. Rousseau, *Lettre à M. d'Alembert*, 168–69, 190, 199; D. F. Norton, "Hume, Human Nature, and the Foundations of Morality," in D. F. Norton, ed., *The Cambridge Companion to Hume* (Cambridge, 1993), 148–81.

11. Rousseau, *Lettre à M. d'Alembert*, 196–200.

12. Rousseau, *Rêveries du promeneur*, 31.

13. Ibid., 41, 88, 95, 98.

14. Georg Jonathan Holland, *Réflexions philosophiques sur le* Système de la nature (1772). 2 vols. (Paris, 1773), 2:239–40.

15. [Paul Thiry, baron d'Holbach], *System der Natur oder von den Gesetzen der physischen und moralischen Welt* (Frankfurt and Leipzig, 1783), translator's preface, vii–viii.

16. Ibid., vi.

17. E. N. Hiebert, "The Integration of Revealed Religion and Scientific Materialism in the Thought of Joseph Priestley," in L. Kieft and B. R. Willeford, eds., *Joseph Priestley. Scientist, Theologian and Metaphysician* (London, 1980), 34.

18. Ibid., 37.

19. Ibid., 33; Joseph Priestley, *Autobiography*, ed. J. Lindsay (Bath, 1970), 111.

20. Ibid., 18–19, and ms Harris Manchester College, Oxford ms Joseph Priestley i, sermon, Leeds, Nov. 1771, 64–66v.

21. A. Page, "The Enlightenment and a 'Second Reformation': the Religion and Philosophy of John Jebb (1736–1786)," *Enlightenment and Dissent* 17 (1998): 70, 77; M. Sonenscher, *Sans-Culottes* (Princeton, 2008), 381–82.

22. Harris Manchester College, Oxford ms Joseph Priestley i/ii, sermon, Leeds, 7 Jan. 1771, 13–14, 17–18.

23. Ibid., 47, 50, 222–23.

24. Page, "Enlightenment and a 'Second Reformation,'" 70–72, 81.

25. Denis Diderot, *Commentaire sur Hemsterhuis*, ed. G. May, in F. Hemsterhuis, *Lettre sur l'homme*, 44–51 (New Haven, 1964), 45.

26. d'Holbach, *Système de la nature*, 1:1–2, 16–17.

27. Michel-Ange Marin, *Le Baron Van-Hesden, ou la république des Incrédules.* 5 vols. (Toulouse, 1762), 1:250, and 2:11–13; Richard, *Défense de la religion*, 47–48, 50–51, 52–54; Holland, *Réflexions philosophiques*, 1:184.

28. Condorcet, *Esquisse*, 136, 157; D'Holbach, *Système social*, 78, 232.

29. d'Holbach, *Politique naturelle*, 81.

30. Abbé Joseph Nicolas Camuset, *Principes contre l'incrédulité à l'occasion du* Système de la nature (Paris, 1771), 99, 104–5.

31. Bergier, *Apologie*, 2:7–9.

32. Diderot, *Political Writings*, 211.

33. Rousseau, *Lettre à d'Alembert*, 203–8.

34. Richard, *Défense de la religion*, 111.

35. Marin, *Baron Van-Hesden*, 1:lxii–lxiv; Jean-Nicolas-Hubert Hayer, *La religion vengée ou réfutation des auteurs impies.* 21 vols. (Paris, 1757–1763), 6:310; Richard, *Défense de la religion*, 26–27, 85–88.

36. d'Holbach, *Système social*, 26–27, 75; Helvétius, *De l'homme*, 2:579; Helvétius, *De l'Esprit*, 258.

37. d'Holbach, *Essai*, 321; Richard, *Défense de la religion*, 92, 97–98.

38. Marin, *Baron Van-Hesden*, 5:196–98; Raymond Trousson, "Michel-Ange Marin et les *Pensées philosophiques*," *Recherches sur Diderot et sur l'*Encyclopédie 18 (1992): 47–55; here 54–55.

39. d'Holbach, *Système social*, 446–48; Richard, *Défense de la religión*, 85.

40. Camuset, *Principes contre l'incrédulité*, 106; [Francois Xavier de Feller, S.J.] "Flexier de Reval," *Catéchisme philosophique* (1772; Liège-Brussels, 1773), 125, 127, 130.

41. Marin, *Baron Van-Hesden*, 3:11–12.

42. Ibid., 24–27.

43. Ibid., 1:1–2, 39–40.

44. [Abbé Guillaume-Thomas Raynal], *Histoire philosophique et politique des établissements et du commerce des Européens dans les deux Indes*. 6 vols. (Amsterdam, 1774), 1:149–50.

45. Diderot, "Japonois, philosophie des," in Diderot and d'Alembert, eds., *Encyclopédie*, 8:457–58.

46. Ibid.

47. Marin, *Baron Van-Hesden*, 1:xv.

48. Ibid., 1:xvi–xviii, xxii–xxiii; Trousson, "Michel-Ange Marin," 52–53.

49. Marin, *Baron Van-Hesden*, 1:ix, 2:196–98, 201–2, 213–14, 226, 323–24, 405; Nicolas-Sylvestre Bergier, *Apologie de la religion chrétienne* 2 vols. (1769; 2d ed. Paris, 1776), 2:27–28, 49, 57.

50. Brissot, *Lettres philosophiques*, 110.

51. Bergier, *Apologie*, 2:28, 49, 57–58; Jacques Domenech, *L'Éthique des Lumières* (Paris, 1989), 12.

52. d'Holbach, *Système de la nature*, 1:6–7, 22, and 2:5, 9, 15.

53. Bergier, *Apologie*, 2:2; Richard, *Défense de la religion*, 50–51.

54. Père Nicolas Jamin, *Pensées théologiques, relatives aux erreurs du temps* (1768) (2d ed. Riom, 1798), 27–28, 31, 34–35.

55. Bergier, *Apologie*, 2:11, 22–23.

56. Jamin, *Pensées théologiques*, 88, 351, 353, 356.

57. Bergier, *Apologie*, 2:49–50.

58. Diderot, *Essai*, 1:95–102.

59. Ibid., 2:11; Rousseau, *Lettre à d'Alembert*, 196–99; [d'Holbach], *Le Bon-Sens*, 177–78.

60. Bergier, *Apologie*, 2:11.

61. Ibid., 2:589.

62. d'Holbach, *Système social*, 64, 66, 107, 114, 168n.; Jean-Baptiste Del-isle de Sales, *De la philosophie de la Nature*. 6 vols. (1770; "à Londres" [Amsterdam], 1777), 1:8–9, 272–73.

63. Smith, *Theory*, 266, 457–63; D. F. Norton and M. Kuehn, "The Foundations of Morality," in K. Haakonssen, ed., *The Cambridge History of Eighteenth-Century Philosophy*. 2 vols. (Cambridge, 2006), 2:941–86, here 941–42, 978; Jerrold Seigel, *The Idea of the Self* (Cambridge, 2005), 146–47.

64. Seigel, *The Idea of the Self*, 147; Smith, *Theory*, 284.

65. Smith, *Theory*, 294.

66. Ibid., 284.

67. Delisle de Sales, *De la philosophie*, 1:466.

68. Witherspoon, *Lectures*, 17–18, 21; Kuklick, *History of Philosophy in America*, 47–49, 59–60.

69. Joseph Priestley, *An Examination of Dr. Reid's* Inquiry into the Human Mind on the Principles of Common Sense (London, 1774), 230.

70. Ibid., 232–33.

71. [James Oswald], *An Appeal to Common Sense In Behalf of Religion*. 2 vols. (Edinburgh, 1766), 1:190.

72. Priestley, *An Examination*, xvi, xxvii.

73. Ibid., 2:590–91.

74. d'Holbach, *La morale universelle*, 2:2; d'Holbach, *Système social*, 41, 75–76, 82; Condorcet, *Esquisse*, 205.

75. d'Holbach, *Système social*, 408–9.

76. Helvétius, *De l'Esprit*, 135–46; Helvétius, *De l'homme*, 1:361–62, 466–70; Fréron, *L'Année littéraire* (1770), 8:319, 323.

77. d'Holbach, *Système social*, 77, 197, 221.

78. Ibid., 254; d'Holbach, *La morale universelle*, 2:2.

79. d'Holbach, *Essai*, 322–23.

80. Delisle de Sales, *De la philosophie*, 1:325.

81. Ibid., 323.

82. Helvétius, *De l'Esprit*, 150.

83. Helvétius, *De l'homme*, 2:902.

84. Ibid., 2:732–34; Domenech, *L'Éthique*, 45–48.

85. Helvétius, *De l'homme*, 2:907, 912, 923.

86. Helvétius, *De l'Esprit*, 211, 217–28; Domenech, *L'Éthique*, 18.

87. Helvétius, *De l'Esprit*, 258.

88. Ibid., 216–17.

89. Ibid., 140–46; Wootton, "Helvétius," 314.

90. Helvétius, *De l'homme*, 2:731–32; Helvétius, *De l'Esprit*, 135.

91. Helvétius, *De l'Esprit*, 144.

92. d'Holbach, *La morale universelle*, 1:11 and 3:53; Helvétius, *De l'Esprit*, 190, 230, 233, 553–63; Diderot, *Réfutation*, 297–98, 316; d'Holbach, *Système social*, 29–31, 78; d'Holbach, *Politique naturelle*, 456–57.

93. Helvétius, *De l'Esprit*, 84; Smith, *Helvétius*, 210.

94. Diderot, *Réfutation*, 300–303.

95. Ibid., 192–95; Diderot, *Réfutation*, 276–77; Ann Thomson, *Bodies of Thought. Science, Religion and the Soul in the Early Enlightenment* (Oxford, 2008), 221–22.

96. Diderot, *Réfutation*, 287–88.

97. d'Holbach, *Essai*, 335; Richard, *Défense de la religion*, 83–84.

98. d'Holbach, *Système social*, 82.

99. Ibid., 81–83; d'Holbach, *La morale universelle*, 1:25.

100. d'Holbach, *Système social*, 92; Richard, *Défense de la religion*, 97–98.

101. d'Holbach, *Politique naturelle*, 49; Helvétius, *De l'homme*, 2:903–7.

102. Ibid., 15–16; Domenech, *L'Éthique*, 49.

103. d'Holbach, *Politique naturelle*, 30; d'Holbach, *Système social*, 31–32; Richard, *Défense de la religion*, 1–2.

104. d'Holbach, *Système de la nature*, 1:7.

105. Paine, *Rights of Man*, 67.

106. d'Holbach, *La morale universelle*, 1:xi.

107. Ibid., 1:ix, 3; Holland, *Réflexions philosphiques*, 106.

108. d'Holbach, *Politique naturelle*, 76; d'Holbach, *La morale universelle*, 3:240.

109. Richard, *Défense de la religion*, 204–5.

110. d'Holbach, *La morale universelle*, 1:22.

111. [d'Holbach], *Le Bon-Sens*, 198; d'Holbach, *La morale universelle*, 1:22.

112. d'Holbach , *Politique naturelle*, 458; Jimack, "Obéissance à la loi," 153–68, here 153.

113. [d'Holbach], *Le Bon-Sens*, vi–viii, 7.

CHAPTER VI
VOLTAIRE VERSUS SPINOZA: THE ENLIGHTENMENT
AS A BASIC DUALITY OF PHILOSOPHICAL SYSTEMS

1. d'Holbach, *Politique naturelle*, 175–77, 328–29; Helvétius, *De l'homme*, 1:81–90.

2. d'Holbach, *Système social*, 506–8.

3. Matthew Turner, *Answer from a Philosophical Unbeliever to Dr Priestley's Letters to a Philosophical Unbeliever* (London, 1782), xxvi.

4. Herder, *Another Philosophy*, 47–48.

5. Diderot, *Essai*, 1:100–102.

6. d'Holbach, *Essai*, v.

7. d'Holbach, *Système social*, 57–62.

8. Ibid., 59–60, 103; d'Holbach, *La morale universelle*, 1:ii–iii.

9. d'Holbach, *La morale universelle*, 2:197.

10. d'Holbach, *Système de la nature*, 1:8.

11. d'Holbach, *Essai*, 96.

12. *Esprit de Guillaume-Thomas Raynal*, 1:339.

13. Ibid., 291.

14. Ibid.

15. Jonathan Israel, "Introduction," in Spinoza, *Theological-Political Treatise*, xxv–xxvi, xxix–xxx; d'Holbach, *Politique naturelle*, 288–89.

16. d'Holbach, *La morale universelle*, 2:209–10; d'Holbach, *Essai*, 19, 24, 28.

17. Frederick the Great, "A Critical Examination," 166; D. Mornet, *Les origines intellectuelles de la révolution française (1715–1787)* (1933; 6th ed., Paris, 1967), 420–21.

18. Voltaire, *Questions*, 5:333.

19. Voltaire, "Tout en Dieu," in Voltaire, *L'Évangile du jour contenant Paix pérpetuelle [. . .] Tout en Dieu [. . .]* ("Londres" [Amsterdam], 1769), 54–70; here 32.

20. Voltaire, *Il faut prendre un parti ou, le principe d'action. Diatribe* (1772), in *Oeuvres Complètes de Voltaire* (Mélanges no. 7) (Paris, 1879), 28:517–54; here 533.

21. Voltaire, *Lettres de Memmius à Ciceron* (1771), in Voltaire, *Oeuvres complètes*, 28:442–43.

22. Ibid., 28:460–62; Voltaire, *Questions*, 4:279–80.

23. Voltaire, *Questions*, 4:277–84; Voltaire, *Lettres de Memmius*, 437–63, 457–58.

24. Voltaire, *Questions*, 4:260.

25. Ibid., 3:59–63, 4:281, and 5:330–32.

26. Ibid., 4:278–79.

27. Ibid., 4:281–84; Voltaire, *Lettres de Memmius*, 458; Voltaire, *Il faut prendre*, 523.

28. d'Holbach, *Système de la nature*, 2:61–62, 65–66; d'Holbach, *Le Bon-Sens*, 31–32, 36–37.

29. Diderot, *Essai*, 2:24; Roland Mortier, *Diderot en Allemagne (1750–1850)* (1954; repr. Geneva, 1986), 33–35.

30. Voltaire to Frederick, 20 Aug. 1770, in Voltaire, *Correspondance*, 36:406–7; Voltaire, *Dieu. Réponse*, 10, 12, 17; Voltaire, *Questions*, 4:290–91; Frederick the Great, *A Critical Examination*, 155.

31. Quoted in Pierre Naville, *Paul Thiry d'Holbach et la philosophie scientifique au XVIIIe siècle* (3d ed., Paris, 1943), 111–12.

32. Voltaire to Grimm, 10 Oct. 1770, in Voltaire, *Correspondance*, 37:24.

33. Naville, *Paul Thiery d'Holbach*, 112; André Robinet, *Dom Deschamps* (Paris, 1994), 74–75, 78–79.

34. Roland Mortier, *Les Combats des Lumières* (Ferney-Voltaire, 2000), 201.

35. Voltaire to marquise Du Deffand, 21 Oct. 1770, in Voltaire, *Correspondance*, 37:40.

36. Voltaire, *Questions*, 2:287.

37. Ibid., 5:330–32.

38. Ibid., 2:287.

39. David Williams, *Condorcet and Modernity* (Cambridge, 2004), 3.

40. *Correspondance inédite de Condorcet et de Turgot 1770–1779*, ed. Ch. Henry (Paris, 1882), 192.

41. Poirier, *Turgot*, 266–67.

42. Ibid.; d'Holbach, *Système de la nature*, 1:18–23.

43. Poirier, *Turgot*, 150, 267; Turgot to Condorcet, Paris, 18 May 1774, in *Correspondance inédite de Condorcet*, 172–73.

44. Ibid.; Condorcet to Turgot, undated May 1774, and Turgot to Condorcet, Paris, 24 May 1774, in *Correspondance inédite de Condorcet*, 177–78.

45. Ibid., 178.

CHAPTER VII
CONCLUSION

1. Constantin-François Volney, *Voyage en Syrie et en Égypte, pendant les années 1783, 1784, et 1785*. 2 vols. (Paris, 1787), 1:183, 391–93, 436.

2. Baker, *Inventing*, 18.

3. François Furet, *Revolutionary France 1770–1880* (1988; repr. Oxford, 1995).

4. Baker, *Inventing*, 25–27.

5. Jamin, *Pensées théologiques*, xiv.

6. Ibid., xiii.

7. *Archives Parlementaires de 1787 à 1860. Recueil complet des débats législatifs et politiques des chambres françaises*, ed. J. Mavidal and E. Laurat. First series: *Cahiers des États Généraux*, 2:1–2.

8. Ibid., 2:64.

9. Morellet, *Mémoires*, 1:364–65, 378–85, 390.

10. Ibid., 1:410.

11. Ibid., 1:148–51 and 2:33.

12. M. S. Staum, *Cabanis: Enlightenment and Medical Philosophy in the French Revolution* (Princeton, 1980), 147–50; Livesey, *Making Democracy*, 63–72; Ruth Scurr, *Fatal Purity. Robespierre and the French Revolution* (London, 2006), 218, 244, 281, 290–91; G. Garrard, *Rousseau's Counter-Enlightenment* (Albany, 2003), 38–39, 119–20.

13. W. C. Proby, *Modern Philosophy and Barbarism* (London, n.d. [1794?]), 67–68.

14. Ibid., 79.

15. Israel, *Radical Enlightenment*, 3–58, 230–41; Israel, *Enlightenment Contested*, 3–60.

16. Ultán Gillen, "Varieties of Enlightenment," in R. Butterwick, S. Davies, and G. Sánchez Espinosa, eds., *Périphéries*, 163–81; here 179–80.

17. Barlow, *Advice*, 2:10–11.

18. Foner, "Introduction," 16.

19. Paine, *Rights of Man*, 68.

20. Abbé Claude Adrien Nonnotte, *Dictionnaire philosophique de la Religion* (Liège-Brussels, 1773), 26–27.

Index

abolitionism. *See* slavery

Adams, John (1735–1826), American Founding Father, 44

adultery, 121, 166–67, 172

Alembert, Jean le Rond d' (1717–1783), French *philosophe*, 5, 84, 212, 225

Alexander the Great, 136–37

Alfieri, Vittorio (1749–1803), Italian poet, 88

America. *See* Spanish America; United States of America

American Revolution, viii, 16, 38–40, 42–47, 49, 64–65, 87, 89, 131; as example to Europe and Ibero-America, 40, 48–51, 59, 147–48; radical critique of, 41–47, 99

Amerindians, 43

Amsterdam, 22. *See also* Dutch Republic

Anglican Church. *See* Britain: Church of England

anti-colonialism, 15, 222

anti-philosophes, 103, 122, 162, 164–75, 217, 240

anti-Trinitarianism, 23. *See also* Unitarianism

apostates, xi, 121

Arabia, 222–23

"argument from design," 9–10. *See also* Voltaire, François-Marie-Arouet de: Newtonianism

Arianism, 25, 27

aristocracy (nobility), 10, 34, 39, 45–46, 58–59, 65, 133, 136, 240; abolition of, 95–99, 105, 144, 146–47, 150; as system of social oppression, 104, 121, 144–45

asceticism, 203

atheists and atheism, 19–20, 26, 80, 82, 159, 173, 175, 177, 208, 210, 236

Bahrdt, Carl Friedrich (1741–1792), German theologian and radical, 73–75, 80–81, 90, 207

Baker, Keith Michael, historian, 225, 227–28

Barlow, Joel (1754–1812), radical publicist, 17, 40–41, 44, 132, 135–36, 140–42, 145–46, 227, 237

Bayle, Pierre (1647–1706), 1–2, 21, 92, 154, 218, 235, 239–40; *Dictionnaire historique et critique* (1697), 239; and (pseudo-) critique of Spinoza, 211; and moral philosophy, 93–94, 169–70, 178, 238; and toleration, 92, 239

Beccaria, Cesare (1738–1794), Italian legal reformer, 106